INTERACTIVE SOFTWARE

INTERACTIVE SOFTWARE

Tools for Building
Interactive User Interfaces

JAMES A. LARSON

YOURDON PRESS
Prentice Hall Building
Englewood Cliffs, New Jersey 07632

Library of Congress Cataloging-in-Publication Data

Larson, James A.
    Interactive software : tools for building interactive user
interfaces / by James A. Larson.
        p.   cm.
    Includes bibliographical references and index.
    ISBN 0-13-924044-6
    1. User interfaces. 2. Computer software. 3. Human-computer
interaction.   I. Title.
QA76.9.U83L37 1992
005.1--dc20   91-9087
                                                      CIP

Editorial/production supervision
  and interior design: *Mary P. Rottino*
Cover design: *Wanda Lubelska Design*
Original Illustrations: *Michael J. Larson*
Manufacturing buyer: *Susan Brunke*
Prepress buyer: *Mary E. McCartney*
Acquisitions editor: *Paul W. Becker*

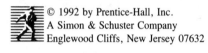 © 1992 by Prentice-Hall, Inc.
A Simon & Schuster Company
Englewood Cliffs, New Jersey 07632

Printed in the United States of America
10 9 8 7 6 5 4 3 2 1

ISBN 0-13-924044-6

Prentice-Hall International (UK) Limited, *London*
Prentice-Hall of Australia Pty. Limited, *Sydney*
Prentice-Hall Canada Inc., *Toronto*
Prentice-Hall Hispanoamericana, S.A., *Mexico*
Prentice-Hall of India Private Limited, *New Delhi*
Prentice-Hall of Japan, Inc., *Tokyo*
Simon & Schuster Asia Pte. Ltd., *Singapore*
Editora Prentice-Hall do brasil, Ltda., *Rio de Janeiro*

To my wife, Carol, who
is also my best friend

Contents

PREFACE   *xiii*

1 INTRODUCTION   *1*

   1.1   User Interfaces Are Important   1

   1.2   Major Problems Face User Interface Designers and
Implementers   2

   1.3   Tools Help Overcome User Interface Problems   3

   1.4   Users Require a Variety of User Interface Styles   7

   1.5   User Interface Designers Use a Variety of Tools   12

   1.6   Specialized Skills Are Needed to Implement User
Interfaces   15

   1.7   User Interface Life Cycle Has Several Phases   19

   1.8   Summary   22

**2 FRAMEWORK FOR DESIGNING USER
    INTERFACES**   *24*

   2.1   A Framework Helps User Interface Designers Make
Design Decisions   24

2.2   Criteria Determine Decision Partitioning   25

2.3   User Interface Design Decisions Are Partitioned into Classes   26

2.4   Help, Prompting, and Echoing Provide the User with Context   32

2.5   The Decision Classes Form a Useful Framework   33

2.6   Summary   35

3   END USERS' CONCEPTUAL MODEL   36

3.1   The Conceptual Model Forms the Bases for User Interfaces   36

3.2   A Metamodel Describes End Users' Conceptual Models   39

3.3   Conceptual Objects Represent Real-World Objects   40

3.4   Relationships Describe Associations Among Objects   45

3.5   Functions Describe What the End User Can Do with Applications   50

3.6   End Users' Conceptual Models Clarify Applications   53

3.7   Summary   55

4   DIALOGS AND SCRIPTS   56

4.1   Script Execution Engines Control Semantic Token Exchange   56

4.2   A Script Describes Several Possible Dialogs   58

4.3   Dialog Designers Specify Scripts   64

4.4   Events Are Processed Asynchronously   69

4.5   Dialogs May Be Multithreaded and Concurrent   69

4.6   Script Specification Techniques Should Satisfy Criteria   71

4.7   Summary   72

5   INTERACTION OBJECTS   73

5.1   End Users Use Interaction Objects to Manipulate Conceptual Objects   73

5.2   Interaction Objects Perform Several Functions   74

5.3   Signal Interaction Objects Transfer Messages   79

5.4   Selection Interaction Objects Are Used for Prompting and Selecting   83

5.5   Editable Interaction Objects Support Information Entry and Modification   91

5.6   Composite Interaction Objects Are Composed of Other Interaction Objects   95

5.7   Interaction Objects Are Built, Modified, and Generated   102

5.8   Dialog Designers Customize Interaction Objects   103

5.9   Designers Use Tools to Design Interaction Objects   107

5.10   Pragmatic Aspects Influence Interaction Objects   108

5.11   Summary   109

6 WINDOW MANAGERS AND USER INTERFACE MANAGEMENT SYSTEMS   111

6.1   User Interface Software Is Modularized   111

6.2   Device Drivers Are Transducers   113

6.3   Window Managers Provide Viewports to Applications   113

6.4   User Interface Management Systems Provide Additional Features   121

6.5   Architectures for Applications and User Interface Management Systems   124

6.6   Summary   131

7 STATE TRANSITION DESCRIPTIONS   132

7.1   State Transition Systems Represent Scripts   133

7.2   Subgraphs Are Factored Out of State Transition Graphs   138

7.3   Redundant Transitions Can Be Factored Out of a State Transition Diagram   140

7.4   A Merged State Replaces Many States   141

7.5   Supernodes Encapsulate Subgraphs   144

7.6   State Charts Represent Multithreaded Dialogs   147

7.7   Transformations Improve Scripts   150

7.8   Dialog Designers Use Many Techniques for Specifying
        Scripts   150

7.9   Summary   152

8 GRAMMARS FOR REPRESENTING DIALOGS   153

8.1   Grammars Represent Monologs   153

8.2   Grammars Are Extended to Represent Dialogs   158

8.3   Top-Down Processing Using a Grammar   165

8.4   Bottom-Up Parsing Using a Grammar   168

8.5   SYNGRAPH Is a Grammar-Driven User Interface
        Generator   169

8.6   Summary   172

9 RULES AND CONSTRAINTS   173

9.1   Rules Support User-Driven Dialogs   174

9.2   Languages Are Used to Specify Rules   180

9.3   Rules Support Error Correction   181

9.4   Rules Can Be Applied Eagerly or Lazily   184

9.5   Two-Way Constraints Support Dynamic Interaction
        Objects   186

9.6   Constraints Enforce Spatial Relationships and
        Appearance   188

9.7   Summary   192

10 MULTIAGENT TECHNIQUES   193

10.1   Shared Memory Controls Dialogs   194

10.2   Event Handlers Respond to Events   200

10.3   Event Loops Support Multithreaded Dialogs   206

10.4   Model, View, and Controller Objects Implement the
        User Interface in SmallTalk.   208

10.5   Object-Oriented Techniques Are Used to Implement
        User Interfaces   210

10.6   Multiagent Approaches Are Used for Implementing
        Direct Manipulation User Interfaces   211

10.7   Summary   212

11 OTHER DIALOG SPECIFICATION TECHNIQUES   **213**

   11.1   Existing Programming Languages Are Extended   214

   11.2   Special Programming Languages Are Designed   215

   11.3   Petri Nets Describe Concurrent Dialogs   217

   11.4   A Knowledge Base Helps Script Design   219

   11.5   Evaluation   220

   11.6   Summary   224

12 USER INTERFACE DEVELOPMENT ENVIRONMENT   **225**

   12.1   A User Interface Design Environment Contains Useful
          Tools and Facilities   226

   12.2   Guidelines and Advisors Help Designers   227

   12.3   Interaction Object Libraries May Be Open or Closed
          229

   12.4   Designers Use Scripts to Predict Ease of Use   230

   12.5   Designers Iteratively Revise User Interface Prototypes
          231

   12.6   Multimedia User Interfaces Require Tools   233

   12.7   Summary   239

**APPENDIX A   RELATIONSHIPS BETWEEN OBJECTS IN THE SAME
          CLASS**   **240**

APPENDIX B   CONCEPTUAL MODEL REFINEMENTS   **243**

   B.1   Merging Object Classes   245

   B.2   Horizontal Partitioning   248

   B.3   Aggregation and Normalization   255

   B.4   Join   263

   B.5   Cross-Product   266

   B.6   Vertical Partitioning   269

   B.7   Atomitize and Concatenation   276

   B.8   Cluster and Collapse Set   278

   B.9   Other Transformations   279

Contents

**APPENDIX C GUIDELINES FOR CHOOSING INTERACTION
               OBJECTS**   *281*

APPENDIX D CONSTRUCTING INTERACTION OBJECTS   *291*

D.1   Artists Use Editors to Coinstruct the Appearance of Interaction
       Objects   291

D.2   MICKEY Generates Default Interaction Objects Using Hints
       Embedded in the Application Code   294

D.3   The Petoud-Pigneur System Generates Interaction Objects from
       Database Design   298

D.4   Designers Use Prototyper to Generate Interaction Objects by
       Demonstration   300

D.5   TAE PLUS Connects Component Interaction Objects into
       Composite Interaction Objects   303

D.6   NeXT Interface Builder Links Interaction Objects with
       Application Objects   304

D.7   Peridot Generates Interaction Objects by Demonstration and
       Inference   305

D.8   User Interface Designers Use Simple Programming Languages
       to Construct Interface Object Behavior   307

D.9   User Interface Style Experts Provide Rules Used to Generate
       Default Interaction Objects by ITS   309

APPENDIX E WINDOWING SYSTEMS   *310*

E.1   Microsoft Windows   310

E.2   The X Window System   312

APPENDIX F SCHEMATIC EDITORS   *316*

GLOSSARY   *321*

BIBLIOGRAPHY   *333*

INDEX   *337*

Preface

PURPOSE OF THIS BOOK

The user interface is one of the most important components of any computer system. The success of a computer system is often dependent on how easily the user can learn and use the user interface. Computer systems often lack good user interfaces for a variety of reasons, including lack of a good user interface design methodology and lack of good tools to implement the user interface.

This book describes how to provide an environment in which good user interfaces can be constructed. It describes a framework and methodology for designing user interfaces. It also describes and evaluates a wide range of languages and tools for specifying and building user interfaces. This book concentrates on the "how" of building user interfaces.

INTENDED AUDIENCE

This book is designed for individuals who wish to understand user interface design and implementation environments. These include user interface designers, software engineers and designers, managers of user interface projects, and commercial programmers. After reading this book, readers should be able to understand, evaluate, and use user specification languages and user interface design tools.

This book has been used for a senior-level and first-year graduate-level course in interactive user interface design and implementation environments. It assumes that the reader understands the basic human-computer interface design principles, such as those found in Brown (1988), Smith and Mosier (1986), Shneiderman (1982), or similar books. It also assumes some familiarity with undergraduate computer science topics such as compilers, data structures, data bases, programming languages, and numerical analysis. Brown and Cunningham (1989), Bass and Coutaz (1991), Harrison and Thimbleby (1990) contain additional information supplementing this book.

CONTENT SUMMARY

Chapters 1 through 11 provide the theory behind tools for building user interfaces. Chapter 1 sets the background for user interface tools. Chapter 2 presents a framework for making decisions during user interface design. Chapters 3 through 11 explore components of this framework in greater detail. Chapter 3 describes the structural aspects, Chapter 4 describes the dialog aspects, Chapter 5 describes interaction objects, and Chapter 6 discusses architectures.

Chapters 7 through 11 discuss various approaches for specifying dialogs of information exchanged between end users and applications. Chapter 7 describes the use of state transition systems for describing dialogs, and outlines several approaches for managing large numbers of states and transitions. Chapter 8 describes how grammars can be extended to describe dialogs. Chapter 9 describes the use of rules and constraints, both for describing dialogs and for describing the appearance and behavior of interaction objects. Chapter 10 overviews the use of object oriented techniques for dialog specification. Chapter 11 discusses various language approaches for describing dialogs. Chapter 12 concentrates on user interface design tools.

BACKGROUND

This book is based on material from courses in interactive software design and implementation which I have taught at the University of Minnesota, Beijing University, College of St. Thomas (St. Paul, Minnesota), and Portland State University.

1

Introduction

This chapter discusses

- What the three major problems are with user interface designs.
- What the major dialog styles are.
- What tools can be used to build user interfaces.
- Who are the users of user interface tools.
- What the user interface life cycle is.

[A computer] is limited not by its power to compute, but rather by its power to communicate with its human users. —H. R. Hartson and D. Hix
(Hartson and Hix, 1989)

1.1 USER INTERFACES ARE IMPORTANT

Computer applications are judged by many factors, including robustness, functionality, speed of performance, and ease of use. Ease of use includes how easily users are able to learn to use the application, how easily users are able to apply the application, and the frequency of user errors when interacting with the application. Ease of use is one of the major factors that influences how users perceive and work with an application. The user interface is almost always discussed in reviews of software products. Very simply stated, if the application is not easy to use, some users become frustrated and abandon the application. Others may tolerate difficult-to-use systems, but are not as productive as they could be. The success of an application is largely determined by how easily the application can be learned and used.

Computer users should be able to use the computer to perform tasks as easily as people can use other modern conveniences. Applications should be as easy to use as telephones, adding machines, typewriters, and other devices designed to make us more efficient. All too often computer applications fail to do this. One of the frequent tragedies of software development is the amount of time and effort implementors spend to design and implement software that is seldom used because it has a poor user interface.

Computers perform calculations at speeds much faster than do humans, execute commands often expressed in a form incomprehensible to most humans, and generate results in a form that is frequently difficult for humans to grasp and analyze. While programmers, engineers, and other computer specialists have extensive training to deal with the computer's speed, language, and data formats, the majority of computer users are not able to easily interact with the computer. The user interface provides the mechanism for overcoming the differences in processing speed and information format between users and computers.

A user interface is a set of protocols and techniques for exchanging information between a computerized application and its human user. The user interface is responsible for soliciting commands from the user, and for displaying application results in a form comprehensible to the user. The use interface is not, however, responsible for application calculations, data storage, retrieval, and transmission.

This introductory chapter provides the context for user interface systems. It first describes some of the reasons why user interfaces are often unsatisfactory and how design and implementation tools can partially overcome these problems. Next, it briefly overviews the major types of user interfaces and the tools used to design, build, and execute user interfaces. We then discuss the various roles which individuals assume as they develop user interfaces. Finally, the life cycle of user interfaces is described.

1.2 MAJOR PROBLEMS FACE USER INTERFACE DESIGNERS AND IMPLEMENTERS

There are several major problems with user interfaces to application systems.

Poorly designed user interfaces   Reasons why applications have poor user interfaces include the following:

- Application developers do not understand the user's degree of computer literacy and familiarity with the application domain, and thus develop user interfaces which are not appropriate for the intended user.

- Application developers design user interfaces which they themselves find convenient. Unfortunately, most end users do not find the types of user interfaces used by professional programmers easy to use. Programmers spend years learning how to write programs for computers, not in how humans use computers to accomplish work.

- Application developers do not take the time necessary to design, prototype, and test good user interfaces. User interfaces must be prototyped and carefully tested and evaluated several times before they are usable by their intended users.

There is often little time or too few resources for evaluating user interface prototypes and for modifying them so that they are easier to use. Modifying a user interface design is difficult because of (1) the difficulty in identifying the code to be modified, which is often intertwined with the application program logic, and (2) the large amount of programming code that must be modified to make even minor changes in the user interface.

Single-user interface for all users   Most application systems are used by a variety of users with differing habits, preferences, idiosyncrasies, training, and working styles. Most users use a single interface to an application system, even though they could be more productive if the interface were customized to their individual needs. This is especially necessary for users who are physically handicapped.

Inconsistencies among user interfaces for multiple applications   Not only must users learn different sets of commands for each application, they must deal with similar commands that may do very different things in different applications. It is difficult to apply the techniques of operating one application to other applications. Each user needs a uniform and consistent user interface to all the applications which he or she uses.

This text discusses methodologies and describes tools for overcoming these three problems. Methodologies and approaches will be presented which can be used to design user interfaces that are easy to use, are tailorable, and can be used to access multiple applications. Tools make these methodologies practical by enabling user interface designers to perform easily and quickly the various tasks necessary to design, implement, test, evaluate, and modify user interfaces.

1.3 TOOLS HELP OVERCOME USER INTERFACE PROBLEMS

There are many types of tools in the marketplace that can be used to build user interfaces. These tools include command processors, menu systems and menu formatters, form systems and form designers, data entry systems and screen formatters, windowing systems, user interface tool kits, and user interface management systems. This section covers a short overview of these tools.

As illustrated in Figure 1.1, most user interface tools have two major components: a user interface execution engine and a user interface authoring tool. Using the *user interface authoring tool*, a user interface designer specifies the description of the user interface. This user interface description includes the format of information to be displayed to the user, the manner in which the user enters information, and the sequence of information exchanges between user and application. Typically, the user interface

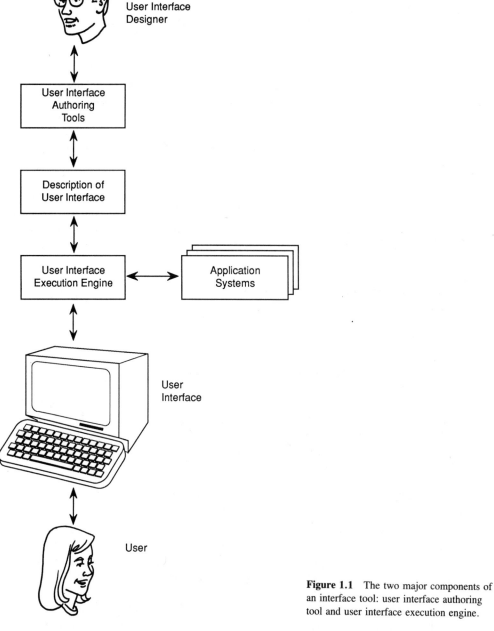

User Interface
Designer

User Interface
Authoring
Tools

Description of
User Interface

User Interface
Execution Engine

Application
Systems

User
Interface

User

Figure 1.1 The two major components of
an interface tool: user interface authoring
tool and user interface execution engine.

designer uses an editor to create and modify fragments of the user interface design. User
interface design fragments may be saved in a library for later reuse by designers of other
user interfaces. The user interface designer may apply various design and evaluation tools

to proposed designs. These tools help the user interface designer specify the design, check the design for completeness and consistency, simulate parts of the design, evaluate the design against designer-specified criteria, and convert the design into a format appropriate for the user interface execution engine. The authoring tool produces either program code or a declarative description of the user interface which is used by the user interface execution engine.

The *user interface execution engine* manages and controls the dialog between the end user and one or more application systems by processing user interface program code or description and producing user interface dialogs in which users exchange information with application functions. The user interface execution engine solicits information from the user and displays information to the user according to the interface design specifications.

User interface tools help to solve the three major problems with user interface to current application systems.

User interfaces can be rapidly constructed and modified   Much of the effort of designing and building application programs goes into designing and coding the user interface. While designing the user interface must always take place, designs take less time to implement if high-level user interface languages and tools are used. User interface languages can be thought of as fourth-generation programming languages in which the user interface designer specifies what the user interface should do without specifying all of the details about how the user interface should be implemented. The effort required to modify an existing user interface can also be reduced by using these languages and tools, which hide many of the time-consuming details that must be specified when using a programming language. User interface tools generate much of the low-level code, decreasing the amount of low-level code which the designers need to write and debug.

In addition, the code generated by user interface authoring tools is frequently more reliable than code created by human implementers, and thus takes less time to debug. As a result, designers have more time to evaluate the human factor aspects of the user interface and modify the user interface when appropriate. Sometimes the same user interface can be used for more than one application system, saving the designers even more time.

Different user interfaces can be constructed for different user classes
End users each have unique habits, preferences, idiosyncrasies, and working styles. Attempts to force end users to change these styles usually result in end user frustration and decreased productivity. All end users of an application system should not be forced to use the same user interface; user interface designers can customize the user interface to the habits and styles of user classes, rather than force the user to tailor his or her working style to the user interface.

For example, users may be classified as either novice or experienced depending upon their familiarity with computing. Novice users may prefer menu or form fill-in styles of user interface, while experienced users may prefer keyword-oriented commands. Jarke and Vassiliou (1985) present several categories of database users and recommend styles of user interfaces for each category.

Multiple styles of user interfaces can be supported by careful design of an application's functional operations and by customizing the user interface to the needs of end users in each class. User interfaces should be designed in two phases. In the *end users' conceptual model specification* phase, the designer defines the functions that the user can invoke. In this phase, the designer is not concerned with how the user will supply this information but with which parameters the user must supply and what information to display to the user. In the *interface description* phase, the user interface designers define a user interface for each class of users. Each user interface description describes the form and manner in which a user in the class enters requests and the format of the information displayed to the user. User interface designers repeat the second phase for each class of users who will use the application.

A user interface designer may create a different user interface for each user class during the interface description phase. For example, question and answer interfaces for novice users, menu interfaces for intermediate users, and command languages for experienced users can all be designed and implemented as interfaces to a single application. User interface tools enable user interface designers to quickly implement user interface designs for each class of users.

Standard user interfaces for each end user class One of the most frustrating aspects of computing is when users must learn different interfaces for different applications. Not only must users learn new sets of commands, they must deal with similar commands that may do very different things. Users have little interest in the peculiarities of different applications and no desire to learn the syntax and semantics of different command languages. User interfaces with a similar *look and feel* are needed for each user class. The user interface *look* refers to the manner in which the computer presents information to the user; similar information should be presented to the user using similar symbols, using a similar format, and positioned in a similar location. The user interface *feel* refers to the manner in which the user enters information and requests.

Standardizing the user interfaces to several applications for each user class permits positive rather than negative transfer of experience. This enables users within each user class to learn new applications easily and rapidly. Once a user learns something about one application, he or she already knows something about how to use other applications. *Interoperability* is the end user's ability to apply operating techniques of one application to another. User interface tools enable the user interface designer to specify and implement standard interfaces for multiple applications, thus providing interoperability among applications for users within the same user class.

There are two general approaches for encouraging designers to create standard user interfaces. The first is to provide a style guideline document to all user interface designers. However, style guidelines are often too general and open to misinterpretation, or too detailed and not generally applicable. The second approach is to encode or embed the user interface style guidelines into the authoring tools, so that all user interfaces generated by the authoring tools adhere to the guidelines. User interface tools are well suited to support this second approach.

1.4 USERS REQUIRE A VARIETY OF USER INTERFACE STYLES

To accomplish a task, users normally iterate the following steps:

- Establish a goal.
- Specify a sequence of commands to the computer to accomplish the goal.
- Examine the results of the commands to determine if the goal has been achieved.

Different end users may prefer different user interface styles when specifying commands and reviewing results of command execution. Five general user interface styles are illustrated in Figures 1.2 through 1.6. These styles, often called dialog styles, differ not only in the appearance of the user interface, but in the sequencing and timing of information exchanges between the user and computer applications.

1.4.1 Command Dialog Style

Figure 1.2 illustrates the command style of dialog. This style requires that users be able to formulate commands and specify their parameters using a formal syntax. The user enters commands into a command box by typing the commands using a keyboard. This style of dialog is frequently useful for experienced users who use the application frequently.

User to UI: WithdrawAmount=110, AccountNumber=137
UI to User: Newbalance=90

Figure 1.2   Command dialog style.

1.4.2 Question and Answer Dialog Style

Figure 1.3 illustrates the question and answer style of dialog. In this style, the user interface execution engine prompts the user to enter commands and parameters by asking questions to which the user enters simple responses. The user interface execution engine directs the user by asking the user specific questions as the user is led through the task of formulating a command. Experienced users may find this dialog style tedious and

Welcome to the automatic bank teller.
What is your account number?
›137
How much do you wish to withdraw?
›$110.00
Your new balance is $90.00
Remove your money from the slot
to the right of this screen

Figure 1.3   Question and answer dialog style.

condescending. This dialog style is more appropriate for novice users who are not familiar with all of the commands and options.

1.4.3 Menu and Form Fill-in Dialog Style

Figure 1.4 illustrates a form fill-in. When using this style, the user interface execution engine prompts the user with menus and fill-in forms rather than questions. The user responds by selecting options from menus and entering simple responses into the slots of the form fill-in. This dialog style is appropriate for novice users who may need to be prompted to enter parameter values. It is especially useful for data entry.

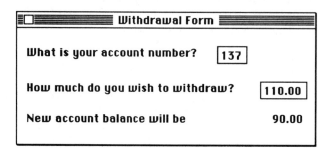

Figure 1.4   Form fill-in.

1.4.4 Natural Language Dialog Style

Figure 1.5 illustrates a natural language interface, in which the user enters a request using English or some other natural language. The system responses are also formulated using the same natural language. Typically users enter requests via a keyboard. The execution engine displays results on a computer screen. Voice synthesis may be used for natural language output in emergency situations or for visually impaired users. Voice recognition and handwriting recognition are beginning to be used for natural language input. Because of the processing necessary to understand general natural language, this dialog style is currently used only in situations where the dialog is constrained to a small subset of the possible natural language sentences and utterances which end users might construct.

> User to UI: Withdraw 110 from account 137
> UI to User: Your new balance is 90. Remove your
> money from the slot to the right of this screen

Figure 1.5   Natural language dialog style.

1.4.5 Direct Manipulation Dialog Style

Commands, questions and answers, menus and forms, and natural language dialog styles are collectively referred to as *conversational styles* because the user engages in a conversation about the actions which the computer should perform. In the past few years, another major category of user-computer dialogs has become popular, called *direct*

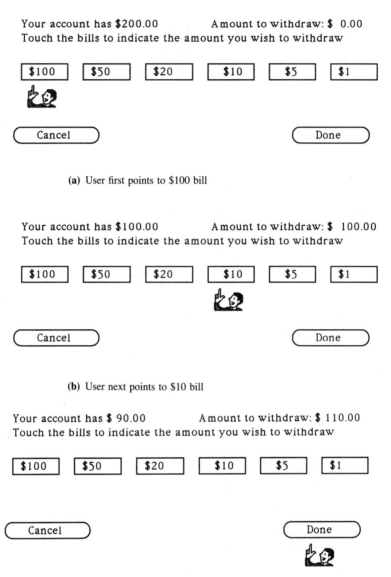

Your account has $200.00   Amount to withdraw: $ 0.00
Touch the bills to indicate the amount you wish to withdraw

| $100 | $50 | $20 | $10 | $5 | $1 |

(Cancel)   (Done)

(a) User first points to $100 bill

Your account has $100.00   Amount to withdraw: $ 100.00
Touch the bills to indicate the amount you wish to withdraw

| $100 | $50 | $20 | $10 | $5 | $1 |

(Cancel)   (Done)

(b) User next points to $10 bill

Your account has $ 90.00   Amount to withdraw: $ 110.00
Touch the bills to indicate the amount you wish to withdraw

| $100 | $50 | $20 | $10 | $5 | $1 |

(Cancel)   (Done)

(c) User indicates that transaction is complete

Figure 1.6 Direct manipulation dialog style.

manipulation. Figure 1.6 illustrates a direct manipulation dialog. In direct manipulation dialogs, users operate directly on objects that are visible on the screen, performing rapid, reversible, incremental actions. Direct manipulation allows immediate feedback on many types of errors which are immediately observed and corrected by the user. The result of one action can be used as input to the next action. When using a direct manipulation dialog style, the user does not need to learn language syntax. Instead, the user selects from

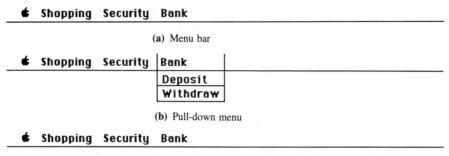

(a) Menu bar

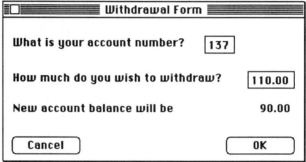

(b) Pull-down menu

(c) Window

Figure 1.7 WIMP dialog style.

alternative options represented by graphical objects called *icons*. Direct manipulation interfaces are usually easy to learn because they are based on metaphors with which the user is familiar. On the other hand, the meaning of some icons may be unclear to some users. Also, a large-screen display space may be necessary to display all of the icons.

Many dialogs are combinations of the above five basic dialog styles. Figure 1.7 illustrates one combination, often called WIMP (windows, icons, menus, pointing devices) user interfaces or GUI (graphical user interface). This style of user interface is based on a desktop metaphor in which the screen resembles the top of a desk on which objects may be placed. Each object is represented by an icon. The user manipulates a device called a mouse to move a cursor across the desktop. When the cursor is on top of an icon, the user may press a button on a mouse (''click'' the mouse) to select the object. The user invokes commands by clicking options on menus which appear on the screen after the user clicks the menu name from a menu of menus. The WIMP style of user interface, made popular by the Macintosh^{TM} computer, is now widely available on many computers.

1.4.6 Computer-Directed and User-Directed Styles

The five dialog styles just introduced fall into two broad classes, computer directed and user directed.

The question and answer and menu form fill-in styles are computer-directed dialogs. In *computer-directed dialogs,* the following two steps are performed repeatedly:

1. A request is displayed to the user prompting the user to enter information.
2. The user enters the requested information.

Because they may be unfamiliar with the options available to them, novice and casual users often prefer computer-directed dialogs. However, applications with computer-directed dialogs may appear to be condescending to experienced users who must wait impatiently while the computer displays instructions. To overcome this perception, experienced users should feel that they are in control by taking the initiative in setting the direction of the dialog. Rather than being directed by the computer to enter some piece of information, the experienced user can take the initiative by selecting and entering pieces of information without direction from the computer.

The keyword, natural language, and direct manipulation dialog styles are user-directed. In *user-directed dialogs,* the following steps are performed repeatedly:

1. The user indicates the next type of information or command to be entered.
2. The user enters the appropriate information or command.

The user interface designer first determines if the dialog style should generally be computer or user directed. Novice users perform better with computer-directed user interfaces, while experienced users perform better with user-directed user interfaces. Some systems provide multiple styles of user interfaces to satisfy the needs of several classes of users.

The user interface designer selects one or a combination of the user interface styles available. Choosing the appropriate dialog style is a complex process involving economics, human factors, computer hardware, and political considerations. Often a user interface contains a mixture of dialog styles. Factors which influence the choice of a dialog style include the following:

- *The capabilities of the hardware to be used.* Some devices (teletype terminals and glass teletype terminals) can only accept and display single lines of text. Menu and form fill-ins and direct manipulation interfaces are not possible on this hardware.
- *The requirements of the application.* Some applications need only a few input parameters and display only a few values as results. A sophisticated direct manipulation dialog style may not be needed in order for the user to interact with these applications.
- *Vendor or enterprise standards and conventions.* Switching among applications is easier if all applications support the same dialog style.
- *The physical capabilities of the intended end users and the environment in which the end user will be working.*

After selecting the dialog style, the user interface designer may use any of several user interface tools to specify, test, and debug a user interface. Some of these tools are described in the next section.

1.5 USER INTERFACE DESIGNERS USE A VARIETY OF TOOLS

User interface tools can be categorized in order of increasing sophistication and complexity as follows: command processors, menu systems and menu formatters, form systems and form generators, user interface tool kits, window managers, and user interface management systems. Let's take a brief tour of these tools and discuss how they can be used.

1.5.1 Command Processors

A *command processor* is a software execution engine which accepts a string of characters entered by the end user, determines the intent of the character string, and invokes the appropriate application functions. Examples of command processors include UNIX® command shells and SQL database query language processors.

1.5.2 Menu Systems and Menu Formatters

Because many users find it easier to "recognize" the name of the desired option from an option list than to "recall" and enter the name of the desired option from memory, menus have become popular, especially for novice users. A *menu* is a displayed collection of options from which the user selects one or more choices.

One technique used by user interface designers to describe menus is a menu specification language. Designers use a *menu specification language* to specify the title of each menu, the options to appear on each menu, and the actions taken when the user chooses each option. Designers may also use specification languages to define the format and arrangement of options within a menu. Another technique for specifying the appearance of menus is to draw each menu using a facility similar to a screen editor. The specifications are processed by a *menu formatter* that generates the code for execution by a menu execution engine. The *menu execution engine* executes the generated code to display a menu to the end user, who selects one or more options. Based on the input, the menu execution engine may either (1) display another menu in order to solicit additional information from the user or (2) invoke an application function that performs the task specified by the options selected by the user.

1.5.3 Form Fill-in Systems

A menu system presents options to the user using one or more menus. The user can only choose from the displayed options and can not enter options or values that do not appear in the menu. For some applications, it is more convenient for the user to enter values directly rather than select them from a menu. This is the case when the set of options is very large. For example, the user should enter a birth date directly from the keyboard rather than select from a large menu of possible birth dates.

Systems which support the direct entry of values into electronic versions of paper business forms are called *form fill-in systems.* A form fill-in system displays form fill-ins containing user-oriented instructions and boxes, called *data boxes,* into which the end user enters values. The user moves a cursor to a data box and then uses a text editor to

```
┌──────────────────────────────────────────────────────┐
│ ▤□ ▦▦▦▦▦ Withdrawal Form ▦▦▦ ▦▦▦▦▦ │
├──────────────────────────────────────────────────────┤
│                                                        │
│  What is your account number?      ┌──────┐            │
│                                    └──────┘            │
│                                                        │
│  How much do you wish to withdraw?   ┌──────┐          │
│                                      └──────┘          │
│  New account balance will be                           │
│                                                        │
└──────────────────────────────────────────────────────┘
```

Figure 1.8   Form fill-in.

enter an alphanumeric string into the data box. Figure 1.8 illustrates a form fill-in which is used to solicit information from a bank customer who wishes to make a withdrawal from his or her account. Form fill-ins can also be used to display function results to users. The form fill-in in Figure 1.4 illustrates the results of a banking customer withdrawing $110 from the account numbered 137.

User interface designers may use a *form generator* to construct form fill-ins. Just as there are two types of authoring tools for menus, there are two types of form fill-in generators. A form specification language is sometimes used by designers to specify the appearance of form fill-ins. Alternatively, form drawing tools can be used interactively to paint the layout and appearance of form fill-ins.

Most form fill-in systems also support a constraint language to specify constraints on values which may be entered into the data boxes of the form fill-in. For example, the user interface designer can specify constraints such as the value of a person's age must always be a nonnegative integer.

1.5.4. User Interface Tool Kits

A *user interface tool kit* is a collection of library functions that displays information to users and solicits information from users. The functions in the user interface tool kit can be used to perform a wide variety of tasks, including the following:

- Display text, menus, forms, graphics, and other types of data within a window
- Obtain information entered by the user via a keyboard, mouse, or other input device

User interface tool kit functions are often invoked from application programs. Figure 1.9 illustrates the relationship between an application program and some of the functions in a user interface tool kit. In this example, the application first invokes a function which displays a menu to the user, who selects an option which is returned to the application. Later, the application invokes a function that displays a final result in a data box.

Application programmers may include references to user interface tool kit functions directly in application code. When invoked, these functions cause information to be presented to the user on a display screen or via a sound-generation mechanism such as a bell, buzzer, tone generator, or voice synthesis device. Tool kit functions also obtain information from the user via input devices such as keyboards, mice, touch-sensitive screens, and various types of pointing devices.

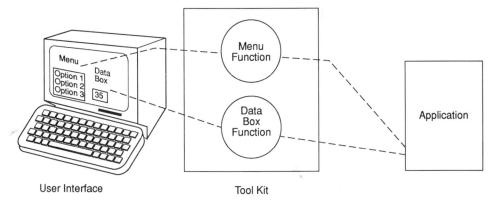

Figure 1.9 Use of user interface tool kit. Application invokes tool kit functions that produce the user interface.

Most tool kits have functions for displaying menus, and can thus be used as a menu system. Similarly, most tool kits can also be used as a forms system. Some tool kits also support command processors.

The user interface tool kit makes the application programmer's job easier because he or she needs only to select the appropriate functions and supply the appropriate parameters in order to create the user's interface to an application program. User interface tool kits are becoming quite popular for this reason. By consistent use of tool kit functions, multiple application programs can have similar user interfaces.

Tool kits contain functions that are invoked from within an application. There is no support for user interface functions to be invoked directly by the user. The user has little direct control over the appearance of the user interface. Window managers overcome this disadvantage.

1.5.5 Window Managers

Many tool kits are associated with a window manager which manages regions of the display screen called *windows*. The application programmer uses the functions of a tool kit to solicit information from the user and to display results to the user within a window.

Window managers provide the user with the ability to have control over some of the appearance of the user interface. Users may open, close, reposition, resize, and scroll the contents of a window. With multiple windows, a user can invoke, monitor, and control several applications which execute at the same time. The window manager is responsible for managing the windows, each of which may correspond to a different application.

Users can also use information displayed in one window as input to another application system by moving the information between windows. For example, Figure 1.10 illustrates a screen with two windows. After the user creates part of the memo in one window using a text editor, the user uses another window to invoke a spreadsheet application. There, the user instructs the spreadsheet to produce the desired table. Finally, the user instructs the window manager to transfer the table from the spreadsheet window to the text editing window where it becomes a part of the memo.

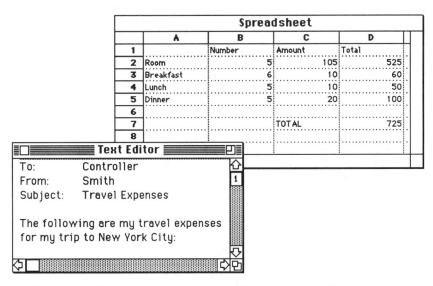

Figure 1.10 Use of user interface tool kit. Application invokes tool kit functions that produce the user interface.

1.5.6 User Interface Management Systems

A *user interface management system* is a collection of software tools used to design, represent, prototype, execute, and evaluate user interfaces to one or more application systems. Figure 1.11 illustrates the major components of a user interface management system. We will call the execution engine in a user interface management system a *script execution engine*. It executes a special program which we will call a script. A script invokes both application functions and functions provided by a user interface tool kit. The result of executing a script is called a dialog, the sequence of exchanges of information between the user and application functions. In the example of Figure 1.11, the dialog solicits instructions from the user via a menu, invokes a DBMS (database management system) to access the database, invokes an application module to perform statistical summaries, and then displays the result in the data box on the user's screen. Different dialogs result when users enter different information during the execution of a script. User interface designers use a *script authoring tool* to design scripts.

A user interface management system contains two important features missing from user interface tool kits and window managers: a script builder and a script execution engine.

1.6 SPECIALIZED SKILLS ARE NEEDED TO IMPLEMENT USER INTERFACES

Several skills are needed to design useful user interfaces. There are several roles [variations of roles suggested by Olsen (1984)] into which user interface design and implementation skills can be categorized. Each role may be filled by a different person.

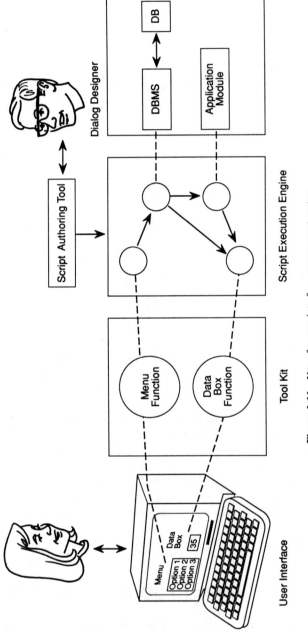

Figure 1.11 Use of a user interface management system.

16

However, there may be several individuals who fill a single roll, and one person may perform several roles. These roles are discussed in detail in the remainder of this section.

1.6.1 End User

Role. End users use the user interface to interact with applications to perform tasks in their job functions. User interfaces are built to be used by end users.

Characteristics. The end user needs user interfaces to interact with the computer applications. Often the end user has little knowledge about computers or programming. End users often conceive of a user interface by analogy and may be strongly influenced by other user interfaces with which they are currently familiar. End users often have strong opinions about what is appropriate and inappropriate with user interfaces.

Requirements. The chief requirement for end users is an easy-to-learn, easy-to-use, and efficient user interface. End users are expected to understand the purpose of the functions provided by the application, be able to invoke those functions by formulating requests using the user interface, and evaluate function results presented by the user interface.

1.6.2 Application Analyst

Role. The application analyst is responsible for identifying the potential end users of the application, defining the problems that end users need to solve, defining the domain-dependent tasks end users perform, and identifying the conceptual objects and functions of the task domain. The application analyst is responsible for designing the end users' conceptual model of the application. This model describes the conceptual objects and functions that end users apply to conceptual objects.

Characteristics. An application analyst should thoroughly understand the application domain. An application analyst should be able to converse easily with end users in order to obtain requirements and construct the conceptual model. An application analyst should be able to formalize end user requirements and the conceptual model and present them to potential end users for review.

Requirements. An application analyst needs a methodology for designing the end users' conceptual model and tools to support the design methodology.

1.6.3 Graphics Designer

Role. A graphics designer develops the visual aspects of *interaction objects,* objects that are displayed on computer screens and which the end user observes and modifies.

Characteristics. The graphics designer is artistic in nature and understands visual appearance, appropriate use of color, appropriate use of line style, pattern, and fonts. It is not necessary that a graphics designer understand programming, but it is necessary that the graphics designer understand what can and cannot be supported by the available user interface programming tools.

Requirements. The graphics designer needs interactive drawing and sketching tools to design the appearance of interaction objects. These tools must be able to store and retrieve appearances so that they can be saved and reused.

1.6.4 Dialog Designer

Role. The dialog designer understands the intended users of the application, how they think about their problems, and how they go about problem solving. The dialog designer designs the metaphor that the user interface presents to the end user and the mechanisms with which the end user interacts with applications. The dialog designer chooses the appropriate interaction objects (designed by a graphics artist) and specifies the sequence of information exchanged between the user and the application functions. The dialog designer designs the set of possible dialogs by authoring scripts.

Characteristics. The dialog designer is skilled in human factors and is experienced in a wide variety of user interfaces. While not necessarily a programmer, a dialog designer is concerned with designing illusions that hide the computational aspects of the application.

Requirements. The dialog designer needs script specification tools and a collection of interaction objects. He or she uses these tools to specify scripts, simulate the user interface, demonstrate the user interface to perspective users, and to modify and refine the user interface rapidly .

1.6.5 Application Programmer

Role. An application programmer implements the nonuser interface portions of the application.

Characteristics. The application programmer is skilled in programming techniques and is responsible for the computation aspects of the application. Usually an application programmer has only a passing familiarity with the application domain and is not trained in human factors or visual design.

Requirements. An application programmer needs a clear, simple description of how the user interface and the computational functions relate. A programmer uses a programming language to implement the computational functions. If the dialog designer does not use a script authoring tool which generates executable code, then the application programmer codes the script as part of the application code.

1.6.6 User Interface Evaluator

Role. The user interface evaluator predicts whether or not a proposed interface design satisfies established guidelines and conventions and determines the effectiveness of the user interface. He or she designs and conducts experimental evaluations of the design and implemented software to determine its quality (how well it solves the domain-specific problems), usability (how easy it is to learn and use), and robustness (how frequently it fails).

Characteristics. The interface evaluator is skilled in human factors and in creating and evaluating experiments to evaluate user interfaces. The interface evaluator may also determine whether the user interface satisfies safety requirements (e.g., electromagnetic radiation is below an acceptable limit) and if the user interface hardware is ergonomically sound (e.g., the position and arrangement of hardware are convenient for human use). Usually a single individual should not perform both the dialog designer and interface evaluator roles. It is easy for a dialog designer to develop a mind-set to a specific design which is difficult to overcome during evaluation.

Requirements. The interface evaluator needs tools for analyzing the human factors' properties of user interface specifications and prototypes.

1.6.7 User Interface Tool Builder

Role. The user interface tool builder determines the need for, describes, designs, and builds tools for designing and building user interfaces.

Characteristics. The user interface tool builder is a skilled systems analyst and programmer.

Requirements. The user interface tool builder is familiar with existing user interface tools and uses them and various software development environments to design and build improved user interface design and implementation tools.

Other roles from traditional software development projects may also be applicable. Project managers, documentation specialists, training specialists, and marketing specialists are useful and necessary in any development project. Just as many organizations have standards for requirements specification, design specification, coding and documentation, standards for user interfaces are desirable to ensure ease of use and consistency among multiple user interfaces. A user interface standards specialist role may be useful for establishing and enforcing user interface guidelines and standards.

All of these user interface roles come into play during the phases of a user interface life cycle, discussed in the next section.

1.7 USER INTERFACE LIFE CYCLE HAS SEVERAL PHASES

Figure 1.12 illustrates the four major phases in the life cycle of a user interface. The heavy arrows between each phase illustrate the ''waterfall'' nature of how the completion of one phase leads to the beginning of the next phase. However, in real-life projects there are often iterations within each phase and feedback between phases. These are illustrated by the light arrows in Figure 1.12. In user interface design, it is common practice to develop several rapid prototypes by iterating over the last three phases several times. Table 1.1 summarizes the four phases of the user interface life cycle, the role of the individuals responsible for each phase, and the results of each phase. Each phase is discussed in greater detail in the paragraphs that follow.

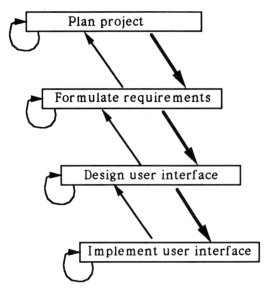

Figure 1.12 User interface life cycle.

1.7.1 Phase 1: Develop the User Interface Design and Implementation Plan

The application analyst defines the scope and goals of the user interface. The analyst determines what applications the user interface should support and determines the compatibility requirements with existing user interfaces.

The application analyst also determines the resources available for designing and implementing the user interface, what types of designers and implementers will be needed during the project, what role the potential users of interface will play in the design and development of the user interface, and what tools are needed during the design and development effort.

TABLE 1.1 Four Phases of a User Interface's Life Cycle

Phase number	Phase	Responsible role	Result
1	Develop design and implementation plan	Application analyst	Plan
2	Formulate and analyze requirements	Application analyst	Requirements and conceptual model
3	Design user interface	Application analyst, graphics desinger, dialog designer	User interface design
4	Implement user interface	Dialog designer, application programmer	Working user interface

The application analyst analyzes the costs of implementing and maintaining the proposed user interface. The potential benefits of the proposed user interface are analyzed. The application analyst uses this information to justify the user interface development plan to management and to obtain their approval.

The application analyst also determines the relationship between user interface and application design and development. The application analyst establishes the priorities among the major user interface and application design and development tasks, and the dependencies among these tasks. The degree of overlap between user interface and application development and planning is determined. The application analyst is responsible for developing a plan for performing these tasks.

1.7.2 Phase 2: Formulate and Analyze Requirements

The application analyst identifies the potential users of the application and the problems they will need to solve. The application analyst then categorizes the potential users into classes based on their understanding of the application and their familiarity with computers.

The application analyst determines the domain-dependent goals of the application, analyzes the user tasks necessary to achieve those goals, and specifies the end users' conceptual model of the application. The *end users' conceptual model* consists of the major conceptual objects which the user may manipulate, the types of operations which the user may perform on the conceptual objects, and the relationships and constraints among the conceptual objects. The application analyst reviews the conceptual model with the potential users to verify its correctness and completeness. A technique for representing the end users' conceptual model is described in Chapter 3.

1.7.3 Phase 3: Design the User Interface

The graphics artist designs a collection of interaction objects with which the user will interact. Examples of interaction objects include menus, dialog boxes, command boxes, icons, windows, and other types of objects that present information to the user and into which the user can enter information. Interaction objects are the mechanisms by which users manipulate conceptual objects in the end users' conceptual model. Most interaction objects present information by displaying it visually to the end user. Some interaction objects offer information by presenting audio messages. Interaction objects are discussed in Chapter 5.

The dialog designer specifies the script which describes the exchange of information between the user via interaction objects and the underlying applications. Scripts are discussed in Chapter 4. Script representation techniques are described in Chapters 7 through 11.

1.7.4 Phase 4: Implement the User Interface

Dialog designers, possibly aided by application programmers, use the available prototyping and implemention tools to implement the user interface. If the dialog designer did not use a user interface development tool which converts script specification to an executable code, then a programmer constructs an executable script as part of the application system.

The application analyst and dialog designer conduct user training in how to use the user interface. They train the potential users in when and how to use the underlying application effectively to perform their tasks. They both work with the potential users to define new office procedures involving the application and the system.

User interface rapid prototyping   No one expects to write programs correctly without debugging. Similarly, no one should expect to design perfect user interfaces without debugging. With the increased availability of user interface development tools, user interface prototyping is becoming popular. A *user interface prototype* is a quickly developed and easily modified working model of the user interface. It presents the user interface appearance and behavior without requiring the underlying application logic. User interface prototypes are very helpful in testing the usefulness of the user interface and determining the appropriateness of the application functions. By using user interface development tools, the last two phases can be quickly performed and a user interface prototype rapidly constructed. The prototype is then iteratively exercised, evaluated, and either modified or replaced by another prototype until the final user interface is designed. Dialog designers almost universally agree that rapid prototyping is necessary to produce quality user interfaces.

The user interface evaluator monitors users as they test user interface prototypes. The evaluator tunes and modifies the user interface to improve the performance of users as they work with the application. Tuning can occur in several forms: (1) changing, enhancing, or introducing interaction objects; (2) changing or enhancing the script; and (3) changing or enhancing the end users' conceptual model. If the users' conceptual model is modified, then the underlying application may also need to be enhanced and extended.

The dialog designer may also demonstrate the user interface to the developers of the underlying application or system. The application programmers may use the user interface to test the underlying application function for correctness and completeness.

1.8 SUMMARY

User interfaces are important because end users need them to interact with computer applications. There are three major problems with user interface designs. They are often poorly designed. Each application is supported by a different user interface, making it difficult for users to switch between applications. And user interfaces are not easily customized to fit the needs of various user classes.

Five general styles of dialog are command, question and answer, menu and form fill-in, natural language, and direct manipulation. Dialogs often contain aspects of several of these styles. User-directed dialogs give the user the feeling that he or she is directing the progress of the dialog. Computer-directed dialogs give the end user the feeling that the computer is leading the user through the dialog.

There are a variety of tools in the marketplace that can be used to build user interfaces. These tools include command processors, menu systems and formatters, form systems and form designers, window managers, user interface tool kits, and user interface management systems.

Users of interface tools can be categorized into several roles, including end users, application analysts, application programmers, dialog designers, graphics designers, interface evaluators, and user interface tool builders. These are the players in the user interface life cycle.

The user interface life cycle consists of four phases: determining the design and implementation plan, formulating and analyzing requirements, designing the user interface, and implementing the user interface. The last three phases are iteratively repeated until the resulting user interface is determined to be complete and easy to learn and use.

2

Framework for Designing User Interfaces

This chapter discusses

> - What a design decision framework is.
> - What criteria to use in choosing a design decision framework.
> - What five useful design decision classes are.

Phase 3 of the user interface life cycle (Chapter 1), deals with designing the user interface. This chapter outlines the issues involved in developing user interface designs and offers a framework for dealing with these issues. Each of these issues will be explored in greater detail in later chapters.

2.1 A FRAMEWORK HELPS USER INTERFACE DESIGNERS MAKE DESIGN DECISIONS

Designing and implementing an easy-to-use user interface subject to the available time and labor constraints is a difficult job. However, by partitioning this large problem into multiple, smaller problems, and then assigning specialists to solve each of the subproblems, it is possible to design and implement a user interface in an efficient and timely manner.

2.2 CRITERIA DETERMINE DECISION PARTITIONING

There are many decisions that designers must make during the design of a user interface. As with any complex decision-making process, it is useful to partition the set of decisions into classes and concentrate on the decisions in each class, seperately. A *design decision framework* consists of a collection of design decision classes. When decisions in each of the design decision classes are combined, an overall design is synthesized. The following criteria may be used for identifying and constructing decision classes.

Separability. Decisions in each class can be identified and separated from one another. Criteria for establishing design decision classes include the following:

- Design decisions specified at different times can be placed into different classes. For example, the information content of messages between the user and the computer can be (and should be) specified before the representation format, display techniques, and input techniques of the messages are specified.
- Design decisions specified by different individuals can be placed into different classes. If the skill and training needed to make decision A are different from the skill and training needed to make decision B, then A and B may be placed into different classes. For example, a dialog designer may specify the message content, while a graphics artist may specify the display and input formats. Several different individuals acting in different roles may be involved in making decisions in the various decision classes. These roles were described in Section 1.7.

Completeness. All necessary decisions fit into some decision class.

Sufficiency. The set of decisions assigned to a class should be large enough to justify a class separate from the other classes.

Understandability. The set of decisions assigned to a class should be small enough so the choices and their impact on the user interface can easily be understood by the human mind.

Independence. The impact of decisions in each class on decisions in the other classes should be minimized. Decisions made in one class should be isolated from decisions made in other classes.

Reusability. Many of the choices made in a decision class for one application can be applied to the corresponding decision class in other applications. Making the same choices in corresponding decision classes increases the uniformity of user interfaces across multiple applications.

Soundness. There is a sound formal basis on which decisions in the class can be made.

This chapter describes a framework consisting of five design decision classes. Sections 2.3 and 2.4 describe these five classes, and Section 2.5 evaluates this framework of design decision classes.

2.3 USER INTERFACE DESIGN DECISIONS ARE PARTITIONED INTO CLASSES

User interface design decisions can be partitioned into several classes. One useful user interface design decision framework consists of the following five classes:

1. Structural
2. Functional
3. Dialog
4. Presentation
5. Pragmatic

Decisions made in the structural and functional classes determine the end users' conceptual model. Decisions made in the dialog decision determine the dialog style. Decisions made in the presentation and pragmatic classes constitute a refinement of the end users' conceptual model and dialog style which can be realized on the available I/O devices such as mouse, keyboard, and screen.*

We will use an example of an automatic teller machine to illustrate the types of decisions made in each decision class of this framework. In this example, a bank customer requests the withdrawal of some funds from a bank account by interacting with a machine called an automatic teller machine (ATM). The bank customer must supply an account number and the amount to be withdrawn from that account. For each decision class, first we will describe the types of decisions to be made, and then illustrate example decisions for the ATM application.

1. Structural decision class. In the structural decision class, the application analyst specifies the structure of the end users' conceptual model. These specifications include a description of the conceptual objects that are consumed, produced, and/or accessed by end users and application functions. These specificatioins also include a description of constraints and relationships that hold among conceptual objects. In this text, we will use the term *end users' conceptual model* to refer to objects in the application domain and the functions which may be applied to them. We will not include application-independent objects such as windows, menus, and other interaction objects that are often part of the user interface. These objects will be added to the conceptual

---

*This is not the only possible decision framework. Foley and VanDam (1990) suggested four levels in the design of a user interface: conceptual, semantic, syntactic, and lexical classes. These levels are frequently used by linguists to describe properties of natural language, and are thus sometimes referred to as the linguistic model for user interface dialogs. [Buxton (1983) partitioned the Foley and VanDam lexical level into two levels, called lexical and pragmatic levels.]

model to form the user interface when decisions about the presentation aspects of the user interface are made.

In the ATM example, the application analyst determines that the customer's account and the banking transaction are two conceptual objects. The customer's account object contains two other objects: account number and balance. The transaction object contains both the date and amount-disbursed objects. The account and transaction conceptual objects are related as follows: each account may be associated with several withdrawals, while each withdrawal must be associated with exactly one account.

2. Functional decision class. In the functional decision class, the application analyst specifies functions (operations), which the user can apply to the conceptual objects. In this class, the application analyst specifies the meanings of functions, but not their format or sequence of invocation. Functional decisions determine what requests the users can express and what results the application functions can present to the user. Functional design includes

- Enumeration of the functions which users may apply to the conceptual objects
- Description of information required to invoke each function
- Description of information produced during the execution of each function
- Description of each possible error which might occur during the execution of each function and the manner in which each error can be resolved

In our ATM example, the application analyst determines that several functions are needed: check, which verifies if a value for account number is valid; withdraw, which debits the account by the amount the user wishes to withdraw; and disburse, which actually disburses cash to the bank customer. To withdraw funds from an account, the bank customer must supply his or her account number and the amount of funds to be withdrawn. If the operation is completed, the user receives cash equal to the amount of the withdrawal. The conditions under which the withdraw operation will fail are enumerated:

- The value for the account number is not valid.
- The funds in the customer's account are less than the amount the customer wishes to withdraw.

If a failure condition is encountered, an appropriate error message is displayed to the bank customer, and no cash is disbursed.

(In a real ATM application, the customer may be required to enter a secret password or other information to verify that he or she is indeed the owner of the account. Also, the ATM may refuse to give cash to any bank customer who has failed to enter an acceptable withdrawal amount after, say, three tries in one day. To keep our example simple, we have omitted this complexity.)

3. Dialog decision class. In this decision class, the dialog designer specifies the content and sequence of information exchanged between the user and applications. In effect, the dialog designer specifies the dialog style. Three important types of decisions are made in this decision class.

- What the units of information exchanged between the user and applications are.
- How these units of information are structured into messages exchanged between the user and applications.
- What the appropriate sequences of message exchange are.

Semantic Tokens. In order to define the concept of a semantic token, we first define the concept of a lexical token. (Lexical tokens are specified as part of the next decision class, the lexical decision class.) A *lexical token* is a keystroke, mouse movement, or mouse click entered by the user or a character, icon, or elementary sound presented to the user. The term "lexical" comes from compiler theory where it originally referred to the symbols or alphabet that make up a computer language. Here we have extended the meaning to include iconic symbols which are displayed on a screen and which the user may manipulate to formulate requests. Individual lexical tokens may be meaningless to a user or an application. However, several lexical tokens can be grouped together to form a semantic token that is meaningful to the user and the application.

A *semantic token* is the smallest unit of information exchanged between the user and applications that can have a formally defined meaning. A semantic token consists of one or more lexical tokens. A semantic token cannot be divided into its lexical tokens and still be interpreted by users and applications meaningfully. Semantic-token decisions concern the content and not the form of the information as entered by the user or as displayed to the user.

The *semantic-token size* is the amount of information contained in each semantic token. Some semantic tokens may be quite large. For example, a single semantic token may contain a command name and several parameter values. Alternatively semantic tokens may be quite small. For example, a command name and each of its parameters may be represented by a separate semantic token.

In this decision class, the dialog designer determines the size of each semantic token obtained from and presented to the user, and the size of each semantic token obtained from and delivered to an application. The dialog designer also determines transformations among user-oriented semantic tokens and the corresponding application-oriented semantic tokens if they are of different sizes or contents.

In the ATM example, the dialog designer determines that the bank customer will enter the account number and amount semantic tokens, which will be delivered to the application functions check, withdraw, and disburse. The application functions, check, withdraw, and disburse, generate semantic tokens to be presented to the user. The content of each of the application generated semantic tokens has the following meanings:

- The account number is valid.
- The account number is not valid.

- There are sufficient funds in the customer's account for the withdrawal.
- There are not sufficient funds in the customer's account for the withdrawal to occur.
- The withdrawal request has been canceled.
- The withdrawal request has been completed.

The following semantic tokens will be presented to the user as prompts:

- Enter account number.
- Enter the amount to be withdrawn.

Messages.   A script specifies the content of messages transmitted between the user and applications. Each message must contain at least one semantic token. Some messages may contain several semantic tokens. For example, the following message:

```
Enter the account number and amount to be withdrawn
```

actually contains the two semantic tokens:

```
Enter account number
```

```
Enter the amount to be withdrawn
```

Likewise, the user may supply messages consisting of multiple semantic tokens. For example, if a command style of dialog is being used, the user may enter, as a single message, the withdraw command and both the account number and amount.

Sequencing.   This is the degree to which the user is forced to exchange semantic tokens with the application in some predefined sequence. Sometimes the application requires that tokens be entered or displayed in a specific sequence. Other applications consume several semantic tokens at the same time. These semantic tokens can be entered by the user in any arbitrary sequence. The dialog designer determines if a sequence is necessary and what that sequence is.

For example, the dialog designer determines that the account number must be entered before the amount. The possible sequences of semantic tokens exchanged between the bank teller and the bank customer constitute a script described by the following steps:

1. The ATM displays semantic tokens representing a welcome message and prompting the customer to enter his or her account number.
2. The customer enters a semantic token consisting of an account number, which is redisplayed to the customer.
3. If the account number is not valid, an error message token is displayed to the customer.
4. If the account number is valid, the customer is prompted to enter the amount to be withdrawn.

5. The customer enters a semantic token consisting of the amount to be withdrawn, which is redisplayed to the customer.

6. If the amount to be withdrawn is larger than the customer's account balance, a semantic token containing an appropriate error message is displayed to the customer.

7. If the amount to be withdrawn is less than or equal to the customer's account balance, a semantic token is displayed to the customer telling him or her that the account has been debited, the value of the new account balance, and how much cash is being given to the user. The cash is also disbursed to the customer.

8. Finally, a semantic token is displayed to the user indicating the end of the dialog.

4. Presentation decision class. In this class, the dialog designer chooses interaction objects which make up the end users' interface. Informally, *interaction objects* are visible objects on a screen which the user manipulates to enter lexical tokens and which the user views to obtain lexical tokens. Examples of interaction objects include menus, command boxes, data boxes, and icons. Interaction objects provide a technique for using a physical input device such as a mouse, keyboard, tablet, or rotary knob to enter a value or command along with the feedback that appears on the screen. Other terms sometimes used for interaction object are *interactor, control,* and *interaction technique.* Interaction objects present semantic tokens to the users by deploying a set of lexical tokens which the user interprets as semantic information from the application. Some interaction objects present lexical tokens to the user in the form of sounds such as rings, buzzers, musical tones, or even synthesized speech.

Interaction objects also obtain semantic information from the user who enters lexical tokens into the interaction objects in the form of keystrokes, mouse movements, and lever movements. Some interaction objects accept voice utterances (speech recognition) and hand gestures.

In the presentation decision class, the dialog designer, often with help from a graphics artist, makes decisions such as the following:

• The visual representation of interaction objects. Graphic designers design the size, shape, color, and font types of visible interaction objects.

• The location of visible interaction objects with respect to other visible interaction objects.

Audio artists may assist the script designer to design audio lexical tokens (sometimes called ''earcons'') consisting of various sounds.

In the ATM example, the dialog designer determines that two interaction objects will be used in the user interface: a message box and a data box. All messages are displayed to the user in the message box. Each piece of information is entered by the user into the data box. The dialog designer specifies the lexical symbols for each semantic token exchanged between the application and the bank customer. Some of these specifications might include the following: The welcome message is ''Welcome to the automatic bank teller.'' The prompt to the customer for entering his or her account number is "Please enter your account number." The account number is a sequence of three digits. The message indicating the end of the dialog is "Goodbye."

The presentation decision class deals with the appearance of the user interface. Many of the decisions of this class can be represented graphically.

5. Pragmatic decision class. This decision class deals with issues of gesture, space, and hardware devices. Often these decisions are determined by the hardware designers in conjunction with ergonomics specialists. Pragmatic decisions include the following:

- Does the user enter semantic tokens by pressing sequences of keys on a QWERTY keyboard or by pressing special function keys?*
- Does the user select options from a menu by using a keyboard to enter the number corresponding to his choice, touch the desired choice displayed on a touch-sensitive screen; point a light pen to his or her choice on the screen; or move a cursor to his or her choice by using a joystick, tablet, mouse, track ball, or step keys?

In our ATM example, the bank customer enters all semantic tokens by pressing numbered buttons on a keypad similar to a touch-tone telephone keypad.

Another Example. To illustrate decisions in each class, consider the example of turning a piece of equipment on and off.

The structural decision class consists of an object which we will call a switch which can be in two states: "on" and "off."

The functional decision class consists of two functions:

1. turn on, which is applicable only when the switch is in the "off" state. The equipment becomes operational when the user performs turn on.
2. turn off, which is applicable only when the switch is in the "on" state. The equipment becomes nonoperational when the user performs turn off.

The dialog decision class describes the possible sequence of commands. In this case, the user turns on the equipment, which becomes operational; later the user turns the equipment off, and it becomes nonoperational. This sequence may be repeated an arbitrary number of times. Note that in this dialog, it is impossible to turn on the equipment if it is already operational, and impossible to turn it off if it is already nonoperational.

In the presentation decision class we choose the vocabulary used by the user to enter the turn on and turn off commands. Possible vocabularies include

- the commands, On and Off,

*The QWERTY keyboard is the standard used on most English-oriented keyboards. The name QWERTY comes from the first five letters above the "home" position of the left hand.

- two icons, one representing turn on and the other turn off,
- two physical positions of a hardware switch.

In the pragmatic decision class, the designers choose the hardware for entering commands and displaying messages. If On and Off commands are to be used, the designers might include two special On and Off keys for entering the two commands. If icons are to be used, the designers might determine that the icons are selected by moving a mouse and clicking the left button on the mouse. If a physical switch is to be used, the designers determine the location, orientation, and type of physical switch.

2.4 HELP, PROMPTING, AND ECHOING PROVIDE THE USER WITH CONTEXT

The third, fourth, and fifth decision classes each involve decisions about prompting, feedback, and help.

Prompts A prompt is a message displayed to the user which reminds or encourages the user to perform some action. Prompts inform the user of what actions are appropriate and when to perform those actions. Dialog designers specify prompts as they make decisions in each of the last three decision classes:

- *Dialog prompts.* In this decision class, the dialog designer determines if and when the user should be prompted for each semantic token to be entered. These prompts may consist of textual messages to the user which explain the meaning of the semantic token that the user should enter.
- *Presentation prompts.* In this decision class, the dialog designer determines if and when the user should be prompted to enter each of the lexical symbols which collectively form a semantic token. Lexical prompts may consist of automatic movement of the cursor to the next position so that the user can enter the next lexical symbol. Lexical prompts may also show the currently allowable options available to the user, perhaps in the form of a menu.
- *Pragmatic prompts.* In this decision class, the dialog designer determines if and when the user should be prompted with instructions about how to use the system's input and output devices to enter lexical symbols. Pragmatic prompts are sometimes used to train a novice user in using hardware, for example, how to select menu options using a mouse.

Feedback Feedback is a message which confirms the acceptability of entered information.

- *Dialog feedback.* Dialog feedback indicates that a semantic token entered by the user is acceptable. For example, after an end user enters the command *delete file13*, the message "deleting file13" is displayed, or a wrist-watch or hour-glass is displayed indicating that the end user's command is being processed.

- *Presentation feedback.* Presentation feedback indicates that a lexical token is accepted. For example, an option selected from a menu is highlighted by brightening, changing color, displaying using reverse video, surrounding by a box, or using some other method to show the option has been selected. As the end user enters each character or digit via a keyboard, the character or digit is displayed on a screen. This type of feedback is sometimes called "echoing."

- *Pragmatic feedback.* Pragmatic feedback indicates that the user has successfully manipulated the hardware to enter information. For example, the pressing of a key on a keyboard results in a clicking sound. The movement of a mouse is reflected by the movement of the cursor on the screen.

It is possible for a feedback message and the following prompt message to be combined into a single message. For example:

- *Dialog feedback and prompts.* The display of a menu of options can indicate both that the previous entry has been accepted (feedback) and that the user should now select one of the options from the dialog menu (prompt).

- *Presentation feedback and prompts.* The letter which the user enters via a keyboard is displayed on the screen (feedback) and the cursor is repositioned following the displayed letter (prompt indicating enter another letter).

- *Pragmatic feedback and prompts.* The movement of a mouse is reflected by the movement of the cursor on the screen, which in turn indicates that the user may move the mouse again.

Help Help messages are displayed when requested by the end user. Help messages may also be displayed automatically during error processing. Help messages can be specified within each of the last three design decision classes.

- *Dialog help.* Help messages in this decision class describe the purpose of application functions and the meanings and effects of each of the semantic tokens to be entered by the user or displayed by the system.

- *Presentation help.* Help messages in this decision class describe how lexical symbols are combined to formulate valid semantic tokens, for example, descriptions of currently valid options associated with a partially entered command.

- *Pragmatic help.* Help messages in this decision class describe how to use the hardware available to enter or select lexical symbols.

2.5 THE DECISION CLASSES FORM A USEFUL FRAMEWORK

How well do the five decision classes of the framework we have presented satisfy the criteria for partitioning suggested in Section 2.2? Some of the criteria are satisfied better than others.

Separability Different individuals make decisions for each class. A person skilled in data modeling develops the end users' conceptual model of objects and their relationships. The meaning of each of the functions is specified formally by a person with a background in formal function specification techniques. A human factors specialist is a good candidate for specifying aspects of sequencing and prompting and other dialog properties. An individual who understands the capabilities of a terminal or workstation and the software that operates the terminal may be in the best position to specify the lexical decisions. Pragmatic decisions are best made by individuals trained in hardware design and ergonomics.

Independence Decisions made in latter decision classes can often be changed without affecting decisions made in earlier decision classes. For example, the manner in which the user constructs a command (pragmatic decision class) can be changed without changing the lexical form of the command itself.

Sufficiency and understandability The number of decisions in each class appears large enough to justify the existence of that class, yet small enough so that the effects of decisions made in any one class can be understood by the person making those decisions. (The boundaries between adjacent decision classes are sometimes fuzzy. What one individual interprets as dialog may be viewed as presentation by another. Designers often choose arbitrary boundaries which may vary from application to application rather than argue exactly where each boundary should fall for general cases.)

Reusability Decisions made in earlier decision classes are the most application dependent and may need to be modified before being reused in another application. For example, the end users' conceptual models of two applications might overlap only slightly, and thus little reusability is possible. Decisions made in latter decision classes are less application dependent and may frequently be reused. For example, the manner in which users construct semantic tokens can be used across several applications. Such commonality is desirable because it makes the user interfaces to multiple applications more consistent.

Completeness Experience suggests that all necessary decisions fit into one of the five decision classes, even though in which decision class they fall may on occasion appear arbitrary.

Soundness With the exception of techniques from database normalization theory and software design theory for formulating and validating the conceptual model, formal theories for formulating decisions in each decision class do not exist. However, there are several formal techniques available for documenting the results of decisions in each decision class.

- Formal techniques for specifying semantics can be used to specify the operations and functions in the functional decision class.
- Techniques from language theory can be used to determine and specify the semantic tokens in the dialog decision class.

- Several formal techniques, including state transition diagrams, context-free grammars, constraint-based techniques, and multimodel techniques can be used to describe decisions made in the dialog decision class. These techniques are reviewed in Chapters 7 through 11.
- Techniques from compiler theory can be used to describe the lexical aspects of interaction objects used to capture information from the user. These techniques can be extended to describe lexical aspects of interaction objects used to display information to the user.

It is quite conceivable that additional design aspects will be recognized as researchers and practitioners in user interface design, specification, and implementation techniques gain more experience and insight. The framework should be flexible and able to accommodate future enhancements.

2.6 SUMMARY

A "divide and conquer" approach can be applied to the problem of designing user interfaces. User interface design decisions can be partitioned into the following five classes:

The structural decision class defines the conceptual objects consumed, produced, and accessed by the end user. The functional decision class defines the functions and their parameters which the user can invoke. The dialog decision class defines the style of interaction between the user and application, including the nature and sequence of information exchanged. The presentation decision class specifies the form and appearance of information. The pragmatic decision class specifies how the user uses physical devices to enter and observe information. Help, prompting, and feedback decisions exist in each of the dialog, presentation, and pragmatic decision classes.

3

End Users' Conceptual Model

This chapter discusses

- What an end users' conceptual model is.
- What notation to use to specify a conceptual model.
- What the components of a conceptual model are.
- Why a conceptual model is important.

3.1 THE CONCEPTUAL MODEL FORMS THE BASES FOR USER INTERFACES

Before a person can drive a car, he or she needs to understand some basic functions about how to drive. The person needs to be familiar with objects such as steering wheel, brakes, gear shifts, and off-on switches. The person needs to understand what happens when he or she turns the steering wheel left, presses his or her foot on the brake, changes gears, and turns on the windshield wipers. These concepts and functions constitute the driver's conceptual model of how to use the car. Application software users need a similar model of the objects and functions they can perform.

The *end users' conceptual model* consists of a description of the functions which the user can perform and the objects to which those functions apply. The end users' conceptual model is the result of decisions made by the application analysts about the structural and functional decision classes, the first two of the five decision classes described in Chapter 2.

The car designer builds a blueprint describing the objects within the car and how they relate to each other. Software developers need a similar blueprint of the software they develop. The *application conceptual model* is developed by application analysts to describe the implementation of the objects and functions in the end user's conceptual model. The application conceptual model frequently contains additional objects and functions that are part of the application's implementation but which the end user cannot directly access or perform. We will leave the problem of specifying the application conceptual model and the design and implementation of the application functions to texts on general software engineering. In this chapter, we will concentrate on the end user's conceptual model and its representation.

An understanding of end users' conceptual model is vital to the end user. User documentation should describe the end users' conceptual model. With this information, the end user should be able to accomplish the following:

- *Understand the application in terms of the objects and relationships with which the end user may interact*. The end users' conceptual model contains the application specific terms and concepts used by the end user when interacting with the application. Without these terms and concepts, it is difficult for an end user to understand the application and its use to perform meaningful tasks.
- *Predict the future*. After understanding the end users' conceptual model, the end user should be able to predict what the application's response will be when he or she invokes a function.
- *Interpret the results*. The user must understand the conceptual model in order to interpret the results of an application and apply those results to the task at hand.
- *Find causes for displayed information*. The end user will be able to explain why the application produced a displayed result.
- *Develop plans*. The end user should be able to construct sequences of operations which lead to obtaining the desired result.

A well-constructed end users' conceptual model helps users to understand what applications can do and how to use the applications.

The end users' conceptual model describes classes of objects which end users view and manipulate using the user interface. The objects are not real objects that the user can touch and hold, but instead represent objects, events, concepts, persons, and ideas from the domain of the application which the end user can observe and manipulate via the user interface.

Example 3.1

The conceptual model of a typical word processing application contains classes of objects such as documents, paragraphs, sentences, words, and characters. Users may create, modify, and delete these objects using functions provided by the word processor. Users conceptualize what the computer does and how they interact with the computer in terms of these objects and functions. ∎

The end users' conceptual model is one of the results of analyzing the tasks which users must perform to achieve the goals of an application. This process, known as task analysis, should be performed for each proposed application. Briefly, it contains the following three steps:

1. Identify the goals to be achieved when using the application. Develop criteria for determining when each goal is achieved.
2. Identify the functions performed by the user to achieve each goal. Verify that the functions to accomplish the goal according to the criteria developed in step 1.
3. For each function identify

   - the object produced when performing the function,
   - the objects required to perform the function.

From this set of objects and functions we will construct the end users' conceptual model. Note that the objects and functions should be in the application domain and should not refer to window management functions and objects such as scroll bars, window open and close buttons, and window resize and repositioning functions. These objects and functions are part of the windowing system which will be constant across all applications.

The end users' conceptual model includes the following:

- Objects which are presented to the end user and the object classes to which they belong
- Relationships between pairs of objects and the relationship classes which contain these relationships
- Functions which the end user can apply to objects and relationships
- Constraints on applying functions to objects and relationships

The following criteria can be used for determining what constitutes a useful end users' conceptual model.

Sufficiency.   All of the application-specific information needed by end users is described in the conceptual model. An end user can accomplish goals by applying sequences of functions to objects in the end users' conceptual model.

Necessity.   Each class in the conceptual model is needed to describe some object or relationship important to the user. Each object class is referenced by some function.

Understandability.   The classes and functions are easy to learn, easy to use, and easy to understand by the end user. The conceptual model can be used to convey quickly the description of the objects and relationships, functions, and constraints among designers and end users. Each function must be precisely defined so that it can be clearly understood by the end user who will not be surprised at the results of performing the function.

Independence.   Each construct (object class, relationship class, function, or constraint) in the end users' conceptual model can be modified with minimal changes required to other constructs in the conceptual model.

Reusability   The objects and the relationship classes in the end users' conceptual model of an application can be reused in the end users' conceptual models of similar applications.

Consistency.   Each function is applied consistently across all applicable objects and relationships. It is important that the user perform the same activity involving different objects in the same manner. This makes learning the system easier because the user can apply what he or she has learned in one situation to similar situations.

Minimality.   No two pairs of classes in the conceptual model describe the same object or relationship. Keeping the number of classes and operations as small as possible has two advantages: there are fewer functions which the user must learn and remember, and there are fewer functions which the implementer must design and implement.

Orthogonality.   Each function is used to accomplish a different task. Two functions do not perform the same activity. The activities performed by one function cannot be accomplished by one or more other functions.

Compatibility with general software design methodologies.   Both the end users' conceptual model and the application model should use similar concepts and notations. Much of the design of the end users' conceptual model is the by-product of applying general software design methodology.

Implementability.   It must be possible to design and implement user interfaces based on the conceptual model within the time and resources available.

3.2 A METAMODEL DESCRIBES END USERS' CONCEPTUAL MODELS

We need terminology to describe structural aspects of end users' conceptual models. A *metamodel* is a modeling technique which contains a set of terms which designers use to describe the object classes and relationships in conceptual models.

There are many possible metamodels (Webster, 1988). The reader may already be familiar with metamodels such as entity relationship diagrams (Chen, 1976) and conceptual graphs (Sowa, 1984). Metamodels differ in the degree and manner in which objects, relationships, and constraints are described.

It is possible to use English, German, or some other natural language as a metamodel for describing the conceptual models. A natural language is easy to use because the application analyst is already familiar with it. However, natural language descriptions can be quite lengthy and are often ambiguous. Except for the most simple conceptual models, most designers have abandoned natural languages for more precise specification techniques.

There is yet no widely used metamodel to describe end users' conceptual models. The metamodel described in this chapter is a synthesis of constructs from other metamodels which the author has found useful for describing end users' conceptual model. This metamodel is based on the concepts of object-oriented modeling. We will, however, apply some techniques from database modeling theory to develop conceptual models which have desirable properties.

Rather than present the metamodel using a keyword-oriented syntax, we will use a graphlike notation to represent object classes and relationships which are easy for humans to draw and comprehend. This graphical notation must, of course, be converted into strings of symbols if it is to be used by user interface tools for analysis and code generation.

3.3 CONCEPTUAL OBJECTS REPRESENT REAL-WORLD OBJECTS

A conceptual object is data which represents a single person, entity, concept, idea, or event. In the end users' conceptual model, we will be interested only in conceptual objects that are visible to the end user. Thus, the end users' conceptual model will contain only objects which are transmitted between the end user and application functions. Either the end user enters information about the conceptual object using the user interface, or the end user interface presents information about the conceptual object to the user.

Example 3.2

> In a banking application, each customer's account is an object which represents the amount of money which the bank holds on behalf of the customer. Information from the customer's account can be displayed to the customer, who may modify that information. Each transaction is an object which represents the deposit or withdrawal of some of the customer's money from the account. Users enter transactions and thereby change information about their accounts. Accounts and transactions are objects in the end users' conceptual model. ∎

A *simple conceptual object* consists of a type and a value. The *type* describes a domain of possible values which the simple object may assume. The *value* is an encoding of information which characterizes the object. Some designers use the term *attribute* or *field* to refer to a simple conceptual object. Figure 3.1 illustrates the graphical representation of some simple conceptual objects. Each object is represented by an oval.

Several objects may have the same type but different values. The term *object class* is used to refer to all of the objects with the same type. Figure 3.2 illustrates several object classes. Object classes are represented by rectangles containing the type name of objects in the class.

Example 3.3

> The banking application has the following simple object classes:
>
> • AccountIdentifier, which assumes the value of the identification number of the account

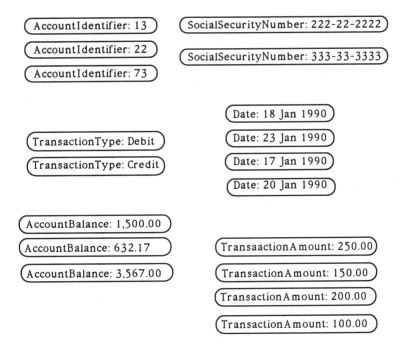

Figure 3.1 Simple objects.

- TransactionType, which assumes the value of either "Credit" or "Debt," depending on whether the transaction is a deposit or withdrawal
- TransactionAmount, which assumes the value of the deposit or withdrawal which the bank customer performs
- SocialSecurityNumber, which assumes the value of the customer's social security number
- Date, which assumes a value which represents a calendar date
- AccountBalance, which assumes the dollar value of the account which the bank holds on behalf of the customer ∎

To distinguish object class names from functions, we will adopt the following conventions: The type name is used as the object class name. The first letter of each word in the object class name is capitalized. No blank spaces are used to separate words making up a name. Function names will begin with a lowercase letter.

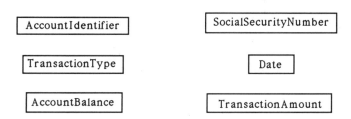

Figure 3.2 Object classes for the simple objects of Figure 3.1.

Simple objects are used to describe individual information units which can be exchanged between a user and an application by a user interface. However, many conceptual objects consist of several such units of information. *Composite conceptual objects* relate multiple conceptual objects together.

Example 3.4

An Account object is formed by relating the AccountIdentifier, SocialSecurityNumber, AccountBalance, and Transaction objects. A Transaction object is formed by combining the TransactionAmount, Date, and TransactionType objects. Figure 3.3 illustrates three Account objects and four Transaction objects. One Account object has value 13 for AccountIdentifier, 222-22-2222 for the value of the customer's SocialSecurityNumber, and 500.00 value for AccountBalance. Another Account object has value 22 for AccountIdentifier, 222-22-2222 for the value of the customer's SocialSecurityNumber, and 632.17 value for AccountBalance. Both these accounts belong to the same customer. A third Account object, belonging

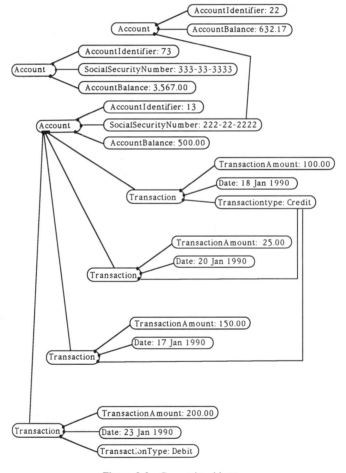

Figure 3.3 Composite objects.

to a different customer, has value 73 for AccountIdentifier, 3,567.00 for AccountBalance, and 333-33-3333 for SocialSecurityNumber. Also shown in Figure 3.3 are four transaction objects. Each of these transaction objects is related to the Account object with Account-Identifier 13. ■

We will use an arc with a circular dot at the end to indicate a commonly used relationship called *IsPartOf*. Generally, we read the name of the object at the end of the arc without the dot, then the relationship name IsPartOf, and finally the name of the object at the end of the arc with the dot. For example, the top relationship in Figure 3.3 is read ''AccountIdentifer IsPartOf Account.'' Other names used for this relationship include ''Is AttributeOf'' and ''BelongsTo.'' We will use an are with a small black rectangle at the end to indicate another commonly used relationship called IsMemberOf. We will discuss relationships further in Section 3.4.

Composite objects also form classes. Figure 3.4 illustrates the Account and Transaction composite object classes and their relationships to the simple object classes of Figure 3.2.

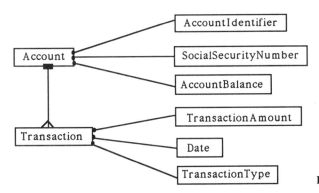

Figure 3.4 Complex object classes.

Objects in end users' conceptual models should satisfy the following two properties:

P1. Each object is uniquely identified.

P2. Each simple object has at most one value.

Each object is uniquely identified   If it is important enough to be an object, then it is important enough to have a unique identifier. In order for the user to manipulate an object, the user must be able to identify the object to be manipulated. Even if the user selects the object from a menu, it still must be uniquely identified so that functions can be applied to it.

The type-value pair of each simple object uniquely identifies the simple object. This implies that two simple objects of the same type must have different values.

Composite objects may be identified by the composition of one or more of its component objects. For example, each Transaction object is identified by the composition of values for Date and AccountIdentifier (assuming that a bank customer can submit at most one transaction per day).

Each simple object has at most one value   If a simple object has more than one value, then we need functions to manipulate each of the values separately. Such commands might include

- Insert a value into the *n*th position.
- Delete a value from the *n*th position.
- Interchange the values in the *n*th and *m*th position.

We will avoid this complexity with simple objects by requiring that each simple object have exactly one value. Figure 3.5 illustrates two approaches for dealing with a simple object with multiple values.

- Grow the object class so that it is related to several new object classes. For example, in Figure 3.5, the PersonName object class is grown into a composite object relating three new object types, LastName, FirstName, and MiddleInitial.
- Grow the object class so that it is related to a new object class with multiple objects.

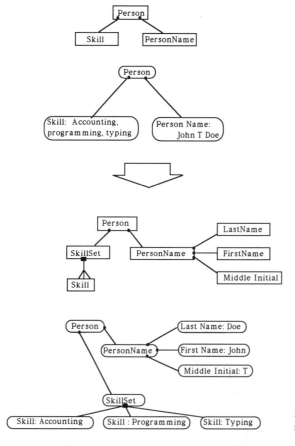

Figure 3.5 Growing an object into several different objects.

For example, in Figure 3.5, the Skill object class is grown to a composite object class, SkillSet, which contains multiple Skill objects.

Figure 3.5 illustrates another convention which we will use in this text. The set of object classes and their relationship classes are at the top of the illustration and one or more examples of individual objects and their relationships are at the bottom of the illustration.

3.4 RELATIONSHIPS DESCRIBE ASSOCIATIONS AMONG OBJECTS

Objects by themselves are not enough to capture the structural aspects of the end users' conceptual model. Relationships describe associations among objects. Relationships are useful for reasons including the following:

- Relationships describe the structure and organization of objects. End users need to understand the object structure in order to use the application.
- Relationships may imply constraints among objects. For example, if Wheel IsPartOf Bicycle and Bicycle is deleted, then Wheel also should be deleted.
- Relationships may reduce the apparent complexity of the end users' conceptual model. An object may inherit information from some other related objects. Inherited information is represented only once rather than replicated multiple times.

A *relationship* is a typed association between two objects. Each relationship is represented by an arc connecting the two related objects. We have already seen two types of relationships, IsPartOf and IsMemberOf. There may be many other types of relationships among objects.

Like objects, relationships also form classes. A relationship class contains relationships of the same type which relate objects from two object classes. Each relationship class has a name and a special type of arc to represent it (sometimes we use labels on arcs to distinguish between relationships of different classes.) Relationship classes have several properties.

P3. Each object class which participates in a relationship class may be total or partial.

P4. Each relationship class may be one to one, many to one, or many to many.

P5. Each relationship class has an implicit, equivalent relationship class in the opposite direction.

Each of these properties is discussed in greater detail in the paragraphs that follow.

Total and Partial. Let A and B be object classes and R be a relationship class which relates objects from A to B. If each object in A is related to some object in B, then A is said to be *total* with respect to the relationship R. If some objects in A are not related to any object in B, then A is said to be *partial* with respect to the relationship R.

Figure 3.6 illustrates a relationship class that is both total and partial. If it is possible for an employee to work for a company without being assigned to a department, then

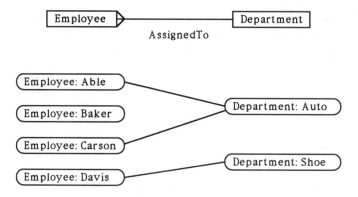

Figure 3.6 Partial relationship class. Employee is partial with respect to AssignedTo. Department is total with respect to AssignedTo.

Employee is partial with respect to AssignedTo. If each Department must have at least one Employee assigned to it, then Department is total with respect to AssignedTo.

One-to-one, many-to-one, and many-to-many relationship classes Let A and B be the names of two object classes. Let R be the name of a relationship class which contains relationships between objects in A and objects in B. R is said to be *one-to-one* if no object in A is related to more than one object in B and no object is B is related to more than one object in A.

Example 3.5

> Let CentigradeTemperature and FahrenheitTemperature be two conceptual object classes. Let the relationship class SameTemperature contain relationships between CentigradeTemperature objects and FahrenheitTemperature objects. Because each CentigradeTemperature corresponds to a single FahrenheitTemperature and each FahrenheitTemperature corresponds to a single CentigradeTemperature, the relationship class SameTemperature is one-to-one. ∎

If R is a relationship between A and B, then R is said to be *many-to-one* if no object in A is related to more than one object in B and an object in B may be related to more than one object in A. We will use three small lines to form a "hen's foot" or "broom" at the end of an arc to denote which object class is the "many" part of the relationship.

Example 3.6

> As illustrated in Figure 3.6, the AssignedTo relationship relates Employee objects from the Employee object class to Department object for which the employees work. Each Department may employ several Employees, but each Employee works for at most one Department. The AssignedTo relationship class is many-to-one. ∎

R is said to be *many-to-many* if an object in B may be related to more than one object in A and an object in A may be related to more than one object in B.

Example 3.7

> Let Student and Course be two object classes and Registered be a many-to-many relationship between objects in Student and Course. As illustrated in Figure 3.7, each Student may be

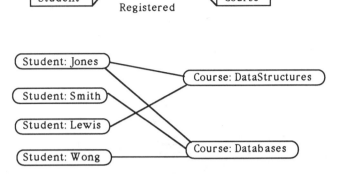

Figure 3.7 A many-to-many relationship class.

registered in several Courses. Several Students may register in each Course. Registered is a many-to-many relationship class. ∎

Usually we try to avoid many-to-many relationship classes because dealing with them is difficult. Any many-to-many relationship class can be replaced by two many-to-one relationship classes as follows.

If R is a many-to-many relationship class between object classes A and B, then we create a new object class, C, and two many-to-one relationship classes: R_1 from C to A and R_2 from C to B. For each relationship in R between a_i in A and b_j in B, we create a new object c_{ij} in C with a relationship from c_{ij} to a_i in R_1 and a relationship from c_{ij} to bj in R_2.

Example 3.8

The many-to-many relationship Registered of Figure 3.7 can be replaced by two many-to-one relationships, BelongsTo and EnrolledIn, and a new object class, Registration, as illustrated in Figure 3.8. ∎

Equivalent relationships The names of many relationships often imply a direction. For each such relationship there is usually another, equivalent relationship with a name that implies the opposite direction, for example, the pairs of relationships IsPartOf and Contains, IsParentOf and IsChildOf, and IsA and Generalizes. We will consider each such pairs of relationships as a single relationship and use one of the two names. Thus, rather than deal with the two eqivalent relationships IsPartOf and Contains, we will use just the single relationship, IsPartOf.

Famous relationship classes Many types of relationships are possible. Figures 3.9 and 3.10 illustrate three types of relationships which occur frequently in end users' conceptual models: IsPartOf, IsA, and IsMemberOf relationships. We now examine these relationships in detail.

IsPartOf relationship IsPartOf relationship is illustrated by a line with a dot at the end; it is frequently used to characterize an object by describing its parts. For example,

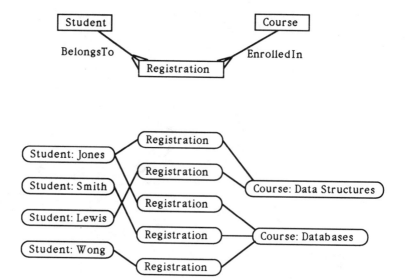

Figure 3.8 Total relationship classes. Student and Registration are total with respect to EnrolledIn. Course and Registration are total with respect to Offered.

in Figure 3.9, an Account is characterized by its parts, SocialSecurityNumber, AccountIdentifier, and AccountBalance.

IsA relationship Object classes can often be placed in a hierarchy of IsA relationships, illustrated by a double line with an arrowhead. The head of the arrow indicates the more general object. The relationship is read by first saying the name of the

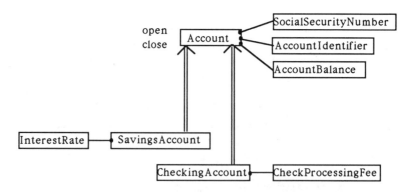

Figure 3.9 Object classes and relationships.

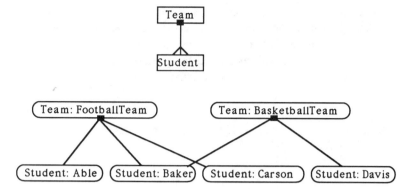

Figure 3.10 Example IsMemberOf relationships.

object at the tail of the arrow, followed by "IsA," and finally the name of the object at the head of the arrow. CheckingAccount IsA Account implies that each CheckingAccount object is also an Account object; SavingsAccount IsA Account implies that each SavingsAccount is also an Account object. The Account object class is more general and is thus higher in the hierarchy. In Figure 3.9 CheckingAccount and SavingsAccount are specializations of Account, and thus are related to Account by IsA relationships.

Inheritance simplifies the conceptual model in that relationships that are shared by objects related by an IsA relationship are expressed only once, within the parent object (at the head of the arrow), and are automatically inherited by the children objects (objects at the tail of the arrow) via the IsA relationship. In Figure 3.9, the CheckingAccount object class is related to four object classes

- CheckProcessingFee
- SocialSecurityNumber
- AccountIdentifier
- AccountBalance

The last three IsPartOf relationships are inherited from Account. Similarly, the SavingsAccount object class is related to four object classes

- InterestRate
- SocialSecurityNumber
- AccountIdentifier
- AccountBalance

Again, the last three IsPartOf relationships are inherited from Account.

IsMemberOf relationship   This relationship is used to indicate which objects are members of a set. We will use a small rectangular dot to represent the object type acting as a set. For example, Figure 3.10 illustrates four Student objects and two objects which represent sets, FootballTeam and BasketBallTeam. Three Students belong to the FootballTeam and two Students belong to the BasketballTeam.

Relationships between objects in the same object class deserve special consideration because they are often represented by special interaction objects. Special properties of these types of relationships are described in Appendix A.

3.5 FUNCTIONS DESCRIBE WHAT THE END USER CAN DO WITH APPLICATIONS

Functions are the basic operations which the user may perform on objects in the conceptual model. Functions enable users to manipulate conceptual objects in order to solve problems. Constraints specify when a function is applicable and describes the conditions under which it can be applied. We will use a keyword-oriented notation to represent functions and constraints because most application analysts use keyword notation for this purpose.

Users may perform functions or operations on conceptual objects. Categories of functions include the following:

- *Construction functions*. Functions which create a new object in an object class or create a new relationship in a relationship class are construction functions, and often perform initialization of object values.
- *Destruction functions*. Functions which destroy or remove existing objects from object classes and destroy or remove relationships from relationship classes are destruction functions.
- *Save functions*. Functions which make objects permanent are save functions. Permanent objects will continue to exist after the user has quit using the current application.
- *Retrieve functions*. Functions which retrieve objects made permanent during the earlier execution of an application are retrieve functions, and may involve query and browsing operations.
- *Transformation functions*. These functions perform transformations on objects, often producing new objects or sets of objects. While construction, destruction, save, and retrieve functions may be supported by an underlying database management system or file system, application-specific transformation functions are usually designed and developed specially for each application.

In a conceptual model, we often position the name of the function by the principle object to which it is applied. For example, Figure 3.11 illustrates that the apply function (a transformation function which modifies Account based on Transaction information) is associated with the Transaction class and that open and close (creation and distribution functions) are applied to the Account class.

Each function has a name and zero or more parameters. We will adopt the following naming conventions: The name of each function begins with a lowercase letter; The name of each parameter will begin with a capital letter.

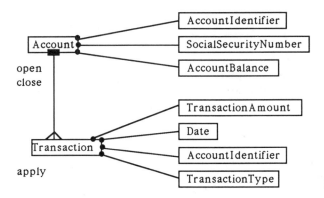

Figure 3.11 Conceptual model classes.

We will use a formal notation to describe functions. This notation will be useful when generating error and help messages. Because some end users may find this notation awkward to use, a more English-like version may be more appropriate for the user documentation. Associated with each function is a set of *preconditions*, statements about objects in the object class which must be satisfied before the function can be performed. Also associated with each function is a set of *postconditions* which must be satisfied after the function is performed. Preconditions will be used in the generation of error messages for presentation to the user when a function cannot be executed. Postconditions will be used in the generation of help messages which explain the purpose and effect of a function to the user.

Example 3.9

Figures 3.12 and 3.13 illustrate the preconditions and postconditions associated with the three functions in Figure 3.11. The names of each parameter associated with a function begins with

```
open ($AccountIdentifier, $SocialSecurityNumber)

Precondition: There does not exist an Account object whose
value for AccountIdentifier is equal to $AccountIdentifier.

Postcondition: There exists an Account object whose
AccountIdentifier = $AccountIdentifier and
SocialSecurityNumber = $SocialSecurityNumber and
AccountBalance = 0.00.

close($AccountIdentifier)

Precondition: There exists an Account object whose
AccountIdentifier = $AccountIdentifier and AccountBalance =
0.00.

Postcondition: There does not exist an Account object whose
AccountIdentifier = $AccountIdentifier.
```

Figure 3.12 Preconditions and postconditions for open and close functions.

```
apply($AccountIdentifier, $Date, $TransactionAmount,
$TransactionType)
```

```
Precondition: There exists an Account object whose
AccountIdentifier = $AccountIdentifier. If
$TransactionType is ''WITHDRAW'' then the value of
AccountBalance of the Account with AccountIdentifier =
$AccountIdentifier must be greater than or equal to
$TransactionAmount.
```

```
Postcondition: There exists a Transaction whose
AccountIdentifier = $AccountIdentifier, Date = $Date,
TransactionAmount = $TransactionAmount, and TransactionType
= $TransactionType. If $TransactionType is ''DEPOSIT'' then
$TransactionAmount is added to AccountBalance of the Account
with AccountIdentifer = $AccountIdentifier. If
$TransactionAmount is ''WITHDRAW'' then $TransactionAmount is
subtracted from AccountBalance of the Account with
AccountIdentifier = $AccountIdentifier
```

Figure 3.13 Preconditions and postconditions for apply functions.

a dollar sign ($). Figure 3.12 illustrates the pre- and postconditions associated with functions which can be applied to Account objects. The open function creates a new Account object in the Account class. A value for AccountIdentifier must be supplied when an open function is invoked. The single precondition requires that the value of AccountIdentifier of Account to be created cannot already exist in some other Account object in the Account class. If another Account object already has this value, then an error message will be generated. Another precondition requires that the user supply a value for the SocialSecurityNumber object. The postconditions indicate AccountBalance will have a default value of 0.00.

The close deletes an existing Account object from the Account object class. The only value which must be supplied to perform the close function is for AccountIdentifier. The precondition requires that AccountBalance must have a value of 0.00 before the account can be closed. An error message will be generated informing the user that an account with funds left in it cannot be closed. The postcondition indicates that the Account object identified by the value for AccountIdentifier no longer exists after performing the close function.

Figure 3.13 illustrates the preconditions and postconditions associated with functions which can be applied to Transaction objects. The apply function causes a new transaction to be created whose value for AccountIdentifier is the same as that for some Account object in the Account class and adjusts the value of Balance of that Account object. ∎

Functions are also inherited from the parent of an IsA relationship to its child. For example, in Figure 3.9, the functions open and close are inherited by SavingsAccount and CheckingAccount from Account.

3.6 END USERS' CONCEPTUAL MODELS CLARIFY APPLICATIONS

We have already seen an example of a conceptual model. Figure 3.11 illustrates the object classes and relationship classes in the end users' conceptual model for the ATM example. Figures 3.12 and 3.13 describe the pre- and postconditions for each function. Actual objects and relationships at a point at a time are illustrated in Figure 3.3.

Figure 3.14 illustrates another example end users' conceptual model for an application involving a home control unit. A small computer will be used to control various devices in a house, including temperature, radio, intercom, telephone, and various home security mechanisms such as heat, smoke, and motion detectors.

The Label object contains the names of each device which can be controlled by a home owner from the home control unit. The Use object indicates whether a device is in use or not. These devices may take on the values of On or Off. Use is not related to

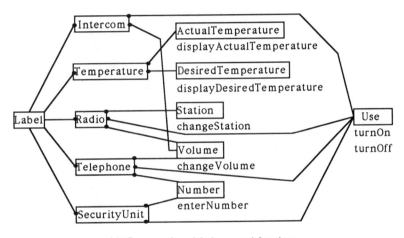

(a) Conceptual model classes and functions

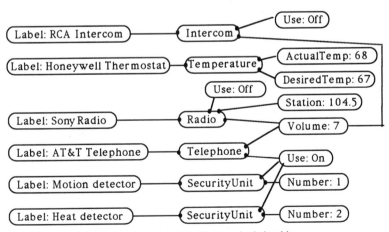

(b) Conceptual model objects and relationships

Figure 3.14 Conceptual model.

Temperature because this device is always on. The Volume object contains a value indicating how loud or quiet the volume should be. Volume is related to Intercom, Radio, and Telephone because the home owner can change the volume for each of these devices. The Number object is a sequence of digits which represents either a telephone number or the identification number of some security device. The home owner may enter a value for Number. The pre- and postconditions for each function are defined as follows:

```
function turnOn()
       precondition: Set = Off
       postcondition: Set = On

function turnOff()
       precondition: Set=On
       postcondition: Set=Off

function displayActualTemperature ()

function: enterDesiredTemperature($Temperature)
       precondition: 35 degrees < $Temperature and
                       $Temperature < 105 degrees
       postcondition: DesiredTemperature = $Temperature

function changeStation ($Station)
       precondition: 700 < $Station and $Station < 1500
       postcondition: Station = $Station

function changeVolume ($Volume)
       precondition 1 ≤ $Volume and $Volume ≤ 10
       postcondition: Volume = $Volume

function enterNumber ($Number)
       precondition: 0000000 < $Number and $Number < 9999999
       postcondition: Number = $Number
```

Because both the radio and telephone cannot be used at the same time, we have the following constraints:

```
constraint: Telephone.Set = On → Radio.Set = Off
constraint: Radio.Set = On → Telephone.Set = Off
```

Now let's use the criteria of Section 3.1 to evaluate this conceptual model.

- *Sufficiency.* All the function names and parameters of the application functions are present in this end users' conceptual model.
- *Necessity.* All object classes are used or seen by the end user. It can be argued that Label information is not needed, but in this case we will assume that the device vendors insist that their brand names be displayed as labels.
- *Understandability.* This conceptual model is probably as simple to understand as possible given the set of functions the home owner can invoke.

- *Independence*. The use of Radio and Telephone interfere with each other, but this is in the nature of the application and thus should be represented as constraints in the end users' conceptual model. Otherwise, the functions are independent of each other.
- *Reusability*. It is likely that other devices used in the home can be modeled using objects in this end users' conceptual model. For example, the conceptual models for controlling an oven, range, and refrigerator can reuse the Temperature and Use objects. The end users' conceptual model for controlling the television may include Volume, Use, and Number objects.
- *Consistency*. The same functions are used on multiple objects. For example, the turnOn and turnOff functions are used uniformly on all composite objects except Temperature, which cannot be turned on or off by the home owner.
- *Minimality*. Again the high reusability results in a minimum number of general-purpose functions such as turnOn and turnOff.
- *Orthogonality*. No two functions can be used for the same purpose.
- *Compatibility with general software design methodologies*. This compatibility depends on the exact notation used for the end users' conceptual model and the notation and concepts embodied within the general software design methodology.

It may be possible to make some improvements to an end users' conceptual model. Appendix B introduces several conceptual model transformations which may be used selectively to improve end users' conceptual models.

The end users' conceptual model is a concise representation of what operations end users may perform and what the parameters of those operations are. It provides a vocabulary to the end user for describing and performing tasks using the application. After understanding the end users' conceptual model, end users should be able to determine what can and cannot be done with the application.

3.7 SUMMARY

A metamodel is used to describe end users' conceptual models. Using a metamodel, system analysts describe object classes, relationship classes, functions, and constraints.

Each object is uniquely identified. Each simple object has at most one value. Each object class which participates in a relationship class may be total or partial. Each relationship class may be one-to-one, many-to-one, or many-to-many. Each relationship class has an implicit, equivalent relationship in the opposite direction.

Functions are used to construct new objects; create, save, retrieve, and destroy existing objects; and transform objects into other objects. Constraints describe the conditions under which functions may be applied. Many constraints can be described using pre- and postconditions.

Users must understand the end users' conceptual model in order to use the application. The end users' conceptual model should be described in user documentation for the application. The end users' conceptual model will form the basis of the application's user interface.

4

Dialogs and Scripts

This chapter discusses

- What a dialog is.
- How scripts describe dialogs.
- What the responsibilities of a script execution engine are.
- What types of information are exchanged during a dialog.
- What the types of scripts and dialogs are and what they describe.
- How to evaluate script specification techniques.

4.1 SCRIPT EXECUTION ENGINES CONTROL SEMANTIC TOKEN EXCHANGE

This chapter discusses the concepts of dialogs and scripts. A *dialog* is a sequence of information tokens exchanged between two or more agents. In general, an agent may be an interaction object or an application function. A *script* is a program which controls the exchange of semantic tokens among agents. A *script execution engine* is a processor that executes a script to control how and when semantic tokens are exchanged among application functions and interaction objects.

A dialog is the specific ordering of a set of semantic tokens exchanged during the execution of a script. A different dialog may result each time the script execution engine executes a script. Irrespective of whether the script execution engine is a stand-alone component or embedded within the application, the script execution engine may perform the following functions:

- *Translating*. The script execution engine accepts user-oriented semantic tokens from interaction objects and translates them to application-oriented semantic tokens for delivery to application functions. It also accepts application-oriented semantic tokens from application functions and translates them into user-oriented semantic tokens for delivery to interaction objects.

Example 4.1

The script execution engine may accept semantic tokens entered by the user into an electronic form interaction object and translate those semantic tokens into a database command to be transmitted to a database management system. ■

- *Routing*. The script execution engine may accept semantic tokens from interaction objects and applications, and route or transfer them to other interaction objects and applications.

Example 4.2

The sequence of semantic tokens to "compile source code," "link source code," and "execute source code" are routed, respectively, to the compiler, the linker, and the loader/initiator. ■

- *Combining*. The script execution engine may accept several semantic tokens and combine them into a single semantic token.

Example 4.3

The user enters several tokens, each containing a value for a parameter needed by an application program. When the script execution engine has collected all the necessary parameters, it constructs a single token containing all the parameter values needed by an application function and then invokes that function and passes the semantic token to it. ■

Example 4.4

A database management system may return a semantic token for each individual record retrieved from the database. The script execution engine bundles the records together into a single semantic token to be presented to the user via a table interaction object. ■

- *Expanding*. The script execution engine may accept a single semantic token and expand it into several semantic tokens.

Example 4.5

An application function generates a semantic token indicating that it successfully completed execution. The script execution engine receives this token and generates two tokens, one is displayed to the user reporting that the application function has completed, and the second contains intermediate results which are transmitted to the next application function within a sequence of application functions to be invoked. ∎

Example 4.6

A database management system generates a semantic token consisting of a file of data to be displayed to the user. The script execution engine partitions the semantic token into several semantic tokens, each consisting of a page of data to be displayed to the user. ∎

Example 4.7

The user enters a token to invoke an application function. The script execution engine builds two tokens, one to be sent to the application function causing it to begin execution and one to be displayed to the user containing the feedback message "application invoked." ∎

- *Planning.* Given a single semantic token, the script execution engine may generate a plan consisting of sequence of semantic tokens to be exchanged among several applications and interaction objects.

Example 4.8

Given a semantic token containing the instruction to calculate a person's retirement benefits, the script execution engine develops a plan to (1) access the employee's personal file, (2) execute an analysis program using information from the employee's personal file and generates raw retirement information, and (3) execute a graphic package function to formulate and display the person's retirement benefits. ∎

As the foregoing examples illustrate, a script and the script execution engine which executes the script can be very complex, performing transformations, routing, combining, expanding, and planning. Often the script execution engine invokes special auxiliary functions to perform some of these functions. These special auxiliary functions may include compilers, parsers, macro processors, command translators, encoders, decoders, and optimizers.

4.2 A SCRIPT DESCRIBES SEVERAL POSSIBLE DIALOGS

We will concentrate on the dialog style aspects of script description without becoming entangled with the physical aspects of the terminal or workstation. Avoiding the device-dependent aspects of script description is accomplished by considering semantic tokens delivered to and from application functions and interaction objects.

We will define the term *semantic dialog* as a sequence of semantic tokens exchanged between interaction objects and applications. There are four ways in which semantic tokens can be exchanged.

1. Semantic token entered by the user via some interaction object
2. Semantic token presented to the user via some interaction object
3. Semantic token generated by an application function
4. Semantic token consumed by an application function

Figure 4.1 illustrates how semantic tokens are exchanged between users and application functions. User-oriented semantic tokens are entered by the user and displayed to the user via interaction objects. Application-oriented semantic tokens are delivered to application functions and generated by application functions.

Each input parameter required by an application function is a semantic token which the script execution engine obtains from the user via an interaction object or is generated from other semantic tokens obtained from the user via interaction objects. Each output parameter generated by an application function is a semantic token which is consumed by another application function as an input parameter, presented to the user via an interaction object, or combined with other semantic tokens by the script execution engine to generate a new semantic token which is presented to the user or used by an application function.

4.2.1 Example dialogs

We will consider the semantic dialogs involved when a banking customer withdraws cash from an ATM. We will assume that a preexisting set of functions is used during a cash withdrawal. The check function verifies that the account number entered by the bank customer is valid. The withdraw function verifies that there are sufficient funds in the account for the withdrawal and calculates the new account balance. The disburse function causes cash to be delivered to the customer via a slot in the ATM.

Four possible banking customer–ATM semantic dialogs are illustrated in Figure 4.2. In semantic dialog A, the customer decides not to withdraw any cash. In semantic dialog B, the customer fails to enter a valid account number. In semantic dialog C, the customer attempts to withdraw more cash than there are funds in his or her account. Finally, semantic dialog D illustrates a dialog resulting in the successful withdrawal of funds. The four dialogs of Figure 4.2 can be described by a single script controlling the exchange of semantic tokens between the banking customer and the ATM.

As illustrated in Figure 4.2, different semantic tokens are exchanged in various circumstances. A script describes any of several possible dialogs which can occur during a conversation between a user and one or more applications. The same script may result in different dialogs, depending on values of semantic tokens supplied by the user and generated by the applications. The four dialogs of Figure 4.2 all result from executing the same script.

Some semantic tokens contain values for variables. The script execution engine obtains values for these variables from the user as is the case for $AccountNumber and $Amount and from application programs as is the case for $NewBalance. The script execution engine is able to remember variable values and use them in semantic tokens which it constructs.

Each of the semantic dialogs in Figure 4.2 is device independent. Nothing is specified about the format or position of information displayed to the bank customer, and nothing is specified about the manner in which the user enters values for the input variables.

Each of the semantic dialogs in Figure 4.2 is also application independent. The implementation of each application function (check, withdraw, and disburse) is hidden from the script execution engine. Any function could be rewritten and, as long as its input and output parameter types do not change, the script does not need to change.

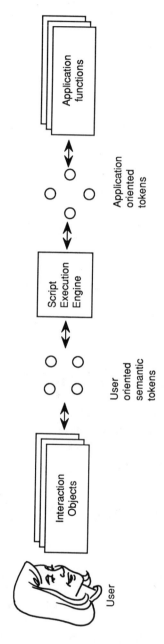

Figure 4.1   Semantic tokens are exchanged between the user and application functions.

```
1. UI to USER:     present ('Welcome to the ATM.
                   Please enter your account
                   number.')
2. USER to UI:     enter ($AccountNumber)
3. UI to check:    check ($AccountNumber)
4. check to UI:    return('Ok')
5. UI to USER:     present ('Enter the amount you wish to
                   withdraw.')
6. USER to UI:     enter ($Amount)
7. UI to USER:     present ('To confirm that you wish to
                   withdraw', $Amount, 'from account',
                   $AccountNumber, 'enter "Yes". If not,
                   enter "No".')
8. USER to UI:     enter ('No')
9. UI to USER:     present ('Your request has been
                   canceled. Goodbye.')
```

(a) Dialog A (user cancels request)

```
1. UI to USER:     present ('Welcome to the ATM.
                   Please enter your account
                   number.')
2. USER to UI:     enter ($AccountNumber)
3. UI to check:    check($AccountNumber)
10. check to UI:   return ('Fail')
11. UI to USER:    present ('The account number',
                   $AccountNumber, 'does not exist. Your
                   request has been canceled. Goodbye.')
```

(b) Dialog B (bad account number)

```
1. UI to USER:        present ('Welcome to the ATM.
                      Please enter your account
                      number.')
2. USER to UI:        enter ($AccountNumber)
3. UI to check:       check ($AccountNumber)
4. check to UI:       return ('Ok')
5. UI to USER:        present ('Enter the amount you wish to
                      withdraw.')
6. USER to UI:        enter ($Amount)
7. UI to USER:        display ('To confirm that you wish to
                      withdraw', $Amount, 'from account',
                      $AccountNumber, 'enter "Yes". If not,
                      enter "No".')
12. USER to UI:       enter ('Yes')
13. UI to withdraw:   withdraw ($AccountNumber, $Amount)
```

(c) Dialog C (insufficient funds)

Figure 4.2 Four dialogs between a blank customer and an ATM.

Sec. 4.2   A Script Describes Several Possible Dialogs

```
14. withdraw to UI: return ('Fail')
15. UI to USER:      present ('There are not sufficient funds
                     in your account to withdraw', $Amount,
                     'Your request has been canceled.
                     Goodbye.')
```

(c) Dialog C (insufficient funds) (continued)

```
 1. UI to USER:      present ('Welcome to the ATM.
                     Please enter your account
                     number.')
 2. USER to UI:      enter ($AccountNumber)
 3. UI to check:     check ($AccountNumber)
 4. check to UI:     return ('Ok')
 5. UI to USER:      display ('Enter the amount you wish to
                     withdraw.')
 6. USER to UI:      enter ($Amount)
 7. UI to USER:      display ('To confirm that you wish to
                     withdraw', $Amount, 'from account',
                     $AccountNumber, enter "Yes". If not,
                     enter "No".')
12. USER to UI:      enter ('Yes')
13. UI to withdraw:  withdraw ($AccountNumber, $Amount)
16. withdraw to UI:  return ($NewBalance)
17. UI to disburse:  disburse ($Amount)
18. disburse to UI:  return ('Ok')
19. UI to USER:      display ($Amount, 'has been withdrawn
                     from your account. Your new balance
                     is', $NewBalance. 'The money will appear
                     in the slot to the right of the screen.
                     Thank you. Goodbye.')
```

(d) Dialog D (successful withdrawal)

Figure 4.2 (continued)

It is possible to replace an application by a user without modifying the script. This might be desirable, for example, if the script is designed before the applications are implemented. In our example, a human bank teller would take the role of the check, withdraw, and disburse functions. In this way, a script can be tested and debugged before the application functions are developed.

It is also possible to replace a user by a function without modifying the script. This might be desirable, for example, if an application is developed to act on behalf of a user. In our example, the application would be an electronic funds transfer system which would communicate with the ATM. Replacing the user with a function may also be useful for exhaustive testing of application function code.

4.2.2 Dialog Viewpoints

There are several viewpoints to a dialog, including

- the user's viewpoint, which includes only the semantic tokens exchanged with the user. For semantic dialog D, this viewpoint contains the following:

```
1. UI to USER:      present ('Welcome to the ATM.
                    Please enter your account
                    number.')
2. USER to UI:      enter ($AccountNumber)
5. UI to USER:      display ('Enter the amount you wish to
                    withdraw.')
6. USER to UI:      enter ($Amount)
7. UI to USER:      display ('To confirm that you wish to
                    withdraw', $Amount, 'from account',
                    $AccountNumber, enter "Yes". If not,
                    enter "No".')
12. USER to UI:     enter ('Yes')
19. UI to USER:     display ($Amount, 'has been withdrawn
                    from your account. Your new balance
                    is', $NewBalance. 'The money will appear
                    in the slot to the right of the screen.
                    Thank you. Goodbye.')
```

While this viewpoint of semantic dialog D contains all of the semantic tokens entered or displayed to the user, it doesn't contain the semantic tokens exchanged with application programs. This viewpoint is of interest to end users, who only need to understand when they exchange semantic tokens with interaction objects.

- The application's viewpoint includes only the semantic tokens exchanged with applications. For semantic dialog D, this viewpoint contains the following:

```
3.  UI to check:      check ($AccountNumber)
4.  check to UI:      return ('Ok')
13. UI to withdraw:   withdraw ($AccountNumber, $Amount)
16. withdraw to UI:   return ($NewBalance)
17. UI to disburse:   disburse ($Amount)
18. disburse to UI:   return ('Ok')
```

This viewpoint describes all the semantic tokens exchanged among the applications but fails to represent the exchange of semantic tokens with the user. This viewpoint is of interest to application programmers, who need to understand when semantic tokens are transmitted to and and from application functions.

- The script execution engine's viewpoint includes all the semantic tokens exchanged with the end user and applications. These are exactly the dialogs shown in Fig. 4.2.

This viewpoint is useful to dialog designers because it is symmetric with respect to both users and applications.

For the rest of this chapter, we will take the script execution engine viewpoint.

4.2.3 Scripts May Permit Users to Retract Previously Entered Information Tokens

Occasionally a user will wish to retract information entered earlier during a dialog and undo any processing involving that information. There are two general approaches for supporting the backup and recovery from incorrectly entered information. Scripts may permit users to retract entered information in either of two ways:

- The user explicitly cancels the effect of the incorrect information by invoking a function which is the inverse of the function which produces the incorrect information. For example, if the user incorrectly executes a command which inserts a value into a database, then the user may execute the inverse of the insert command, the delete command, which removes the data from the database. In this approach, the user must explicitly issue inverse commands for each command being retracted.
- The user invokes the generic inverse function, undo, to cancel the effect of each operation performed by a script.

Some operations cannot be undone. These are operations which cause changes in the world outside of the system in which the script is executing. Examples include disbursing cash from an ATM, launching a missile, and sending or displaying a message to a user who takes action based on that message. Users should not be allowed to undo these types of actions using the generic inverse function, undo. Instead, users must perform the appropriate inverse function (if they exist) and make the corresponding changes to the real world.

Whenever a script executes an operation which cannot be undone, we say that script contains a *commit point*. The effect of operations performed prior to a commit point are considered permanent and cannot be retracted or undone unless their effect in the real world is also reversed.

4.3 DIALOG DESIGNERS SPECIFY SCRIPTS

The dialog designer performs the following three tasks:

- Design the application-oriented semantic tokens consumed and generated by application functions.
- Design the user-oriented semantic tokens consumed and generated by interaction objects.
- Design the mappings and transformations among these semantic tokens.

The dialog designer, system analyst, and application programmer jointly design the application-oriented semantic tokens. Often these semantic tokens are already specified as parameters to functions.

The dialog designer next determines the dialog style for the user interface. Each dialog style implies certain classes of interaction objects. The dialog designer then defines a set of generic interaction objects and the user-oriented semantic tokens which they consume and produce. Often existing interaction objects can be reused by modifying their appearance and behavior. The dialog designer specifies the user-oriented semantic tokens consumed and produced by the interaction objects.

(Some dialog designers design the script before designing the interaction object to be used by the dialog. Some dialog designers design the interaction objects first and then design the script. Other dialog designers intermix the design of interaction objects with script design. In this text, we have separated these two design activities so that we can study the problems involved with each separately. Merely because we present the problems of script design and interaction object design separately should not imply that dialog designers should always perform these tasks separately.)

Finally, the script designer specifies the mappings between the user-oriented semantic tokens and the application-oriented semantic tokens. This mapping may be fairly simple or quite complex, depending on the differences in the functions in the end user's conceptual model and the functions actually available by the underlying applications.

4.3.1 Order-Dependent Scripts

Many scripts require that semantic tokens must be exchanged in a specific sequence.

Example 4.9

In the ATM example, the user must enter a value for AccountNumber before entering a value for Amount. The reason for this is because the first function to be invoked—check—requires only a value for AccountNumber. Both AccountNumber and Amount semantic tokens are needed by the second function to be invoked, withdraw. ∎

Sometimes a script execution engine acts as a buffer, collecting semantic tokens before invoking application functions.

Example 4.10

In another version of the ATM script, the user enters either values for AccountNumber and Amount in either order. The script execution engine waits until both values are entered before invoking the check and withdraw functions. If either of these application functions returns an error, a message is displayed to the user. ∎

Scripts which hide the natural sequence of application function invocation from the user are generally more complex than are scripts which make that natural sequence of application function invocation visible to the user. A script which hides the sequence of application functions must accept semantic tokens from the user and store semantic tokens until they are consumed by application functions.

Whether the user perceives a user-directed or computer-directed user interface affects the sequencing of semantic tokens exchanges. User-directed dialogs generally consist of many individual semantic tokens entered in arbitrary sequences by the user, while computer-directed dialogs may have more fixed sequences of semantic tokens entered by the user.

The following steps outline one possible approach for designing a sequential script.

1. Identify the tasks which the user will perform. Continuing with our ATM example, the application analyst determines that the four major tasks to be performed by users are opening an account, closing an account, depositing funds into the account, and withdrawing funds from the account. We will consider only the withdrawing funds task in the remainder of this example.

2. For each task, determine all the functions in the end users' conceptual model which must be invoked to perform the task. Represent each function as a node in a graph. Represent each of the function's input parameters as an arc pointing to the node. Represent each of the function's output parameters as an arc pointing away from the node. In the ATM example, there are three functions, check, withdraw, and disburse. These functions are illustrated in Figure 4.3(a) as ovals. Input parameters have directed arcs pointing to the function and output parameters have directed arcs pointing away from the function.

3. Determine orderings among the functions. There are two types of orderings:

a. Identify each parameter which is output from one function and is input by another function. Connect the two corresponding arcs. The result is a data flow graph which shows how data flows among the functions. In the automatic banking example, there is no data flow among the three functions.

b. Examine the pre- and postconditions to determine natural orderings among the functions and insert these orderings into the graph as directed arcs. Figure 4.3(b) illustrates natural orderings for the ATM example by heavy arcs: (i) check to withdraw because the AccountNumber must be verified to be valid before the withdraw function can be invoked and (ii) withdraw to disburse because withdraw must verify that there are sufficient funds in the account before the disburse function can be invoked.

4. Determine what parameters should be supplied by and presented to the user. Parameters represented by arcs leading to a function and not connected to an output

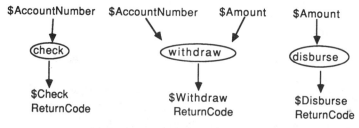

(a) Functions used in the ATM example

Figure 4.3 Design of a sequential script.

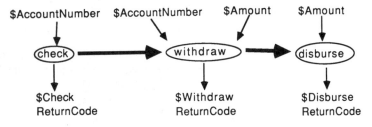

(b) Function orderings

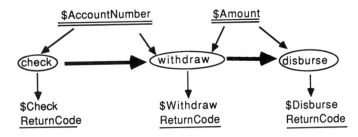

(c) Input and output parameters

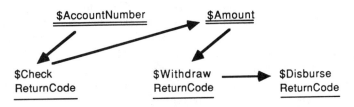

(d) Total ordering consistent with (c)

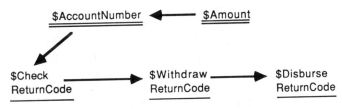

(e) Total ordering not consistent with (c)

Figure 4.3 (continued)

arc must be supplied by the user. In Figure 4.3(c) these parameters are underlined twice. The parameters represented by arcs leading from a function and not connected to an input arc are displayed to the user as results. In Figure 4.3(c), these parameters are underlined once. Some of the parameters represented by arcs which connect two functions may also be displayed to the user as intermediate values.

5. Determine a total ordering of parameter values supplied by and displayed to the user. Several options are possible, including the following:

    a. The total ordering of parameters supplied by and displayed to users is consistent with the partial ordering of parameters implied by the functions. Figure 4.3(d) illustrates a total ordering of parameters which is consistent with the partial ordering of parameters illustrated in Figure 4.3(c). Some of the values must be stored until all the input parameters needed by a function are available. The value of AccountNumber must be saved until the withdraw function is invoked.

    b. The total ordering of parameters supplied by and displayed to users is not consistent with the partial ordering implied by the functions. Figure 4.3(e) illustrates a total ordering of parameters which is not consistent with the partial ordering of parameters of Figure 4.3(c). The script must temporarily store parameter values until they are needed by a function whose execution is delayed until all its input parameters are available.

4.3.2 Order-Independent Scripts

Order-independent scripts permit the user to enter information in arbitrary sequences. For these scripts, the script execution engine must buffer semantic tokens and dynamically determine when to invoke application functions. In general, order-independent scripts consist of a case statement with conditions involving semantic tokens and the corresponding application functions to invoke when those conditions are satisfied.

Let $\{t_1, t_2, ..., t_i, ..., t_n\}$ be a set of points in a dialog during which the user may enter information or observe results. For each t_i, let v_i be the number of variables within a script for which the user may enter a value. Let w_i be the number of variables whose values can be presented to the user. Possible measures of the degree of order independence include the following:

$$\frac{\sum_{i=1}^{n} v_i}{n}, \quad \frac{\sum_{i=1}^{n} w_i}{n}, \quad \frac{\sum_{i=1}^{n} (v_i + w_i)}{n}$$

If the measure has the value of one, then the script produces an order-dependent dialog. The larger the measure, the greater the order independence of dialogs produced by the script.

To construct order-independent scripts, the dialog designer performs all the steps in the order-dependent methodology outlined except for step 5. Because step 5 is not performed, only a partial ordering of input and output parameters may be created. Usually the designer then uses a rule-based (Chapter 8) or multiagent (Chapter 9) specification technique to describe the conditions under which users can enter semantic tokens and the conditions under which semantic tokens are presented to the user.

4.4 EVENTS ARE PROCESSED ASYNCHRONOUSLY

Certain events, or interrupts, can occur at arbitrary times with respect to the processing of a dialog. Examples of such events include the following:

- The user signals a change of script.
- The user signals a request for a help message.
- An executing function returns intermediate status information to be displayed to the user.
- A concurrent process, such as a print routine, signals that the printer is out of paper.

Script execution engines vary in how they deal with asynchronous events. Possible approaches include

- Disregard all interrupts.
- Ignore all interrupts until the script has been executed.
- Process the interrupt at convenient points during the script.
- Immediately stop processing the script and respond to the interrupt.

The first approach is usually considered unsatisfactory. The next two approaches require that events be stored in a queue until they can be processed. The third approach requires that dialog designers indicate points in the script where the dialog can be suspended while events are processed.

The script itself may describe what action is to take place for each interrupt event. This is frequently accomplished with scripts specified using object-oriented and multiagent-model approaches (Chapter 9). The script itself may specify nothing about event processing. This approach is occasionally used when the script is specified using state transition systems (Chapter 6) and context-free grammars (Chapter 7). In these cases, the script execution engine, and not the script being processed, deals with each type of interrupt.

4.5 DIALOGS MAY BE MULTITHREADED AND CONCURRENT

While order-independent scripts permit the user to change interaction objects, users must continue within a single script. In *multithreaded* dialogs users are presented with more than one "thread" of interaction, allowing them to be involved in more than one task at a time. Users may switch among several scripts.

One of the most widely used examples of multithreading occurs in windowing systems. A script which controls a dialog between the user and some underlying application is associated with each window. Within an active window, the user exchanges information with an application according to the flow of control specified by the script associated with that window. Only one window may be active at any point in time. The user switches between scripts by making a different window active. Often this is done by moving a cursor to the window to be activated or explicitly selecting the window to be made active from a menu of inactive windows.

For another example of a multithreaded dialog, consider the windowing system again. The windowing system itself is an application with its own script. This script controls the placement of windows on the CRT screen and the enlarging, shrinking, stretching, overlying, activating, and deactivating of windows. The user switches from the dialog within the window to the windowing dialog by moving the cursor to the boarder of the window. By manipulating the various icons in the boarder of the window, the user interacts with the windowing dialog rather than with the dialog represented by the application within the window.

Let $\{t_1, t_2, ..., t_i, ..., t_n\}$ be the points during a dialog during which the user may enter information. For every t_i, let r_i be the number of scripts into which the user may enter a value, and s_i is the number of scripts which may present a value to the user. Possible measures of the multithreading are

$$\frac{\sum_{i=1}^{n} r_i}{n}, \quad \frac{\sum_{i=1}^{n} s_i}{n}, \quad \frac{\sum_{i=1}^{n} (r_i + s_i)}{n}$$

If the measure is one, then the dialog is single threaded. If the measure is large, then the user may be doing so much multithreading that he or she may have trouble maintaining the mental context for each dialog.

Some windowing systems even support the transfer of information between scripts if the user copies information from one window to a clipboard and then from the clipboard to another window. A *clipboard* is a memory buffer which can be accessed by multiple scripts. It provides a mechanism for dialogs to communicate with each other by sharing data in a clipboard.

A *concurrent dialog* is a multithreaded dialog in which more than one thread is being executed simultaneously. This is possible only if the underlying computer system can execute more than one thread at the same time. Usually, some form of multitasking or parallel processing is needed to accomplish this. A concurrent dialog represents concurrency from end user's point of view because the user can switch among multiple scripts. A concurrent dialog also represents concurrency from the system's point of view in that the system can process multiple threads of different scripts at the same time.

Concurrent dialogs are necessary when user interfaces support more than one stream of output for simultaneous presentation to the user. For example, the user interface displays an animation at the same time it replays an audio clip. Concurrent dialogs are also necessary if the user may enter information at the same time the user interface is presenting information. For example, the user enters answers to a series of questions while the user interface is playing background music and displaying the amount of time left for the user to complete his or her answers. Concurrent dialogs will be widely used in multimedia applications involving temporal data such as audio and video.

4.6 SCRIPT SPECIFICATION TECHNIQUES SHOULD SATISFY CRITERIA

Script representation techniques differ in the degree of dialog complexity which they can represent. Some representation techniques can represent only very simple dialogs. These representation techniques are themselves fairly simple. Script representation techniques used to describe complex dialogs are of necessity themselves fairly complex.

Chapters 7 through 11 present several different techniques for representing scripts. Associated with each representation technique is an execution engine which executes or interprets scripts and produces interactive dialogs. State transition descriptions (Chapter 7) and grammars (Chapter 8) are frequently used to describe simple, order-dependent dialogs. Rule- and constraint-based techniques (Chapter 9) and multiagent techniques (Chapter 10) are useful for representing multithreaded and concurrent dialogs. Chapter 11 discusses other approaches for representing scripts.

A script specification technique should meet as many of the following requirements as possible. We will use these criteria to evaluate each of the script representation techniques discussed in Chapters 7 through 11.

- *Sequencing, multithreading, and concurrency.* The script specification technique should support the description of (1) order-dependent and order-independent dialogs, (2) single-threaded and multithreaded dialogs, and (3) concurrent and nonconcurrent dialogs.
- *Understandability.* The script specification technique should be easy to understand. Little effort should be required to learn and recall how to use the specification technique. There should be no doubt as to the behavior of any dialog resulting from executing the script.
- *Sound formal basis.* The model used for script representation should support well-defined properties on which algorithms for validating and processing dialogs can be based.
- *Reusability.* Common parts of a script specification can be specified once and shared among the remainder of the script specification.
- *Executability.* It should be possible to construct a prototype automatically from the specification. Software should exist that can interpret the specification and produce dialogs for evaluation.
- *Familiarity.* The script specification technique should be as similar to the dialog designer's mental model of the script as possible. The dialog designer should spend as little effort as possible to convert his or her mental model of the script into the notation used to describe the script.
- *Perspicuity.* The notation can be used to develop insight into the user interface.
- *Inconsistent and incomplete specification detection.* The dialog designer should be able to enter incomplete specifications. It should be possible to detect incomplete and inconsistent specifications.
- *Measurability.* The complexity of the script specification can be used as a measure of the complexity of the corresponding dialogs which it describes. It should be possible to evaluate dialogs from their script specification.

- *Backup and recovery*. It should be possible to cancel or undo a sequence of operations not containing a commit point.
- *General control constructs*. The script language should contain language constructs which control the sequential, conditional, and iterative execution of functions and the synchronization and data exchange within multithreaded dialogs.
- *Scalability*. The script language can be used to describe large and complex dialogs.

4.7 SUMMARY

A script is a program which controls the exchange of semantic tokens among interaction objects and application programs. A dialog results when a script execution engine executes a script. A script execution engine may perform transformation, routing, combining, expanding, and planning functions. The script execution engine may be embedded within an application module or may be a module separate from other application modules.

To design a dialog, the script designer determines the application-oriented semantic tokens consumed and generated by applications, the user-oriented semantic tokens consumed and generated by the user via interaction objects, and mappings among these semantic tokens. The script designer also determines the total or partial order in which these semantic tokens are accepted and presented to the user.

A script specification technique should satisfy several criteria. Script specification techniques include state transition systems, context-free grammars, rule-based techniques, and multiagent models.

5

Interaction Objects

This chapter discusses

- What interaction objects are and why they are important.
- What interaction objects do.
- What the major classes of interaction objects are.
- How to compose composite interaction objects.
- How to build, modify, and generate interaction objects.

5.1 END USERS USE INTERACTION OBJECTS TO MANIPULATE CONCEPTUAL OBJECTS

Users manipulate *interaction objects* to interact with applications. Interaction objects are also called widgets, interactors, and controls. Interaction objects can be viewed in different ways by individuals in different roles.

- *Definition 1 (for end users).* An interaction object is a mechanism with which the user interacts directly. The device may be visual (such as an icon on a screen or light on a control panel) or auditory (such as a bell, buzzer, or voice synthesizer). The user manipulates interaction objects using mechanical devices such as a keyboard or pointing devices such as mouse, joystick, track ball, or touch-sensitive pad. End users interact with interaction objects to enter both commands and data to the application which in turn supplies data which the interaction objects present to the user.

- *Definition 2 (for application programmers).* An interaction object is a software module which performs I/O to the end user on behalf of an application. For the application programmer, an interaction object is just a predefined software module which can be invoked to perform I/O functions.

- *Definition 3 (for system designers).* An interaction object is software and hardware components with which the end user communicates. System designers configure hardware devices such as CPU, storage devices such as disk drives, and various types of terminals and workstations. System designers configure software modules such as operating systems, database management systems, application packages, and user interface modules including multiple-interaction objects and possibly a script execution engine.

- *Definition 4 (for graphics and audio artists).* An interaction object is the physical representation of conceptual objects in the end users' conceptual model. The graphics artist designs several appearances for visual interaction objects to display in various situations. Audio experts design sounds for audio interaction objects to convey meanings to the user.

Figures 1.9 and 1.11 illustrated two ways in which interaction objects interact with application functions. In Figure 1.9, interaction objects make up the tool kit and interact directly with application functions. In Figure 1.11, interaction objects interact with a script execution engine which in turn invokes application functions. Whether there is a separate script execution engine or the dialog control is distributed among application functions, interaction objects are the user's gateways to the computational faculties of applications.

Two important aspects of interaction objects are appearance and behavior. Appearance may be specified graphically while behavior is usually specified textually, although recently some behavior has been specified "by demonstration" or "by example."

5.2 INTERACTION OBJECTS PERFORM SEVERAL FUNCTIONS

Chapter 5 discusses the use of scripts to control the exchange of information between users and application functions. Scripts can also be used to control the exchange of information between users and interaction objects. *Interaction object behavior* is controlled by a script which may perform any of several functions, including the following:

- Sensing
- Constraint enforcing
- Translating
- Transmitting
- Buffering
- Formatting
- Echoing
- Presenting

Each of these functions will be discussed in detail.

5.2.1 Sensing

Sensing involves detecting the end user's manipulation of an interaction object and interpreting the manipulation as information entered by the user. Users can perform a variety of gestures and actions using keyboards and keypads, pointing devices, levers, and switches. An *event* occurs whenever such a gesture or action is detected. Lexical tokens representing each event are generated by the device drivers and are placed on an *event queue*. Interaction objects examine the event queue for sequences of lexical tokens and transform them into semantic tokens which are then transmitted to the script execution engine or application.

The following illustrates how two different interaction objects sense different events yet generate the same semantic token for transmission to a script execution engine or application.

Example 5.1

The interaction object is a data box with the label "Enter 'OK' if you want the application to continue." The user presses the keys "O," "K," and "Carriage return" on a keyboard. The device driver detects these events, generates lexical tokens representing "O," "K," and "Carriage return" and transmits them to an interaction object, which translates these lexical tokens to a semantic token indicating that the user has approved the action. ■

Example 5.2

A menu of options is displayed to the user. The user moves the mouse causing the cursor to be repositioned to the "OK" option in the menu. The end user then clicks a button on the mouse. The click event is translated to lexical tokens representing, "cursor is repositioned to location (x, y) within the screen and user clicks select button on the mouse." These lexical tokens are then translated to the same semantic token as the previous example. ■

Some interaction objects also sense events which occur indirectly because of human actions. Suppose that interaction object A is partially hidden by interaction object B. If the user repositions interaction object B on the screen so that it no longer hides interaction object A, the window manager will generate an event for interaction object A informing it that its screen representation is no longer hidden and that it should redisplay itself so that the user can observe the complete interaction object.

5.2.2 Constraint Enforcing

Several types of constraints may need to be enforced. Some constraints are best enforced by applications. Other constraints are best enforced by the script execution engine. However, a large number of constraints can be enforced by interaction objects. This saves the costs of moving data and error messages between the interaction object and the script execution engine or application. However, enforcing constraints within interaction objects do make the design and implementation of interaction objects more complicated.

One technique for enforcing constraints is rule processing. A rule processor examines the input string and verifies that a set of rules is satisfied. The rules may describe a variety of constraints, including

- Check the type of the entered value.
- Verify that the entered value is one of a set of values.
- Verify that the entered value falls within prespecified bounds.
- Verify that the entered value and other values satisfy a prespecified Boolean condition. For example, the value for HighSchoolGraduationDate is greater than the value of BirthDate.

Many interaction objects are designed to reference *callbacks,* application procedures called when some event occurs. Callbacks may enforce semantic integrity constraints, provide information needed to redisplay the interaction object, and check that the precondition of an application function are satisfied before the application is invoked. To minimize the communication costs between interaction objects and application functions, callbacks may be compiled and linked with the interaction object.

5.2.3 Translating

Suppose the user enters the sequence of lexical tokens

```
"select * from emp;"
```

which is an SQL database management system request to display all the columns of a table named emp. An interaction object might convert this sequence of lexical tokens into the following sequence of semantic tokens,

```
<keyword, select>
<keyword, *>
<keyword, from>
<table, emp>
<string, terminator>
```

which are passed to a database management system which in turn converts these semantic tokens into a series of calls to database management system subroutines.

Translating sequences of lexical tokens into sequences of semantic tokens is called *lexical analysis*. The software which performs lexical analysis is called a *lexical analyzer* or *recognizer*. Basically, the lexical analyzer examines sequence of lexical tokens for character patterns, extracts character strings which match these patterns, and then converts the extracted character strings into semantic tokens. A sequence of lexical tokens entered by the user which fails to be recognized by the lexical analyzer is rejected.

5.2.4 Formatting

Transformations may also occur between the form of data received by the interaction object and the form presented to the user. Formatting controls the changes in appearance of interaction objects in response to information received from the script execution engine or application program. The interaction object determines the exact wording, font type, or icons and generates the lexical symbols which are displayed to the user.

The information may be presented to the user using various media, including

- Text (including numbers and character strings)
- Graphics (including pictures, and charts)
- Sound (including alarms and voices)
- Full motion video

(Interaction objects which stimulate our other senses of touch and smell are technically possible but not widely used.)

5.2.5 Buffering

Buffering is necessary to bridge the gap between the speed with which end users enter or observe information and the speed with which computers perform calculations. Interaction objects act as buffers between end users and the script execution engine or application functions. Buffering acts as a type of flow control, collecting pieces of information until it is convenient to present them to the user or transmit them to the script execution engine or an application function. The data structure of the interaction object acts as a buffer or temporary storage structure for this information.

5.2.6 Transmitting

After users have finished entering and editing information into an interaction object, the user indicates that editing is complete by entering a *terminator,* which is a lexical token indicating that the user has completed manipulating the interaction object. The interaction object then transmits the information to the script execution engine or application function and the interaction object may be removed from the screen. Depending on the interaction object, many types of terminators are possible.

- *Command line interaction object.* A carriage return terminates the command.
- *Simple interaction object.* The process of selecting an option also terminates the interaction.
- *Document.* Save and quit commands cause information to be transmitted from the interaction object to the script execution engine or application function.

In addition to transmitting information from the user to the script execution engine or application functions, information is also transmitted in the opposite direction, from application functions to the interaction object which presents the information to the user.

5.2.7 Echoing

Each piece of information entered into an interaction object should be "echoed" or displayed to the user so that he or she can review and possibly edit it. All text editors echo each keystroke entered by the user by displaying the corresponding letter or number on the screen. For selection interaction objects, the appearance of the selected choice is modified in some way, often by replacing the bit map representing the selected option by another bit map in which it is highlighted or marked so that the user can see the option he or she just selected.

Interaction object classes Traditionally, interaction objects have been largely limited to visual representation. However, interaction objects should use as many of the human senses as possible to present information to the user. Multimedia can be used to increase the communication bandwidth between users and applications. In many situations, pictures can convey information faster than can text. Multiple channels of communication involving many of the human senses can increase and improve user application communication.

Interaction object specifications describe two major aspects: (1) presentation and (2) behavior, including constraints that the interaction object checks on data entry, the manner in which users enter either commands or data, and the resulting changes in the presentation of the interaction object.

There are many types of interaction objects and many interaction object taxonomies. We will use the taxonomy illustrated in Figure 5.1. This taxonomy is based on the interactive capabilities of interaction objects.

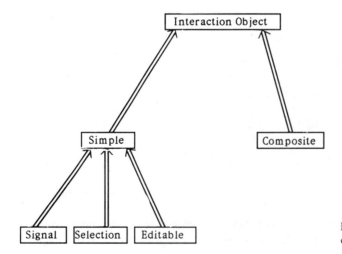

Figure 5.1 Interaction object classification.

Chap. 5   Interaction Objects

- *Signal interaction objects* transmit a predefined message between the end user and the script execution engine or an application function. Signal interaction objects can be classified as input, which the user uses to signal that a predefined message should be delivered to the dialog processor or application function, or output, with which the dialog processor or application function sends a predefined message to the user. An example of an input signal interaction object is a button. Examples of an output interaction object include error boxes, buzzers, blinking lights, and the replay of prerecorded verbal messages.

- *Selection interaction objects* are used to present a small number of choices to the user, who selects one of the choices. Selection interaction objects include radio buttons, toggle switches, and dials.

- *Editable interaction objects* accept information entered by the user using some type of editor such as a text editor or drawing tool. Editable interaction objects include command boxes, data boxes, and bit maps which the user can edit.

- *Composite interaction objects* contain two or more single selection, editable, and/or other composite interaction objects. Users may enter and/or select multiple values which may be buffered within the composite interaction object before being transmitted to the dialog processor or application function. For example, a fill-in form interaction object saves the values entered by the end user into each data box contained in the form and generates a structured record which is transmitted to the script execution engine or application function.

We will examine this taxonomy of interaction objects, starting with signals and proceed to composite interaction objects.

5.3 SIGNAL INTERACTION OBJECTS TRANSFER MESSAGES

Signal interaction objects may be either input or output.

5.3.1 Output Signals

Output signal interaction objects present informative, warning, or error messages to end users. Examples of output signal interaction objects include ringing bells; buzzers; blinking lights; and text, audio, and video messages. Figure 5.2 illustrates a state transition diagram for an output signal. The output signal may be in either of two states, Presenting, or NotPresenting. The output signal transitions from the NotPresenting state to the Presenting state if an application function or script execution engine sends it a Present message. The output signal transitions from the Presenting state to the NotPresenting state when it receives any of three messages:

- Remove from the user.
- Remove from an application function or script execution engine.
- Timeout from a timer mechanism.

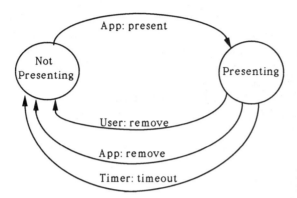

Figure 5.2 States of an output signal interaction object.

When the signal interaction object is in the Presenting state, it may have a visual appearance containing an informative, warning, or error message. It may have an audio presentation, or possibly both an audio and visual presentation. When the signal interaction object is in the NotPresenting state, it may not be visible, or if visible, the previously presented message should not be visible to the end user. (One of the most annoying implementation errors with signal interaction objects is when they continue to present out of date messages.)

Types of output signal interaction objects In addition to the display of textual and graphical information, audio and video output signal information objects are possible.

Audio. Prerecorded sounds may be stored and replayed. Some systems store and replay analog representations of sounds. This approach is not compatible with most digital storage techniques used by computers. An alternative approach is to convert sound to a digital representation for storage on traditional digital storage media. Sounds are produced by converting the digital representation back to analog form for presentation to the user via speakers.

Sounds may be synthesized by preparing a stream of bits which is interpreted by a synthesizer to produce appropriate sounds. The synthesizer may be used to produce nonverbal sounds such as buzzers, bells, sirens, and music, as well as synthesized speech. At least two techniques are used to produce human-like voices.

1. *Sampling and digitizing techniques.* An analog sound is captured by periodically recording samples of its waveform. The samples are digitized and stored. When playback occurs, the digitized bits are reconverted to analog sound waves. This type of audio is occasionally heard on the telephone: "The number you have reached, five, five, five, five, five, five, five, is not a working number." The vocabulary of such synthesizers is limited to the number of prerecorded words and phrases. Quality is good, but this technique requires rather large amounts of storage.

2. *Phoneme synthesis.* A collection of possible sounds in a language is stored. Speech rules are applied to machine-readable text to produce sounds resembling human speech. There is no limit to the vocabulary of this type of speech; however, the

synthesized speech may be highly distorted because of the limitations of the speech production rules.

Video. Humans perceive the rapid display of arrays of pixels as animation of graphical objects or full-motion video. In effect, a window acts as a television. It is also possible to superimpose text and graphics on top of the video. The storage requirements for full-motion color video can be tremendous. Techniques for compressing and decompressing each frame of video, as well as techniques for compressing and decompressing sequences of frames, are used to minimize the required storage [Luther, 1989].

Output signal interaction object characteristics   Output signal interaction objects have the following presentation characteristics:

- Length of time that the message is presented to the user:
  - for a fixed period of time,
  - until replaced by another message,
  - until explicitly removed by the user.
- Frequency with which the message is presented to the user, for example, the number of times per minute a beeping sound is produced, the number of times per minute a voice message is repeated, or the number of times a visual message is blinked.
- Visual appearance, including
  - Shape (usually rectangular)
  - Length
  - Width
  - Border design and color
  - Background pattern and color
  - Type, size, and color of font (or design of an icon)
  - Location on the screen

5.3.2 Input Signals

An input signal interaction object is used by the user to invoke an operation with default parameter values.

Figure 5.3 illustrates the four states of an input signal interaction object and the transitions among those four states.

When an application function or script execution engine initially displays an input signal interaction object, it is either Enabled or Disabled. The application function or script execution engine may change the Enabled state to Disabled and change the Disabled state to Enabled. When the interaction object is in the Enabled state, the user may cause the predefined message to be sent to the script execution engine or application function. This causes the interaction object to enter the Confirmation state, where it remains for a prespecified amount of time before returning to the Enabled state.

An example of an input signal interaction object is a button. Figure 5.4 illustrates the appearance of a typical button in each of the four states.

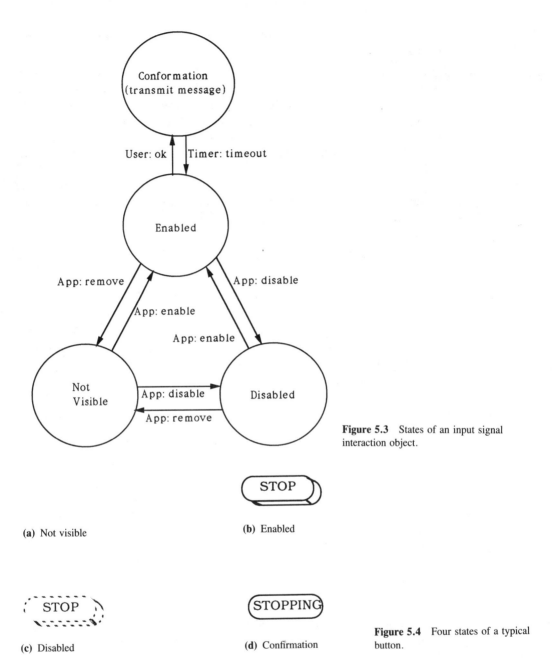

Figure 5.3 States of an input signal interaction object.

(a) Not visible

(b) Enabled

(c) Disabled

(d) Confirmation

Figure 5.4 Four states of a typical button.

When the user selects the button in the Enabled state, the predefined message is transmitted to the dialog processor or application function. If the application does not disable or remove the button, the user may select the button again and transmit the message again after the button returns to the Enabled state.

5.4 SELECTION INTERACTION OBJECTS ARE USED FOR PROMPTING AND SELECTING

Selection interaction objects are used when there exists a small number of predefined options which can be exchanged between the user and the application. First, we will review some of the many selection interaction objects; then we will categorize their important parameters.

The interface designer will use a selection interaction object when it is better for end users to select from presented options rather than to enter the option explicitly. Selection interaction objects are used to prompt the end user to select options and to transmit the user's choice to the script execution engine or application function.

5.4.1 How Selection Interaction Objects Work

Figure 5.5 illustrates the state transition diagram for a selection interaction object with two options. A selection interaction object supports the following behavior:

1. When initially displayed, a default option is automatically selected. When the selection interaction object is presented to the end user, the currently selected option is clearly identified.
2. The end user is constrained to select only from the options presented by the interaction object.
3. The end user may change the selected option by selecting another option. The previously selected option is deselected.

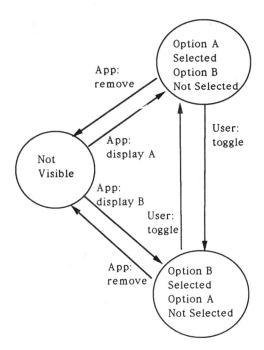

Figure 5.5 States of a selection interaction object with two choices.

When the selection interaction object is visually displayed to the user, the user selects options either by pressing the appropriate key on a keyboard or by moving a cursor to the option to be selected and pressing a accept key. Often the accept key is physically part of the pointing device used to position the cursor.

5.4.2 Examples of Selection Interaction Objects

Examples of visibly displayed selection interaction 'objects include the following:

1. Toggle switch. Figure 5.6 illustrates several types of toggle switches. Each switch has exactly two states. The end user is able to switch, or toggle, between states. Toggle switches are used when the user must choose between two options. Examples of toggle switches include the following:

- Zoom-in and zoom-out pair [Figure 5.6(a)]. This toggle interaction object has two states with two very different appearances: (1) a small icon which represents a closed window—when the user selects the small icon, it is replaced by a

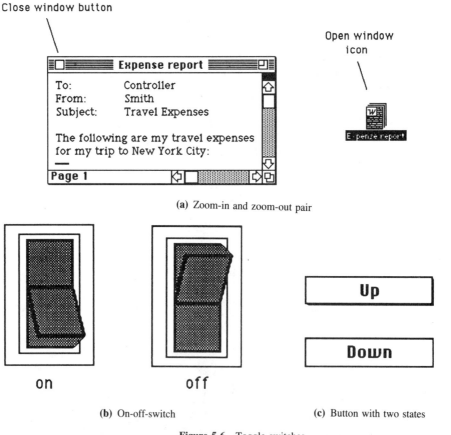

(a) Zoom-in and zoom-out pair

on   off

(b) On-off-switch   (c) Button with two states

Figure 5.6 Toggle switches.

window—and (2) a button within the border of a window that when selected by the end user, causes the window to be replaced by the small icon.

- On-off switch with "on" and "off" appearances similar to the light switches in many buildings [Figure 5.6(b)].
- Button with two states, "Up" and "Down" [Figure 5.6(c)].

2. Exclusive setting menu. Figure 5.7 illustrates several menus with *n* options from which the user can select exactly one option. These menus allow the user to choose

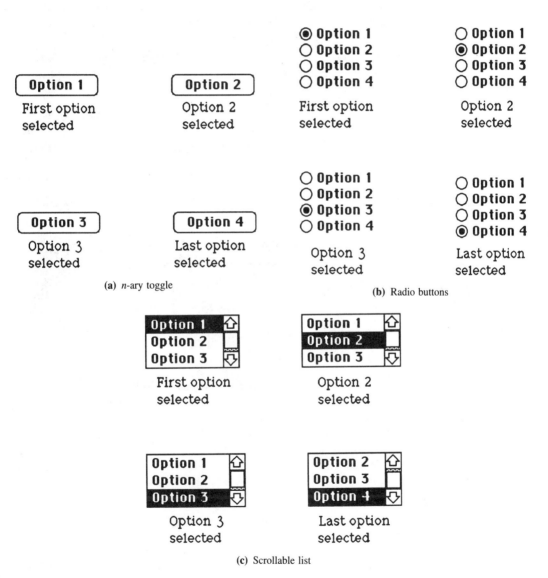

(a) *n*-ary toggle

(b) Radio buttons

(c) Scrollable list

Figure 5.7 Exclusive setting menus.

a single option from among a small number of discreet option values. Examples of menus include the following:

- *n*-ary toggle [Figure 5.7(a)]. With an *n*-ary toggle, the user may step forward through a circular list of options by clicking the *n*-ary toggle. Each time the user clicks the toggle, the current option is replaced by the next option on the option list. Because the list is circular, the first option on the list reappears after the user clicks the toggle displaying the last option on the list.
- Set of *n* radio buttons [Figure 5.7(b)]. Radio buttons are similar to the set of push buttons which are a part of the tuning device used with many car radios. If the user selects a button which is not currently selected, it becomes selected and the previously selected button becomes deselected.
- Scrollable list [Figure 5.7(c)]. User may scroll through the list of options by selecting the scroll up arrow or scroll down arrow. The user selects an option by checking it.

3. Valuator. A valuator displays a scale representing a range of continuous values. The user can change the selected value within the range indicated on the scale by moving a pointer. Examples of valuators include slider bars and gauge shown in Figure 5.8.

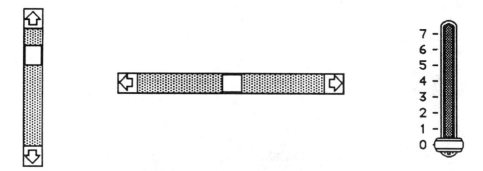

Figure 5.8 Valuators.

Selection interaction objects can also be presented verbally to users. Automatic telephone answering systems frequently verbalize choices to callers, who make selections by pressing buttons on touch-tone telephones. This approach enables the telephone to be used as a primitive computer terminal to many applications.

The QUICK (quick user interface construction kit) system developed at the University of Oregon (Douglas, Doerry, & Novick, 1990) uses a clever type of selection interaction object with four options. The user selects each option by performing one of the following operations:

- Click the interaction object once.
- Click the interaction object twice.
- Drag the interaction object.
- Drop the interaction object.

The user interface designer specifies the actions to be performed whenever the user selects one of the four options. The designer specifies actions by filling blanks and selecting menu options. Educational and training applications have been constructed consisting of a set of QUICK interaction objects. QUICK is further descibed in Appendix D.

5.4.3 Selection Interaction Object Characteristics

User interface designers specify selection interaction object characteristics, including the following:

1. Number of options within a selection interaction object. A frequently used guideline for the number of options in a menu is between 5 and 9, which corresponds to the number of chunks of information that psychologists believe can be held in a human's short-term memory.

2. Arrangement of options within the selection interaction object. Typical arrangements include

- *Vertical.* A single-column list format [Figure 5.9(a)] will aid scanning and assimilation of available options, especially for novice users.
- *Horizontal.* If there are only a few options and there is a shortage of display space, then the options may be displayed as a single row as shown in Figure 5.9(b).
- *Palette.* For menus containing icons, arrange the icons on a palette, as illustrated in Figure 5.9(c).

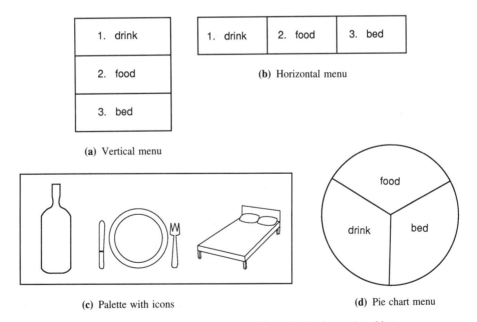

Figure 5.9 Arrangement of options within a selection interaction object.

- *Pie chart format.* Figure 5.9(d) illustrates a pie chart menu. Because the cursor is initially located in the center of the menu, little movement of the cursor is needed to select any option.

3. Position of the selection interaction object with respect to other selection interaction objects. Many user interfaces have a screen area dedicated for the display of selection interaction objects. Macintosh™ has a menu bar (a type of horizontal menu) at the top of the screen. MacPaint® and MacDraw® each have a palette on the left side of the screen. In addition to placing menus within reserved screen areas, there are choices for the spatial relationship among selection interaction objects. Options include

- Overlay previous selection interaction object [Figure 5.10(a)].
- Stacked selection interaction objects [Figure 5.10(b)].
- Tiled selection interaction objects [Figure 5.10(c)].

4. Border design and color.

5. Background design and color.

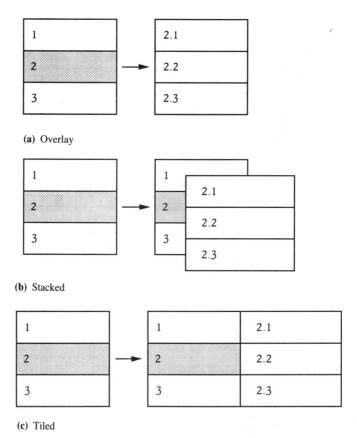

(a) Overlay

(b) Stacked

(c) Tiled

Figure 5.10 Relative positions of multiple selection interaction objects.

5.4.4 Techniques for Displaying Options

Within a selection interaction object, there are several techniques for formatting options.

1. The option is represented by either text or an icon. An *icon* is a pictorial representation of an option.

2. Spatial area, called the sensitive area of the option, causes the option to be selected when the cursor is within the area. The sensitive area can be identified by

- a color and/or texture different from the surrounding area. *Texture* refers to the design displayed in a screen area. Figure 5.11 illustrates several different textures.

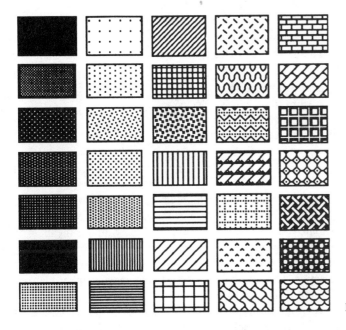

Figure 5.11 Several textures.

- a border which separates the sensitive area from the surrounding screen area. Sometimes the border of the sensitive area is not visible to the user.

3. Placement of messages within the sensitive area:

- Centered, as illustrated in Figure 5.12(a).
- Left justified, as illustrated in Figure 5.12(b).

5.4.5 Option Selection Technique

There are several possible techniques for entering the user's response to select options from a selection interaction object.

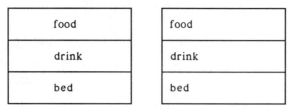

Figure 5.12 Placement of message in sensitive area.

(a) Centered　　　　(b) Left justified

- Move a cursor to the desired option and press an accept key. If a mouse is used to move the cursor, the accept key may be located on the mouse. If step keys are used, the accept key is usually another key, often labeled SELECT, ENTER, or RETURN.
- Each option is labeled with an integer. The user presses the keyboard key with the same integer to select the desired option.
- Each option begins with a unique set of characters. The user enters these character keys via the keyboard to select the desired option.
- Each option is associated with a function key. When the user presses a function key, the corresponding option from the menu is selected.

5.4.6 Indicating the State of an Option

There are three states for each option: not available, available but not selected, and selected.

Some menus have modes during which one or more of the options from a menu are not applicable. An option is said to be not available if the user should not select it. Because users become accustomed to the spatial layout of options within a menu, it is desirable to not change the positions of options in the menu, even if some of the options are not currently available. Therefore, we need some technique to indicate if an option is not currently available for selection. Options that are not available may be either blanked out [Figure 5.13(a)] or grayed out [Figure 5.13(b)].

Because users may select multiple options within some menus, a technique is needed to indicate options which have been selected. Selected options are often shown as highlighted [Figure 5.14(a)], reversed video [Figure 5.14(b)], or checkmarked [Figure 5.14(c)].

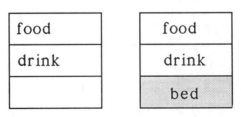

(a) Bed is blanked out　　　　(b) Bed is grayed out

Figure 5.13 Techniques for illustrating nonavailable options.

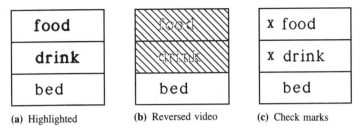

food		x food
drink		x drink
bed	bed	bed

(a) Highlighted   (b) Reversed video   (c) Check marks

Figure 5.14 Selected option.

5.5 EDITABLE INTERACTION OBJECTS SUPPORT INFORMATION ENTRY AND MODIFICATION

5.5.1 How Editable Interaction Objects Work

Editable interaction objects enable end users to enter and edit complex messages to be transmitted to a script execution engine or an application function. Editable interaction objects support the following behavior:

1. A default value exists for editable interaction objects. Often the default of 0.0 is used for a real number data type, 0 for an integer data type, and a string of blank characters for a character string data type.
2. Any modifications to the value of an editable interaction object are immediately echoed to the end user. This enables the user to verify that the value has been modified correctly.
3. The value entered by the user into the interaction object may need to satisfy predefined semantic integrity constraints. For example, the value of a person's age may be constrained to be a positive integer.

Editable interaction objects accept and display the traditional data types: integer, real, character, Boolean, and so on. State transition diagrams for editable interaction objects may be quite complex.

5.5.2 Example Editable Interaction Objects

Examples of editable interaction objects include the following:

- *Data box* (Figure 5.15). Using a text editor, the user can move the cursor left or right within a data box and enter or edit an alphanumeric character string. Most text editors will automatically move the cursor one position to the right after the user enters each character. A special operation, backspace, both moves the cursor one position to the left and removes a single character.

Age 22 **Figure 5.15** Data box.

- *Command box* (Figure 5.16). The user uses a text editor to enter a command with zero or more options into this type of editable interaction object. If the command is too big to fit into the command box, the command can be scrolled within the command box.

Command | delete 5,7; | **Figure 5.16** Command box.

- *Document* (Figure 5.17). The interaction object is basically a long character string. Sometimes the term "text file" is used in place of the term "document." The user views and modifies lines of a document page using a screen editor. The user can cause the text to "page" or "scroll" up or down to reveal text not currently displayed.

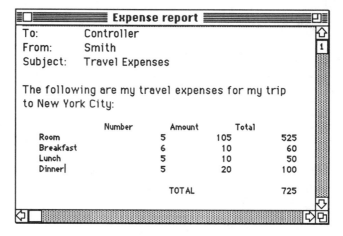

Figure 5.17 Document page.

- *Bit map*. By turning individual cells of a two dimensional matrix on and off, a user can create a visual pattern which can be used as an icon (Figure 5.18).

5.5.3 Input Technologies

Editable interaction objects can accept information from any of several input devices. Currently, the most frequently used input devices are keyboard and mouse. Other input devices include microphones (with speech recognition capabilities) and tablets (with handwriting recognition capabilities). Speech and handwriting recognition are new technologies likely to be available soon. We will examine these two technologies in the remainder of this subsection.

Speech recognition   There are several issues involved with speech recogniton.

- *Speech mode*. In *isolated word recognition*, users must briefly pause between each word. In *continuous speech recognition* it is not necessary for the user to pause between each word.

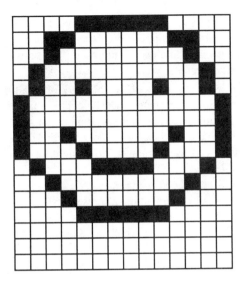

Figure 5.18 Bit map.

- *Vocabulary size.* The number of words that can be recognized.
- *Word confusability.* The similiarity of word sounds.
- *Training.* In a *speaker-dependent* system, the speaker trains the speech-recognition system to recognize words spoken by the speaker. In a *speaker-independent* system, no training is necessary.
- *Perplexity* (the number of choices that can be made at each choice point). Once a word has been recognized, the speech recognition system knows that only a small subset of the vocabulary can immediately follow the recognized word.
- *Noise/signal ratio* (the degree of background noise which the speech recognition system must ignore).

In general, low-end speech-recognition systems support isolated word recognition, small vocabulary, low-word confusability, speaker-dependent training, low perplexity, and no background noise. High-end systems increase the vocabulary size, support continuous speech recognition, enable speaker independence, or offer some combination of these capabilities.

Four major approaches are used in speech-recognition systems.

1. *Template-based approach.* A collection of prototypical speech patterns is stored in a database as reference patterns. The user's utterance is matched with the pattern that it most closely resembles.
2. *Knowledge-based approach.* Speech knowledge is derived from understanding acoustic and phonetic theories of speech, as well as from syntactic, semantic, and discourse properties of spoken sentences. Speech knowledge is used to recognize individual words and meanings.
3. *Probabilistic approach.* A model of the probability of each sound, as well as the probability of two sounds occurring in succession is synthesized from example

speech input. The user's utterance is broken into individual sounds and sequences of sounds. Known words and sequences of words are assigned probabilities which indicate how closely they match the user's utterance. The known words with the maximum probability are selected.

4. *Connectionist approach.* A neural network is a network of small processors which map input parameters to output parameters. Designers train the neural network by presenting it with pairs of input and the corresponding output. The designer selects a set of acoustic attributes that describes patterns of speech. The neural network can then map acoustic attributes of user utterances to recognized words.

Recognized words should be echoed to the user by either (1) displaying the text within a data box, command box, or document or (2) presenting the recognized words as synthesized speech. The user may edit the recognized words, either by using a traditional text editor or by using voice editing commands which are themselves recognized and then executed. Each editing command is preceded by an ''escape word'' which signals that the following word is an editing command rather than data being entered.

Handwriting recognition   There are several issues involved with handwriting recognition. Issues of training, vocabulary size, letter confusability, and perplexity are similar to these issues in speech recognition. An additional issue is writing style. There are basically five levels of recognition difficulty.

1. *Boxed discrete characters.* The characters are written in predefined areas or boxes. No pair of characters may be connected.
2. *Spaced discrete characters.* Each pair of characters must be separated by a blank space, but the characters are not confined to predefined boxes.
3. *Run-on discrete.* Each pair of characters may appear connected, but are formed one at a time with the user lifting the pen off the writing tablet after each character.
4. *Cursive.* Characters are connected.
5. *Mixed cursive, discrete, and run-on discrete.*

Several approaches and combinations of approaches may be used to recognize characters, including the following:

- *Feature analysis.* Characters are represented by a set of features such as descending line or no descending line. The unknown character is classified using a decision tree based on features.
- *Time sequence of zones, direction, or extremes.* By dividing the rectangle that surrounds a character, and examining the order in which the pen tip traverses each zone, the unknown character is identified. Similarly, a character can be described in terms of a sequence of pen directions, such as up, down, left, and right.
- *Curve matching.* An unknown character is matched against prototype curves.
- *Analysis by synthesis.* Models of handwriting generation based on strokes and rules for connecting strokes into symbols are used to classify each unknown character.

Recognized words are echoed to the user by displaying the text within a data box, command box, or document. The user may edit the recognized words, either by writing special proof symbols such as circles, brackets, and arrows to signify actions and commands. For example, to cut and paste some text, the user might specify the scope of the text to be operated on by drawing a circle around it, draw an "X" superimposed on the selected text (thereby deleting it and storing it in a clipboard), and then draw an arrow to indicate where to paste the text.

5.6 COMPOSITE INTERACTION OBJECTS ARE COMPOSED OF OTHER INTERACTION OBJECTS

Composite interaction objects are composed from two or more simple or other composite interaction objects. Description of composite interaction objects includes

- What the component interaction objects are. Component interaction objects represent conceptual objects that are related to another conceptual object by the IsPartOf relationship. For example, in Figure 5.19, the conceptual objects represented by each toggle switch are IsPartOf the conceptual object represented by the nonexclusive setting menu.

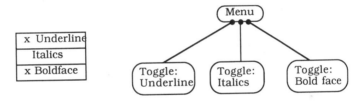

Figure 5.19 Menu of toggle boxes form a nonexclusive setting menu.

- Where the component interaction object is displayed relative to other component interaction objects.
- When the component interaction objects are displayed within the composite interaction object. If all of the component interaction objects are always visible, and their physical arrangement does not change, then composite interaction objects are said to be *static*. Otherwise, the composite interaction object is said to be *dynamic*.
- Composition operators may be used to combine two or more interaction objects and other composite interaction objects into a composite interaction object. Composition operators include union, cross-product, and overlay.

5.6.1 Union Composition

Two or more interaction objects are made part of a composite interaction object without changing the appearance or behavior of the component interaction objects. Examples of composite interaction objects constructed by forming the union of component interaction objects follow:

- *Nonexclusive setting menu,* from which several choices can be made. Several toggle objects are positioned together to form a menu in which the user can toggle each object. For example, Figure 5.19 illustrates the conceptual objects and the corresponding interaction objects for a menu consisting of three toggle boxes. A checkmark indicates that the user has chosen the ''select'' state of the toggle box.
- *Electronic form.* Figure 5.20 illustrates an electronic form consisting of multiple data boxes. In addition to containing basic component interaction objects, electronic forms may also contain composite interaction objects. For example, Figure 5.21 illustrates an electronic form which contains two other electronic forms.
- *Dialog box.* The dialog box illustrated in Figure 5.22 contains two data boxes and two buttons.
- *Spreadsheet.* As illustrated in Figure 5.23, a spreadsheet consists of a two-dimensional matrix of message and data boxes. The message boxes display labels.

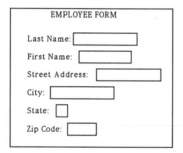

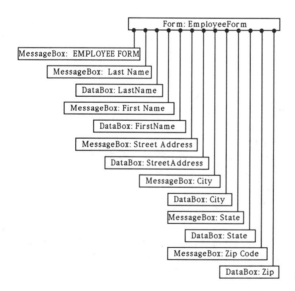

Figure 5.20 Electronic form.

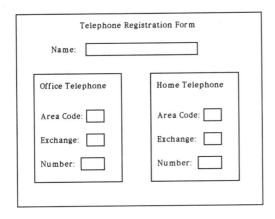

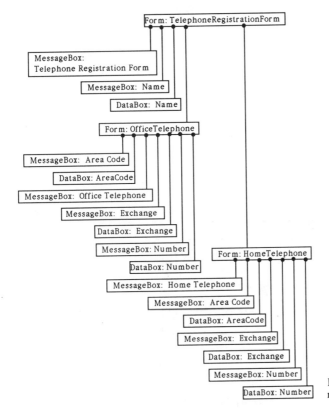

Figure 5.21 Form with two nested forms.

The user enters values into specific data boxes, which causes values in other data boxes to be modified. Spreadsheet constraints specify how derived values are computed from other values. The use of constraints is discussed further in Chapter 9.

- *Geometric figures.* As illustrated in Figure 5.24, geometric figures consist of multiple points, lines, and polygons.

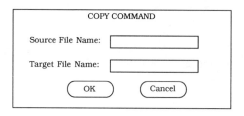

Figure 5.22   Dialog box.

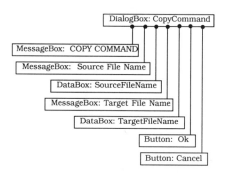

Figure 5.23   Spreadsheet.

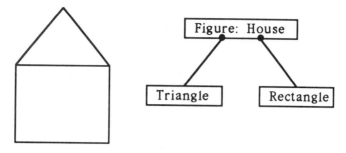

Figure 5.24 Geometric figures.

Constraints are often used to specify the spatial relationship among interaction objects which are composed together to form a composite interaction object. The use of constraints to enforce spatial relationships and appearance is discussed in Chapter 9.

5.6.2 Cross-Product Composition

The cross-product composition combines interaction objects such that the resulting composite interaction object presents the cross-product of the domains of the component interaction objects. Both the appearance and the behavior of the component interaction objects are modified.

- A horizontal and a vertical slider can be composed to create the two-dimensional slider illustrated in Figure 5.25. This slider is used to control both horizontal and vertical scrolling in the interviews tool kit developed at Stanford University. (Linton, Vlissides, & Calder, 1989)
- Two menus can be combined into a checkboard menu as illustrated in Figure 5.26. This checkboard menu could be used by a hotel guest to make restaurant reservations.

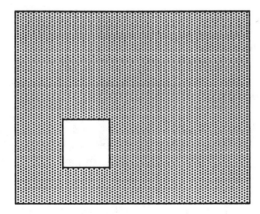

Figure 5.25 Two-dimensional slider.

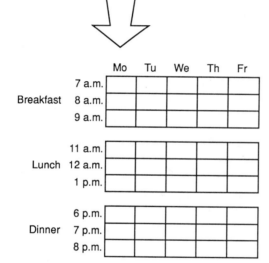

Time
7 a.m.
8 a.m.
9 a.m.
11 a.m.
12 a.m.
1 p.m.
6 p.m.
7 p.m.
8 p.m.

Day
Mo
Tu
We
Th
Fr

	Mo	Tu	We	Th	Fr
7 a.m.					
Breakfast 8 a.m.					
9 a.m.					
11 a.m.					
Lunch 12 a.m.					
1 p.m.					
6 p.m.					
Dinner 7 p.m.					
8 p.m.					

Figure 5.26   Checkboard menu.

5.6.3 Superimpose Composition

In superimpose composition, two or more component interaction objects are represented by the same composite interaction object:

- In Figure 5.27, a single gauge is used to represent both the current temperature and the desired temperature. These two interaction objects are combined so that they share a common grid but different value pointers. In this example, the user may adjust the desired temperature pointer, but may only observe the current temperature pointer.

- In Figure 5.28, a single gauge is used to represent both AM and FM station call numbers of a radio. Both AM and FM grids are displayed, but only one pointer is

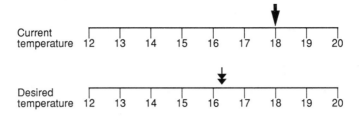

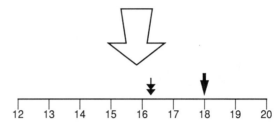

Figure 5.27 Overlayed gauges.

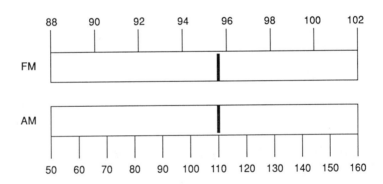

Figure 5.28 AM and FM gauges.

visable. Depending on the state of a toggle interaction object, the station interaction object of Figure 5.28 represents the AM station call numbers (if the toggle is in the AM state) or the FM station call numbers (if the toggle is in the FM state).

5.6.4 Dynamic Composite Interaction Objects Contain a Variable Number of Visible Component Objects

Dynamic interaction objects are composite interaction objects in which some of the component interaction objects may not be visible to the user. A prespecified condition determines whether the component interaction object is visible or not. This condition may involve values entered or selected by the user in sibling or parent interaction objects. Dynamic interaction objects are used when the type of information which must be entered by the user is dependent upon previously entered or computed information. Some examples follow:

- Figure 5.29. Display a data box asking for the maiden name after an end user indicates her gender is female and marital status is married.
- Figure 5.30. Display an error message when the user enters an invalid value into a data box.
- Figure 5.31. Display *n* ChildInfo electronic forms after an employee indicates that he or she has *n* children.
- Figure 5.32. Display a two-level hierarchy of menus whose root menu is a vertical bar with each leaf menu displayed as a pulldown menu. Each leaf menu becomes visible after the user selects the corresponding option from the vertical menu bar.
- Figure 5.33 illustrates a hierarchical representation of a collection of directories and files of a file system. This composite interaction object is dependent on the actual structure of the directories and files in the underlying file system.

5.7 INTERACTION OBJECTS ARE BUILT, MODIFIED, AND GENERATED

There are three general approaches for implementing interaction objects.

1. *Build from scratch.* Specify the interaction object using any of several programming languages. While this is necessary for creative and original interaction objects, many interaction object designers avoid this approach, which can be very time consuming.
2. *Modify existing code.* Select and modify existing interaction object code from an interaction object library. The popularity of interaction object libraries such as the Macintosh user interface toolkit, Microsoft® Windows™ (IBM DOS), Presentation Manager™ (IBM OS/2), and X window system™ (for Unix-based machines) make this a frequently chosen option. This approach is discussed in Section 5.8.
3. *Design tools.* Specify the semantics using high-level specification languages or drawing tools and then automatically generate the executable code. By using design

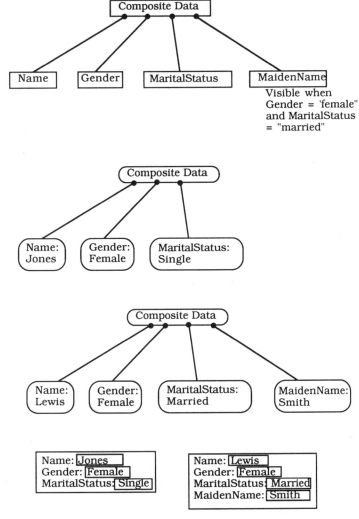

Figure 5.29 Dynamic interaction object in which MaidenName is dependent upon value of MaritalStatus.

tools, interaction object designers can avoid much of the complexity of the first two approaches, yet still generate a large number of interaction objects which automatically adhere to the user interface guidelines implicitly enforced by the generation tools. This approach is discussed in Section 5.9.

5.8 DIALOG DESIGNERS CUSTOMIZE INTERACTION OBJECTS

Many dialog designers have access to libraries containing a variety of interaction objects. The dialog designer selects appropriate interaction objects from a library and includes

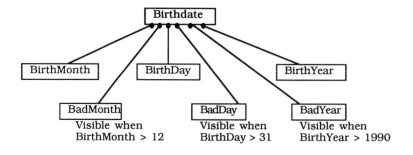

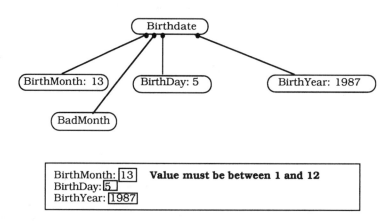

Figure 5.30 Signal interaction object is included in complex object when error occurs.

them in the user interface design. Appendix C describes guidelines which dialog designers may use in selecting interaction objects.

After the dialog designer selects one or more interaction objects from the library, a graphics artist customizes the appearance of the selected interaction objects to meet the needs of the user interface. This customizing can be accomplished in several ways:

Customize the Presentation of an Interaction Object. Each interaction object has a set of parameters for the presentation attributes such as the length and frequency of time the interaction object is presented. Values for these parameters can be displayed on a *property sheet,* an updatable electronic form containing the names of all attributes and the values that can be modified. Some property values (such as position and size) can be changed by directly manipulating the interaction object appearance. Extensive programming experience is not usually necessary to specify parametric values via a property sheet.

Modify the Behavior of an Interaction Object. A programmer may modify the behavior of an interaction object by modifying the software which is used to manage the object. For example, the programmer may specify new constraints which a data box applies to information being entered by the user. Programming experience may be necessary to modify interaction objects in this way.

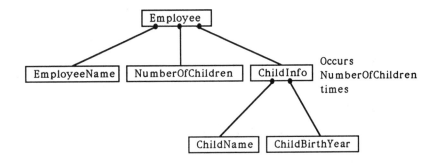

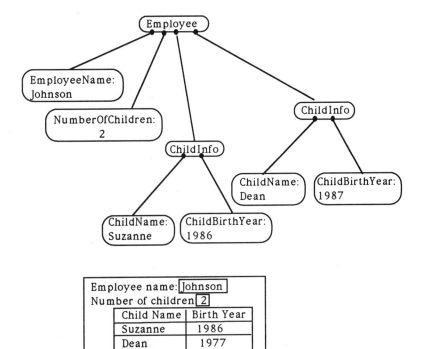

Figure 5.31 Composite object with a variable number of subobjects.

Modify the Common Behavior and Appearance of Several Interaction Objects.
Interaction objects may inherit a common appearance and behavior. For example, the
software which enables users to scroll horizontally within a window and the corresponding appearance of a vertical scroll bar are frequently factored out of all the interaction
objects with horizontal scrolling and placed in a generalized interaction object. All
interaction objects which need horizontal scrolling inherit the scroll bar from this
generalized interaction object. In this way, all interaction objects which support scrolling
have a common appearance (the horizontal scroll bar) and behavior (the manner in which

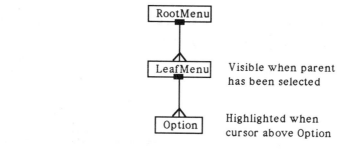

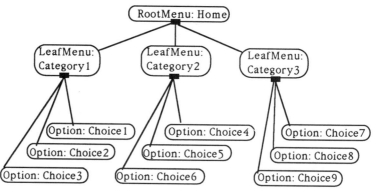

Figure 5.32 Two-level hierarchy of menus.

the user indicates scrolling is desired and the way in which the interaction object responds). By changing the appearance and behavior of the generalized interaction object, the appearance and behavior of all inheriting interaction objects are changed in a uniform and consistent manner. Libraries of interaction objects are frequently organized in such a manner that interaction objects inherit a common appearance and behavior from the generalized interaction object.

Efforts are underway to define an application programming interface (API) for interaction objects. An API defines the data structures and commands by which application functions and script execution engines interact with interaction objects. A uniform API would permit user interface designers to substitute one interaction object with another interaction object with a similar behavior but a different appearance.

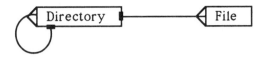

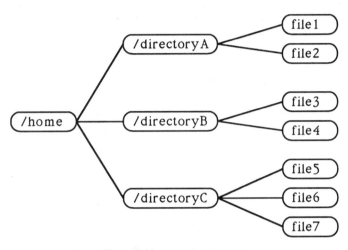

Figure 5.33 Directory browser.

5.9 DESIGNERS USE TOOLS TO DESIGN INTERACTION OBJECTS

Interaction object designers use several mechanisms to specify the appearance and behavior of interaction objects that they design.

- WYSIWYG (what you see is what you get) direct manipulation techniques are used for positioning, orienting, stretching, shrinking, and sizing the visual components of interaction objects.
- Menu selection is used to specify attributes whose possible values form a small set. For example, designers select font type, font size, and color of textual labels and messages from menus.
- Property sheets are used to specify presentation aspects not easily specified by direct manipulation. For example, designers enter labels, titles, and message wording into property sheets.
- Specification and programming languages are used by designers to specify the behavioral aspects of interaction objects. Languages are used to specify control flow

(iteration, conditional branching) and the conditions under which the interaction object presentation changes.

Appendix D reviews some existing tools for designing and creating interaction objects.

5.10 PRAGMATIC ASPECTS INFLUENCE INTERACTION OBJECTS

Nothing affects the useability of a user interface as much as the hardware viewed and manipulated by the user. Individuals with large hands may find keyboards with small keys difficult to use, especially if the keys are arranged closely together. A user's hand will quickly tire after holding a light pen containing a heavy battery. If the terminal screen flickers or displays a fuzzy image, the user may develop a headache. Changing the user interface hardware may dramatically change the way users interact with the user interface.

Ergonomics is a branch of science which studies how humans interact with mechanical objects. Ergonomists have completed thousands of experiments and investigations to characterize the attributes of mechanized objects which make them easy for humans to manipulate and use. A collection of principles and guidelines is emerging which can be applied to the design of hardware used for user interfaces. These principles and guidelines are documented in (Brown, 1988; Smith & Mosier, 1986).

Widely used interaction devices   Often user interface designs are constrained by the available hardware. For example, it may not be economically feasible to replace several hundred teletype-compatible CRTs by graphics-oriented, bit-mapped screens. In these cases, the user interface designers try to design the best interface possible given the hardware available.

Sometimes user interface designers may design or choose the hardware to be used. In these cases, the designer is constrained by the types of hardware currently available and the amount of funding available to design, implement, or buy the hardware.

Currently the widely available hardware supports a range of input and output devices. Input devices generally fall into the following categories:

- Keyboardlike devices, including buttons, keys, and touch-sensitive surfaces
- Piano keyboards which are used to capture musical scores
- Pointing devices, including track ball, joystick, light pen, touch pad, touch screen, touch tablet, and mouse, which enable a user to reposition a cursor on the screen
- Voice recognition devices which recognize one or more human utterances
- Scanning devices which capture raster-oriented images of text, graphics, and pictures
- Devices that capture handwriting and schematic drawings
- Foot-operated devices including foot switches (like the high-beam/low-beam light switch on the floor of some cars), pedals (like the gas pedal of a car), and moles (foot-controlled mice).

Widely used output devices include the following:

- Lights, buzzers, bells, and other devices used to convey a predefined message to the user
- Devices capable of displaying a text string, such as the LCD display on a pocket calculator
- Devices capable of displaying multiple lines of text, such as teletype-compatible CRT screens
- Bit-mapped CRT screens which can display two-dimensional images and animation
- Sound-generation devices which produce a wide variety of sounds including synthetic speech and music

Future interaction devices   Researchers and engineers are currently investigating the use of many technologies for possible use as new devices for interacting with computers. New input technology includes devices that capture human gestures, including

- Data glove, which captures the position of a hand and fingers in three-dimensional space.
- Body suit, which captures the position of a person's body and limbs in three-dimensional space.
- Eye-tracking device, which detects the movement and focus position of the human eye.
- TV camera, which captures and recognizes human gestures, including shrugs and facial expressions.

New output devices are

- Devices that display digitized video images
- Graphics devices that display two-dimensional images, including motion parallax and shadows to simulate three-dimensional images
- Holographic display devices that produce three-dimensional images which can be viewed from multiple observation points

Some scientists and futurists are predicting that some day human brain waves can be captured and interpreted by advanced hardware, and perhaps be generated for consumption by the human brain. Although the idea that a computer can read a human mind seems both frightening and unlikely today, today's human-computer interaction would undoubtedly seemed frightening and unlikely to individuals living just a few decades ago.

5.11 SUMMARY

Interaction objects perform several functions, including sensing the end users' manipulation, enforcing constraints, buffering intermediate data, translating lexical tokens into semantic tokens, transmitting semantic tokens between the script execution engine and applications, echoing information entered by the user, and displaying information received from the script execution engine or applications.

Signal interaction objects transfer messages to and from the user. Examples of output signal objects include bells, buzzers, lights, text, audio, and video messages. A button is an example of an input signal interaction object.

Selection interaction objects prompt users by presenting options and accepting selections made by users. Examples of selection interaction objects include toggle switches, exclusive setting menus, *n*-ary toggles, valuators, slider bars, and voice menus.

Editable interaction objects enable end users to enter and edit information. Example editable interaction objects include data boxes, command boxes, documents, and bit maps. Users enter information into interaction objects by using keyboards and mice, speech recognizers, and handwriting recognizers.

Composite interaction objects are constructed by combining two or more interaction objects. Composite operators include union, cross-product, and superimposition. Dynamic composite interaction objects contain a variable number of visable component objects.

Three approaches for constructing new interaction objects are building them from scratch, modifying existing interaction objects, and generating them from high-level specifications. Existing interaction objects from libraries can be modified by changing default attributes, changing the code within the interaction object, or changing the inherited attributes and code.

Ergonomists study how humans interact with physical devices. Sometimes dramatic improvements in the ability of end users to interact with applications result with only minor changes to physical devices. New I/O devices will enable end users to interact with application functions in new and novel ways.

6

Window Managers and User Interface Management Systems

This chapter discusses

- What device drivers are.
- What window managers are and why they are important.
- What features are provided by user interface management systems.
- What architectures are used for applications and user interface systems.

6.1 USER INTERFACE SOFTWARE IS MODULARIZED

Computer applications often require the creation of large and complex software systems. Software engineers attempt to manage this complexity by partitioning the software into small, independent modules which can be created and maintained separately. This chapter explores approaches for the modularization of user interface software.

User interface system researchers and designers have suggested many different user interface execution software architectures. User interface software architectures differ in the manner in which the user interface software is partitioned and modularized. There is no clear best architecture for all situations, therefore, we will present several alternative architectures and discuss the advantages and disadvantages of each.

The following criteria may be used when evaluating user interface software architectures:

- *Reusability*. Each component should be potentially reusable in other user interfaces.
- *Module simplicity*. Each component should be simple enough to be understandable by individuals who design, implement, and maintain the component.
- *Minimal execution overhead*. The communications among components should be minimized.
- *Interface simplicity*. The interface between each pair of components should be as small and simple as possible.
- *Independence*. User interface design decisions from different design decision classes can be implemented and modified independently.
- *Minimal redundancy*. The same functions should not be implemented in more than one component.

Different user interface software architectures are "best" for different weightings of these criteria. Section 6.5 reviews some of the more widely used user interface software architectures.

User interface software consists of several major components.

- *Input and output devices and their drivers*, which transform electronic information to a form perceivable by users and convert user gestures into electronic information. Input and output devices and their drivers implement decisions from the pragmatic decision class. Device drivers are discussed in Section 6.2.
- *Windows*, an abstraction of input and output devices used to permit several applications to share the same input and output device. For example, a screen can be partitioned into several windows with each window considered a separate output device by several executing applications. Window managers are discussed in Section 6.3.
- *Interaction objects*, the mechanisms by which users interact with the application. Interaction objects implement decisions from the presentation decision class. Interaction objects were discussed in detail in Chapter 5.
- *Script*, the mechanism which controls and sequences the exchange of information between the user and the application. Scripts implement decisions from the dialog decision class. Section 6.4 discusses how user interface management systems execute scripts, and some of the additional features provided by user interface management systems.
- *Application-specific functions*, which perform calculations specific to the application and implement decisions from the functional and conceptual decision classes.

6.2 DEVICE DRIVERS ARE TRANSDUCERS

Basically, an input device is a transducer from physical human gestures values consumed by an application. An output device is a transducer from logical values produced by an application to physical properties that can be sensed by the human perceptual system.

Rather than including the detailed instructions for all input and output devices within every application program, designers have created a library for each device which contains routines to present information to the user and obtain information from users. These libraries contain functions collectively known as *device drivers*. The interfaces between device drivers and application functions have been standardized, so that the specifics of the device can be hidden from application functions. Because the device drivers hide the differences between these output devices from the application, an application function does not need to be changed if its output is displayed on a printer or on a VT100 terminal. Of course, some devices are so different that their differences cannot be hidden from the application program. For example, color graphics cannot be displayed on a VT100 terminal—its device driver library does not contain routines for displaying color graphics nor does it support hardware to display color graphics.

6.3 WINDOW MANAGERS PROVIDE VIEWPORTS TO APPLICATIONS

Window managers manage the devices used to exchange information between applications and users. Output devices include video displays and sound synthesizers. Input devices include keyboards and pointing devices such as mouse, joystick, track ball, or light pen. The window manager interacts with the device drivers of output devices to present information to the user, and with the device drivers for input devices to obtain messages which represent information being entered by the user. Applications and script execution engines pass images expressed as bit maps or PostScript™ notation to the window manager which presents those images to the user. The window manager returns messages to the applications and script execution engine entered by the user via input devices.

Some devices can be shared by several applications. A video display is one such device. Its display surface can be partitioned into windows, with each window associated with an application. The application perceives its window as a display device and is not aware that the physical display device is shared with other applications.

From a user's point of view, a *window* is the portion of the screen which the window manager allocates to an application. Information from several applications may be presented to the user in separate windows on the same terminal screen.

From a programmer's point of view, a window is much more than a portion of a screen; a *window* is a data structure and a unit of executable code to which messages can be sent. Windows accept messages from a variety of sources, including the input devices, from applications wishing to display information to the user, from system routines wishing to display messages to the user, and from other windows. Depending on the messages received, a window may perform actions, including displaying information to the user within the windows boundaries on the screen, presenting audio information (such as alarm bells and buzzers, synthesized voice, and prerecorded sounds), and generating messages to send to other windows. Programmers specify application-specific actions to be performed in response to messages received by the window manager.

It is important to note that a window manager is not responsible for how the application displays information within a window. The application has the responsibility for managing the window contents. The window manager is responsible for mapping the window contents to the video display and providing a border with adornments (such as resize and reposition icons) which the user may manipulate to change the size and position of the window within the video display. Window managers have their own user interface, so that users can rearrange the windows displayed on the video display.

Most window managers are closely tied with one kind of operating system. Several commercially available window managers, and the type of system on which they run, include the following:

- *X Window System* (a public domain package available from MIT), which runs on UNIX® systems. The X window manager is briefly described in Appendix E1.
- *OpenLook*™, a commercial version of X that supports a special look and feel called "OpenLook" from AT&T.
- *Motif*™, a commercial version of X from the Open Systems Foundation. Motif supports a look and feel somewhat different from OpenLook.
- *Microsoft Windows,* which runs on MS-DOS systems, is described in Appendix E2.
- *Presentation Manager* (developed by Microsoft and available from IBM) for OS/2 systems.

6.3.1 Window Manager Features

Window managers have become popular because they support many features which are useful to both end users and application developers.

Users Interact with Multiple Processes.   Window managers allocate windows to each of several processes. Multiple processes can share a video screen if each process is associated with a window displayed within the screen. The user views the progress and controls each process by looking at the contents of the window allocated to the process and issuing commands to the process when its window is in focus.

Users Easily Move Information Between Applications.   Windows provide a convenient way for users to transport information between applications. Figure 6.1 illustrates a screen with three windows. One window is allocated to a text editor, another is allocated to a spreadsheet program, and the third window is allocated to a database program. In this example, the user first retrieves some data from the database using the database application. The user then selects some of the retrieved data and moves that data to the spreadsheet application in the second window. The spreadsheet application calculates aggregate and summary information, which the user then moves to the window allocated to the text editing program. The user uses the text editor to integrate the summary information in a report being prepared using the text editor.

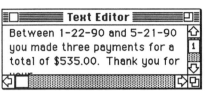

Figure 6.1 Three windows for three applications.

Users Access Remote Applications. Some window managers can allocate a window to a process operating on a remote computer via a communication system. For example, a user at a workstation wishes to access a database on a mainframe. The user asks the window manager to create a window into which the user can enter a request to the database management system on the mainframe. After the request is processed, the window manager displays the results from the database management system in the window.

Users Have Multiple Views to a Process. Some window managers can allocate several windows to an application; each window displays some aspect of the application to the user. Multiple windows can be useful for providing various views of the application to the user. For example, in Figure 6.2, two windows have been allocated to a planning system. One window displays a graph showing the precedence among the tasks of a project. The other window displays the completion percentage for each task.

Users Receive Events. When a process detects some unusual event of which the user should be aware, the process notifies the window manager to display a message

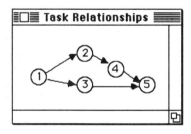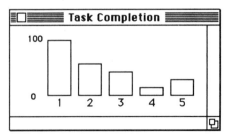

Figure 6.2 Two windows representing two views of an application.

describing the event. A user will notice the appearance of the message and take appropriate action.

Sohisticated User Interfaces Can Be Constructed Using Window Managers. Most window managers have libraries containing a wide variety of reusable interaction objects which can be used to build sophisticated user interfaces.

Terminal Independence. Some window managers work on a large variety of terminals and workstations, and hide the differences between those terminals and workstations from the application. Terminal independence increases the transportability of applications to a wider variety of terminals and workstations.

6.3.2 Window Managers Characteristics

Window managers differ in both the features offered and the manner in which the user and programmer see these features. This section discusses the major features of most window managers.

Window Shape. A few window managers support windows of arbitrary shape. For example, Figure 6.3 illustrates a circular window containing a clock, a screen with a rectangle window containing text, and a rectangle with rounded corners containing a menu. Users can quickly recognize and distinguish windows of differing shapes faster than similarly shaped windows. However, the algorithms that display and manage arbitrarily shaped windows are more complicated, and thus more time consuming, than the algorithms that display only rectangular windows.

Most window managers support only windows that are rectangular. In these systems, different labels, colors, font styles, sizes, and other display characteristics are used to help the user distinguish between different windows.

Rectangular windows may be either tiled or overlapped. *Tiled* windows can only be positioned on the screen in such a fashion that they do not overlap. Figure 6.4 illustrates a tiled screen. Figure 6.5 illustrates a screen with overlapped tiles. *Overlapped* windows can be placed on the screen so that they overlap, giving the user the impression of stacking windows on top of each other. The algorithms used to manage overlapping windows are more complicated than tiled windows and may be more time consuming to execute. Whether tiled or overlapped windows are better, is a personal judgment. However, there appears to be a trend toward overlapped windowing systems.

Figure 6.3 Windows with different shapes.

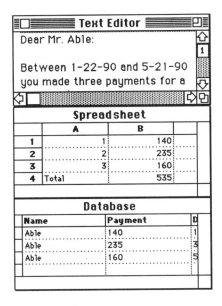

Figure 6.4 Tiled windows.

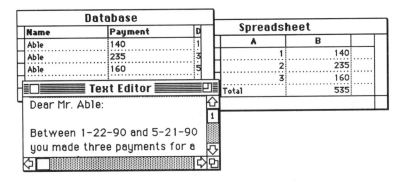

Figure 6.5 Overlapping windows.

Clipping. Sometimes the window is not large enough to contain all the information to be displayed. When this happens, the information is *clipped* so that the unclipped portion of the information will fit into the window. Figure 6.6 illustrates information clipped so that it fits into a window. Clipping is also necessary when windows overlap. As illustrated in Figure 6.7, information in the "underlying window" is clipped so that the user can see all of the information in the "overlying window."

Window Relationships. Some window managers maintain logical relationships between windows. Often the windows form a hierarchy consisting of a root window with children. Each window may have zero or more children windows, but each window (except the root) must have exactly one parent window. Some window managers require that all children windows be physically located within the boundaries of the parent

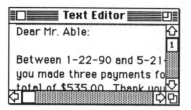

Figure 6.6 Clipped window.

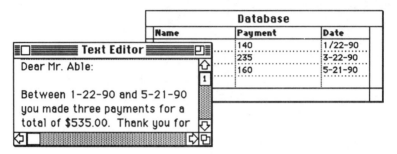

Figure 6.7 Underlying window is clipped.

window (Figure 6.8); other window managers allow children windows to be displayed anywhere on the screen.

Coordinate Systems. When an application instructs the window manager to display information in a window, it must determine where in the window the information should be displayed. A two-dimensional coordinate system is used for this purpose. A single pair of coordinates is used to specify where a spot of color should be displayed within the window. Two pairs of coordinates can be used to indicate where a rectangular

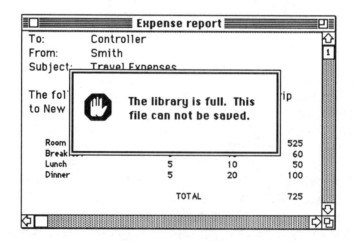

Figure 6.8 Hierarchy of windows.

subwindow should be positioned within a window; the first pair specifies the upper left-hand corner and the second pair specifies the lower right-hand corner.

Window Fragments. In a window manager that supports overlapping windows, the portion of a window overlaid by another window is called a *window fragment*. When the overlaying window is removed, the contents of the window fragment must be redisplayed. Some window managers do this automatically by keeping the contents of the window fragment in a buffer which is copied to the fragment after the overlying window is removed. Other window managers do not maintain buffers containing the contents of window fragments, so when the overlying window is moved, the application program must supply the contents of the window fragments. This increases the complexity of the application program.

Input Handling. Input received by the window manager from various input devices must be routed to the appropriate window. Usually, input is routed to the currently active window (the window on top of other windows on the desktop). Some window managers route keyboard input to a window other than the currently active window. The window receiving keyboard input is said to be the *focus* window. Some window managers route mouse input to a window other than the currently active window. The window receiving mouse input is called the *capture* window. Some windows, called *modal* windows, override other windows and receive all keyboard and mouse input.

Changing the Window in Focus. Some window managers use the current position of the cursor to identify the window in focus. Other window managers require the user to move the cursor inside of the desired window and then enter a refocus command, usually by pressing a key on the mouse, to change the window in focus.

Imaging Model. An *imaging model* is the representation of information passed from the application or dialog processor to the window manager for display to the user. Several models are commonly used including

- *Pixel*. The image to be displayed is an array of dots called *pixels*. The window manager clips the array to fit into the available space provided by the window and moves the array to the available space in the window. This approach is especially fast because the window manager does not have to interpret instructions to create the image to appear in the window. However, this approach may require large amounts of memory to store pixel arrays about to be displayed and large transfer costs and delays to transfer images between the application and the window manager.
- *PostScript*™. PostScript is a language used to describe an image to be displayed on a screen or printed on a printer. The window manager contains a PostScript interpreter which accepts the PostScript notation and generates the pixel array displayed to the user. While images take less space to store and less time to transfer between the application and the window manager than if the image is already represented using pixels, additional time is needed by the window manager to interpret the image and construct the pixels for display.

Other imaging models include GKS, a collection of functions used to describe a flat surface containing lines, polygons, circles, and other graphic objects, and PHIGS, a generalization of GKS which describes a hierarchy of graphic objects which constitute an image.

Resources.   Character strings must be translated to pixel images before being displayed. Each character can be mapped to several alternative pixel images, each displaying a different font and size. Each font and size to which a set of characters are mapped to is called a resource. A *resource* is an interaction object that is defined separately from the window manager. Resources are stored permanently on disk and are made available to the window manager only when needed by the window manager to display information. Users may store new resources on disk storage and have those resources loaded into the window manager without recompiling and linking the window manager. In addition to font types and sizes, resources may also include colors, cursor images, sounds, key bindings, and other mappings between the internal representation of information and the appearance of its display to the user or the manner of its input by the user.

6.3.3 Window Functions

Most window managers support a set of window manipulation functions which users and/or applications can invoke to control the contents of their video screen. The basic functions include the following:

Create and Destroy.   Create causes a new window to be opened on the screen. When creating a new window, its shape, size, and location must be specified. Destroy causes an existing window to be removed from the user's screen.

Move.   Reposition a window (1) within its parent window if the window manager requires that children windows be located within the boundaries of its parent window, (2) within the root window if the window manager requires that no portion of the window be outside the border of the screen, or (3) anywhere on or off the screen if the window manager imposes no restrictions.

Resize.   Make a window larger or smaller.

Reparent.   Change the parent-child relationship of two windows.

Circulate.   Move the top window on a stack of windows to the bottom of the stack or move the bottom window to the top of the stack.

Open and Close.   Closing a window causes the window to be replaced by an icon. Opening the window consists of selecting the corresponding icon from a menu of icons. The selected icon disappears from the menu as the window appears on the screen.

Cut and Paste Functions.   When information is *copied,* it is placed into a buffer, called the *clipboard.* The *cut* operation is the same as a copy in which the copied information also is deleted from its source. The *paste* command copies information from one clipboard to another window. There are two ways in which cut and paste functions can be implemented.

1. Cut and paste operates on the image model only.

2. Cut and paste operates on both the image model and the information structure.

If two applications are integrated in the sense that they support common data structures, then the second type of cut and paste can be supported. If the two applications do not support each other's data structures, then only the first type of cut and paste can be supported.

Stop, Start, Rewind.   Audio and full-motion video are temporal in nature. Special operations such at stop, start, rewind, and play at various speeds (both forward and backward) may be supported.

These functions can be invoked by selecting the function name from menus. Some menus are permanently displayed, often with a set of icons embedded into the border of the window. Other menus are displayed on request, often in the form of pulldown menus from a standard menu bar across the top of the window.

6.3.4 Generalized Windows

Researchers (Clarkson, 1991) have recently generalized the concept of a two-dimensional window to the concept of the three-dimensional room. While a user may scroll up and down, left and right in a traditional windowing system, a user may "turn" left or right, "look" upward or downward, advance forward and retreat backward, and thus reposition the user's perspective within the room. While a user may "open" an icon to see a window and "close" a window which is replaced by an icon in a traditional windowing system, a user may open a door to enter another room and close a door to exit from a room. Thus, a user may navigate from room to room.

Rooms represent a more familiar paradigm for users than windows, but require more sophisticated interaction objects and the corresponding interaction techniques (such as twisting knobs, flipping switches, pushing and pulling objects, and repositioning the user's viewpoint within the room). The currently popular mouse will likely be replaced by data gloves and other gesturing devices as interaction techniques for manipulating objects in rooms. Unfortunately, the hardware necessary to support the interactive, animated graphics is still experimental and is too expensive for widespread acceptance.

6.4 USER INTERFACE MANAGEMENT SYSTEMS PROVIDE ADDITIONAL FEATURES

The previous section described how window managers provide users with a "view port" or window to an application. Users may resize and reposition the window on the screen, and reposition the window over the application's data space by scrolling and paging. Some window managers support the functions cut, copy, and paste so users can move data among applications.

While the window manager manages size and position of windows, a UIMS (user interface management system) controls what happens within one or more windows by executing scripts associated with each application. The UIMS acts as a script execution engine. As it executes a script, it obtains information from users via interaction objects, transmits information to application functions, obtains results from application functions, and presents those results to the user via interaction objects.

A UIMS is the run-time kernel of a user interface system. In some cases, the UIMS is an application skeleton into which the programmer inserts additional specifications and code. In some cases, the UIMS accepts user interface specifications and executes or interprets them directly. In other cases, the UIMS may accept high-level user interface specifications, which it translates to a lower-level representation before execution. In this case, the UIMS can be thought of as a user interface code generator.

If the generated code references one or more modules provided by the UIMS, then these UIMS modules must be present during execution. This implies that at least part of the UIMS must be distributed with the software (and that the UIMS vendors may charge royalties for each copy of the distributed user interface). If the generated code does not contain references to UIMS modules, then the user interface can be distributed provided there is a compiler or interpreter for the code generated by the UIMS.

In addition to accepting commands specific to the application, the UIMS accepts and executes general commands such as undo, redo, and helpAboutFunctions. The remainder of this section discusses these commands.

Undo Function. Some UIMSs maintain a log of functions which it has performed. The log also records the values of all variables modified by each function. Each time the user requests that the undo function be executed, the UIMS replaces the modified values of the most recently executed function by the unmodified values from the log and removes the executed function from the log. The logs maintained by various UIMSs may differ in two aspects:

1. *Length of the log.* Some UIMSs maintain a log containing only the most recent function. Other UIMSs maintain a log containing an arbitrary number of functions.
2. *Scope of functions included on the log.* Some UIMSs include only functions from a particular script. Other UIMSs include functions from all scripts.

Example 6.1

Suppose that a UIMS maintains a log of unlimited length. Further, suppose that user performs the following functions:

```
T1: open(AccountIdentfier = 22, SocialSecurityNumber = 222 22 2222)
T2: apply(AccountIdentifier = 22, TransactionAmount = 300,
TransactionType = Deposit)
T3: apply(AccountIdentifier = 22, TransactionAmount = 300,
TransactionType = withdrawal)
T4: close(AccountIdentifier = 22)
```

After executing these four functions, the log contains the following values:

```
T1: Old.AccountIdentifier = nil; New.AccountIdentifier = 22;
    Old.SocialSecurityNumber = nil;
    New.SocialSecurityNumber = 222-22-2222;
    Old.Account = nil; New.Amount = 0;
```

```
T2: Old.Amount  =  0.0; New.Amount  =  300.00;
T3: Old.Amount  =  300.00; New.Amount  =  0.00
T4: Old.AccountIdentifier  =  22; New.Account Identifier  =  nil;
    Old.Amount  =  0.00; New.Amount  =  nil;
    Old.SocialSecurityNumber = 222-222222; New.Social SecurityNumber = nil;
```

Now suppose that the user changes his or her mind and wishes to undo these four functions. Beginning with the last entry in the log and working toward the first entry in the log, the first execution of undo causes the deleted Account object to be recreated with values of 22 for AccountIdentifier and 0.00 for Amount and 222 222222 for SocialSecurityNumber. The next execution of undo causes the Amount to be reset to 300.00. The next causes it to be reset to 0.00. The final execution of undo causes the Account object to be deleted. ■

Some functions do not have inverses. Such functions usually cause a change to the environment outside of the computer. Once the environment is changed, it is not easily restored to the state it was in prior to the execution of the function.

Exmple 6.2

The launchMissile function does not have an inverse because once launched, a missile cannot be physically stopped in flight and returned to the launching pad. ■

Generic Redo Function.   The *redo* function replaces old values by the corresponding new values.

Example 6.3

Having executed the four functions of Example 6.1 and then executing the undo operation four times, we can now redo the four operations by executing redo four times. The first execution causes 22 for AccountIdentifier and 222-22-2222 for SocialSecurityNumber to be inserted. The next redo causes 300.00 to replace 0.00 for Amount. The third redo replaces 300.00 by 0.00 for Amount. The fourth redo causes the Account to be deleted. ■

Redo should not be executed against functions which change the environment outside of the computer.

Example 6.4

The disburseFunds function of an ATM should not be redone if it delivers cash to a customer. ■

The undo and redo functions enable end users to go forward and backward in time, undoing mistakes and recovering from lost data.

The helpAboutFunction Function.   Function-specific help functions provide the user with specific information about other functions which the user can execute. This function, called helpAboutFunction (FunctionName), displays messages to the user explaining the purpose and effect of FunctionName. One approach for implementing this function is to place prespecified messages into a table. Then helpAboutFunction accesses this table, selects the appropriate prespecified messages, and display the messages to the user. Another approach is for the helpAboutFunction to generate messages from pre- and postconditions associated with each function.

The Halt Function. Some functions may take several minutes or hours to perform. Occasionally end users desire to cancel such functions. The *halt function* causes an executing function to terminate. Often the undo function is then executed, so that all changes made by the halted function are undone.

Semantic Constraint Enforcement. A controversial issue in UIMS design is how much semantic constraint enforcement should the UIMS perform. While enforcing semantic constraints within the UIMS leads to more immediate feedback, it may also lead to redundancy between the UIMS and application functions which may enforce the same constraints. The more semantic constraints enforced by the UIMS, the less independence between the UIMS and the application functions. Resolving this tension between the UIMS and application functions is an open research problem.

6.5 ARCHITECTURES FOR APPLICATIONS AND USER INTERFACE MANAGEMENT SYSTEMS

Sections 6.2 and 6.3 discussed the device drivers and windowing systems used for input and output by applications. This section describes alternative architectures for the rest of the application. The application may be partitioned into components by either of two approaches.

1. Components are based on combinations of the decision classes discussed in Chapter 2. Sections 6.5.1 through 6.5.4 discuss architectures derived using this approach.
2. Components consist of subsets of the application's functions called agents. Each agent is then further partitioned into modules based on combinations of the decision classes discussed in Chapter 2. Section 6.5.5 describes these approaches.

6.5.1 Monolithic Architecture

In the monolithic application all of the decisions of the structural, functional, dialog, and presentation decision classes are implemented within a single component, as illustrated in Figure 6.9(a). Only the pragmatic decisions are implemented separately.

We do not recommend this architecture for the following reasons:

- The software logic which implements the decisions from each decision class is often so intertwined that it is impossible to extract that software for reuse elsewhere.
- The complexity of the single component may be so great and the resulting implementation so large that implementers have difficulty debugging and maintaining the software.
- Changes to one portion of the component may require changes elsewhere in the component because of its unstructured nature.

To overcome these problems, user interface system implementers have partitioned the single monolithic component into several components, giving rise to other architectures.

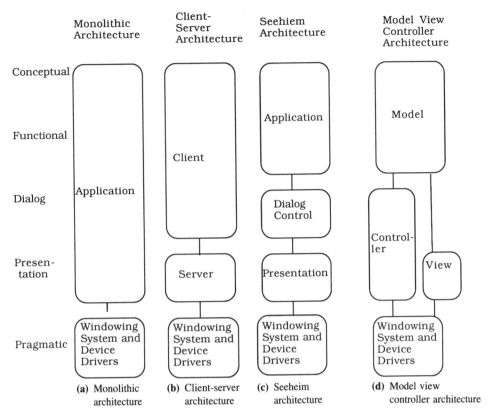

Figure 6.9 Components of four user interface system architectures.

6.5.2 Client-Server Architecture

The client-server architecture divides the monolithic architecture into two major components, as illustrated in Figure 6.9(b).

1. The *client,* which implements the decisions made in the structural, functional, and dialog decision classes.
2. The *server,* which contains a library of I/O routines that implement the presentation aspects of the user interface. This collection of reusable I/O functions is sometimes called a *user interface tool kit.* Typically, tool kits contain I/O functions which implement interaction objects and a window manager. The server is responsible for presenting information from the client to the user and for converting data and commands entered by the user to a form understandable by the server.

Many windowing packages, such as the X windowing system and Microsoft Windows, use this architecture. The client-server architecture has been quite popular for the following reasons:

- It separates much of the user interface from the application code.
- Routines in the server can be reused in multiple applications.

The client-server model has the following possible disadvantages:

- The interface between the client and server may be complex and difficult to learn and use. Servers may contain hundreds of procedures which interact in subtle ways.
- The number of messages exchanged between the client and servers may be large, especially due to the messages from the server that invoke ''callback'' functions in the client.

6.5.3 Seeheim Architecture

Developed by user interface system experts at a 1985 conference in Seeheim, Germany, the Seeheim model (Green, 1983) makes the assumption of modular separation of the application and its interface. The Seeheim architecture [Figure 6.9(c)] consists of the following components:

- The *presentation component* deals with the physical representation of the user interface. This includes the interaction objects and image model. The presentation component implements results of decisions in the presentation decision class.
- The *dialog control component* deals with the dialog between the user and the application. This component is responsible for the structure of the commands and dialog used by the user. The dialog control component implements results of decisions in the dialog decision class.
- The *application component* defines the application itself. It contains all the computational logic to carry out the functions provided by the application. This component implements the functions of the functional decision class and objects and relationships of the structural decision class.

These three components communicate by transferring information tokens. A token flowing from the user to the application is called an input token, and a token flowing from the application to the user is called an output token.

The Seeheim model has the following advantages:

- The Seeheim model supports various types of independence. Because of the numerous components, changes to one component can be isolated from other components, especially between components that are not adjacent to each other.
- The Seeheim model implements each decision classes as a different component, allowing different individuals with different expertise to work independently.

Disadvantages include the following:

- There may be some redundancy among the components. For example, both the presentation and application components may enforce the same semantic constraints.

- The extra levels of software and message passing may introduce inefficiency. Nonadjacent components can only communicate indirectly with each other, using common adjacent components as intermediaries. One possible technique for improving efficiency is to allow the presentation component to interact directly with the application interface.
- It is sometimes difficult to separate the user interface from the application. In applications involving editing, browsing, and inspecting, the user interface needs to be tightly coupled with the application logic. The Seeheim model may not be appropriate for applications like these.

6.5.4 Model View Controller Architecture

The model view controller paradigm (Krasner & Pope, 1988) is used in the Smalltalk (Goldberg & Robson, 1983) object-oriented programming language. The concepts of model, view, and control can also be used as a high-level architecture. This architecture [Figure 6.9(d)] consists of three major modules.

1. Model contains all of the computational algorithms necessary to support the structural and function decision classes.
2. View contains the algorithms and heuristics dealing with the display aspects of the presentational decision class.
3. Controller contains the algorithms and heuristics dealing with the user entry of data and commands (part of the presentation decision class) and all aspects of the dialog decision class.

In the model view controller user interface system architecture, the presentation decision class has been divided into two subclasses, one dealing with output (the view) and one dealing with input (the controller). The input subclass is combined with the dialog decision class to form the controller. Unlike the Seeheim architecture in which there is a stratification of decision classes into layers and with each component interfacing only with components in adjacent layers, in the model view controller architecture the three components interface directly with each other. Thus, a change in a model component can be communicated directly to the view component and bypassing the controller component.

The model view controller has not been widely used as an architecture, but has been used in the SmallTalk programming environment as a multiagent model, described next.

6.5.5 Multiagent Models

The multiagent model partitions an application system into a collection of modules called *agents*. Each agent implements part of the application functions. Each agent has memory which contains a state, receives events, and reacts to events by changing its state and producing other events. Each agent may be implemented as one or more objects:

- Each agent is implemented as a a single object [Figure 6.10(a)]. Each agent is itself implemented using the monolithic architecture. Each agent implements the results

(a) Each agent implemented as a single object

(b) Each agent implemented as two objects

(c) Each agent implemented as three objects

Figure 6.10 Multiagent models.

of the conceptual, functional, dialog, and presentation decisions for its part of the application.

• Each agent is implemented as two objects, one for computation and the other for presentation [Figure 6.10(b)]. Each agent is implemented according to the client-server architecture: each agent is implemented as a client object which is responsible for the conceptual, functional and dialog aspects of its part of the application and a server object which is responsible for the presentation aspects of the agent's partition of the application.

• Each agent is implemented as three objects [Figure 6.10(c)]. One example of this is the model view controller model used in SmallTalk in which the model object is responsible for the conceptual and functional decisions, the view object is responsible for the output presentation decisions, and the controller object is responsible for input and dialog decisions for the agent's part of the application.

Multiagent models have the following benefits:

• *Modularity*. Each agent has its own state and implementation. It is possible to modify an agent without affecting other agents in the application system. The implementation of each agent can be reused to implement other agents.

• *Distributed*. Each agent may be executed on a physical processor different from the processors used for other agents.

- *Multithreaded.* Users may interact with agents at any time, and may switch from agent to agent.

Disadvantages of the multiagent model include the following:

- Communication among the large number of agents necessary to implement an application may become expensive.
- Understanding how multiple agents interact can be difficult for the programmer, especially if the number of agents is large.

6.5.6 Communication Among Components

There are at least three approaches that are used to exchange semantic tokens among architectural components.

1. Subroutine call. Components invoke other components as subroutines. Information tokens are passed from the calling component to the called component in the form of parameters. Information tokens are returned from the called routine in the form of returned parameters. While subroutine calls are the most familiar technique for programmers, subroutines suffer from the following disadvantage: An interaction object can accept information from a user only while it is active (after it has been called). If the script execution engine or some application is active, the interaction object cannot accept information from the user, who is forced to wait until the interaction object is invoked.

2. Shared memory. Components act as co-routines which communicate by shared memory. Figure 6.11(a) illustrates two shared memories, one shared by the script execution engine and interaction objects, and the other shared by the script execution engine and application functions. The interaction objects may place information obtained from the user into one of the shared memories, which can be accessed by the script execution engine. The execution engine places information into the second shared memory for use by an application function. Figure 6.11(b) illustrates a single shared memory (sometimes called a blackboard memory) shared by all three components: the script execution engine, interaction objects, and application functions. Treating the components as separate processors which are all active at the same time enables users to enter information using an interaction object in parallel with the processing of other components. However, each component must explicitly check shared memory to detect any new information placed there by other components.

3. Message passing. Components act as co-routines which communicate by passing messages containing information tokens. For example, an interaction object accepts information from the user and transmits an information token to the dialog component, which receives the information token and examines it, generating a new message containing one or more information tokens for an application function. Usually each processor has a queue (sometimes called a mailbox) which is able to accept and temporarily store multiple messages from other components. Components may work in parallel. Rather than look in shared memory, each component looks in its mail box for messages containing information to process.

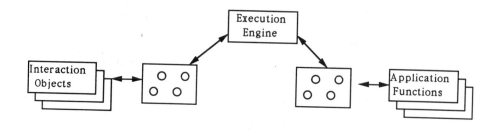

(a) Two shared memories

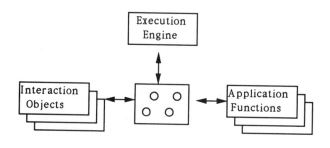

(b) Single shared memory

Figure 6.11 Common data structures.

6.5.7 Current Trends

At least three general trends can be observed in the use of the architectures just described.

1. Fewer and fewer new applications are being implemented using the monolithic architecture. The complexity and lack of flexibility of this architecture has spawned much research activity in proposing and evaluating alternative architectures.

2. With the widespread use of tool sets such as those supported by the X Window System, Microsoft Windows, and IBM's Presentation Manager, many new applications are being developed using the client-server model. However, these applications lack the user interface application independence which can be achieved by the Seeheim model.

3. The Seeheim model remains controversial. While widely used in the early days of UIMS, practioners faced efficiency issues, especially when implementing direct manipulation user interfaces.

4. A trend to multiagent models has recently become widely used in several areas.
   a. Object-oriented programming languages such as SmallTalk, Objective C, C++, and Object-Oriented Pascal are becoming popular programming languages.
   b. Object-oriented database management systems are now commercially available.
   c. Many user interfaces, especially those involving direct manipulation, are being implemented using object-oriented techniques.

While the monolithic architecture is on the wane, the client-server and multiagent models are on the rise. Because none of these architectures appear best for all situations, it appears that all three will continue to be used for some time to come.

6.6 SUMMARY

Device drivers are subroutine packages which hide specific characteristics of devices from applications. Multiple windows enable users to view and control multiple processes, as well as have multiple views to a single process. Window managers support the basic window functions of create and destroy, move, resize, reparent, circulate, open, and close.

A user interface management system is a user interface execution engine which executes user interface scripts. Some UIMSs also support multithreading of dialogs among multiple scripts and functions such as undo, redo, helpAboutFunction, halt, cut, copy, and paste. A UIMS may also enforce semantic integrity constraints on behalf of the underlying application functions.

A user interface system architecture describes the major components of a user interface system. The monolithic application model consists of a single component in which decisions of four of the decision classes are implemented. The client-server architecture divides the monolithic application architecture into two components, one dealing with computation and the other dealing with appearance. The Seeheim model consists of three components, one for each of the conceptual and functional, dialog, and presentational decision classes. Multiagent models in which the application is partitioned into agents, with each agent being implemented as one, two, or three objects in manners similar to the three other system architectures are also possible.

Semantic tokens may be exchanged among the user interface system components by subroutine call, shared memory, or message passing.

7

State Transition Descriptions

This chapter describes

> - How state transition systems are used to represent scripts.
> - How to deal with large state transition systems.
> - How to represent multithreaded dialogs.
> - What tool can be used to specify state transition systems.

A dialog is the exchange of information among two or more parties. A script is a formal description of allowable dialogs. Scripts are useful in many situations, including the description of communication system protocols; commit, abort, and concurrency control protocols in distributed database management systems; and human-computer dialogs in user interface systems. Chapters 7 through 10 present techniques for representing scripts with emphasis on how they are used to describe dialogs between users and application functions.

In this chapter, we consider the use of state transition systems to represent dialogs. We will review several techniques for describing state transition systems. Examples of user interface systems which use state transition systems to represent dialogs are also presented in this chapter.

7.1 STATE TRANSITION SYSTEMS REPRESENT SCRIPTS

A *finite state transition system* is a model of a system which accepts semantic tokens as input and performs actions based on that input. A finite state transition system consists of a finite number of states and a set of transitions that each map a semantic token and a state into another state. There is one special state, called the *start state,* in which an execution engine for the finite state transition system begins processing. There may be one or more final states, called *end states* in which the execution engine stops processing.

Beginning with the start state, an execution engine for a finite state transition system repeatedly performs the following steps:

1. The state transition system execution engine waits in a state until it receives a semantic token from

- an end user via an interaction object,
- an application function,
- a sensor which detects a condition or event in the real world,
- another finite state transition system.

2. The state transition system tests conditions and selects zero or more transitions to other states. A transition may contain zero or more conditions. All conditions associated with a transition must be satisfied in order for the transition to be selected.

- If the current state is an end state, then the execution engine stops.
- If one transition is selected, the execution engine begins to execute the state at the target of that transition.
- If more than one transition is selected, the execution engine chooses one of them, places the remaining transitions on a stack, and begins to execute the state which is the target of the chosen transition.
- If no transitions are selected, the execution engine pops the top transition from the stack and begins to execute the state at the target of that transition. If there are no transitions in the stack, the execution engine stops.

3. The state transition system performs actions associated with the new state. These actions may

- present a semantic token to the user,
- transmit a semantic token to an application,
- modify a variable,
- generate a semantic token for use by another finite state transition system.

Dialog designers use state transition systems to represent scripts. When an execution engine processes a state transition system, the result is a dialog consisting of semantic tokens exchanged between the user and one or more application functions.

A directed graph, called a *transition graph,* is frequently used to illustrate a finite state transition system. The nodes of the graph correspond to the states of the finite state transition system. Each node is labeled with the name of the state to which it corresponds. We will use a double-circled node to represent the start state. Single circles represent states involving actions which exchange information with end users via interaction objects, and small squares represent states whose action is invoking or sending semantic tokens to application functions. The actions associated with a state may be listed inside the node associated with the state, listed in a table associated with the transition graph which contains state names and actions, or listed in pop-up windows which designers can open and close when displaying state transition graphs on a video screen. In order to keep the size of nodes small in the illustrations in this text, we will not list the actions inside of nodes.

There is a directed arc between each pair of states which can be involved in a transition. Each arc is labeled with the condition which must be satisfied for that transition to be used.

Example 7.1

Figure 7.1 illustrates a transition graph representing a very simple finite state transition system. It accepts two parameters, AccountNumber and Amount. Figure 7.1 consists of states named Welcome, EnterAmountToWithdraw, DoCheck, and Finish. Initially, the state transition system is in the start state, Welcome. The actions associated with this state cause a message to be displayed to the user requesting a value for AccountNumber. The user enters

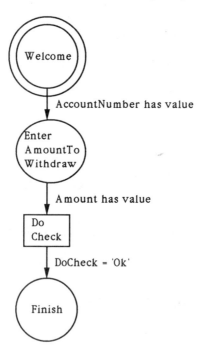

Figure 7.1 Transition graph representing finite state transition system.

a value for AccountNumber, which causes the execution engine to select the transition leading to state EnterAmountToWithdraw, and the execution engine switches to this state. The action associated with this state displays a prompt to the end user to enter a value for Amount. The user enters a value for Amount which causes the finite state transition system to select the transition leading to the DoCheck state. The finite state transition system moves from state the EnterAmountToWithdraw state to the DoCheck state. The action associated with the DoCheck state invokes the Withdraw function and provides it with two parameters, AccountNumber and Withdraw. When the withdraw function is completed, the execution engine selects the Finish state and transitions to it. Because Finish is an end state, the processing stops. The actions performed in each state are summarized in the following table:

State	Action
Welcome	display ('Welcome to the ATM. Please enter your account number.')
EnterAmountToWithdraw	display: ('Please enter the amount you wish to withdraw.')
DoCheck	withdraw (AccountNumber, Amount)
Finish	stop

Example 7.1 is improved in Example 7.2 to be more realistic. ∎

Example 7.2

Figure 7.2 illustrates a transition graph representing a finite state transition system for the ATM dialog of Chapter 4. The actions performed in each state are summarized in the following table:

State	Action
BadAccountNumber	display ('The account number you entered,' AccountNumber, 'does not exist. Your request has been canceled.')
Confirm	display ('To confirm that you wish to withdraw', Amount, 'from account', AccountNumber, 'enter "Yes". If not, then enter "No".')
DisburseFails	display ('This machine cannot disburse cash. Please use another machine.')
DoCheck	check (AccountNumber)
DoDisburse	disburse (Amount)
DoWithdraw	withdraw (AccountNumber, Amount)
EnterAmountToWithdraw	display ('Enter the amount you wish to withdraw.')
Finish:	display ('Goodbye.')
NegativeConfirm	display ('Your request has been canceled.')
Success	display ('Remember to take your money out of slot to the right of this screen. Thank you.')
Welcome	display ('Welcome to the ATM. Please enter your account number.')
WithdrawFails	display ('There are not sufficient funds in your account.')
WithdrawOk	display (Amount, 'has been withdrawn from your account. Your new balance is', NewBalance.)

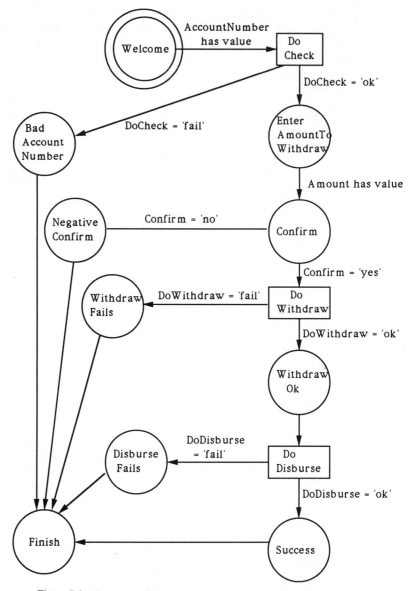

Figure 7.2 Transition graph representing another finite state transition system.

The three application functions implement the following capabilities:

1. check, an application function which searches a database for the account number, returning the result ok if it is found.

2. withdraw, an application function which subtracts the amount to be withdrawn from the current balance and returns ok if the new account balance is greater than or equal to zero.

3. disburse, an application function which disburses cash to the ATM patron.

Each of the dialogs of Figure 4.2 corresponds to a path through the state transition system illustrated in Figure 7.2. For example, dialog trace B of Figure 4.2 corresponds to the path containing the following states:

Welcome
DoCheck
BadAccountNumber
Finish ■

If only one transition is selected at each state, the state transition system is said to be *deterministic*. Otherwise, the state transition system is said to be *nondeterministic*.

In nondeterministic state transition systems, the execution engine chooses one of the several transitions and pushes the remainder onto a stack. If the execution engine reaches a non-end state and is unable to select a transition, then it will pop a transition from the stack and begin executing the state at the target of that transition. In effect, the execution engine made a bad decision when choosing among the alternative transitions and is now revisiting that state. However, actions performed by the execution after making the bad decision must be undone. Some application functions can be undone, and some cannot. Semantic tokens displayed to the user must be retracted. Because of problems like these, scripts represented by nondeterministic state transitions are not frequently used.

Let B denote an arbitrary state in a state transition diagram. Let B* denote the *inverse* state associated with state B that cancels or undoes all actions performed within state B. The transition from B to B* is called the undo transition. There are also transitions from B* to each state that transitions to B. After B transitions to B* and B* has undone all of the actions performed by B, then the execution engine will make a transition to the state that was executed before state B was executed. In order to do this, the state transition execution engine maintains a stack of executed states. The execution engine can "back up" a path of executed states if each state in the path has an undo transition. Of course, the execution of some states cannot be undone. These states have no associated undo state. A state transition execution cannot "back up" beyond a state with no undo transition.

There are three approaches for implementing inverse states.

1. *Explicit inverse operations*. Inverse state B* contains a set of operations that are the inverse of the operations in state B. When B* is executed, variable values of state B are explicitly changed back to the values they had before B was executed.
2. *Implicit undo by stacking*. The state transition system execution engine maintains a stack of old and new (modified) values for each variable that is changed by state B. The inverse state B* pops pairs off of the stack and replaces the new value of the variable by its old value.
3 *Implicit undo by spooling*. The state transition system execution engine does not change variable values directly, but "spools" or records actions in a buffer. When the execution engine reaches a state with no undo transition, the actions are applied. If an undo is executed, the actions in the buffer are discarded.

Robert Jacob (1983, 1986) pioneered the use of state transition diagrams for user interface systems. Where we have used the term semantic token, Jacob used the term event, but the main idea is the same. Also, rather than associate actions with state, he associated actions with transitions between states. The type of state transition diagram used by Jacob is called a Moore diagram. The type of state transition system used at the beginning of this chapter is called a Mealy system. It is possible to convert Moore systems to Mealy systems, and vice versa.

Most dialogs are more complex than our simple ATM example. It is not uncommon to use hundreds of states and hundreds of transitions among states. While state transition execution engines have no trouble dealing with large numbers of states and transitions, the individuals who define scripts may have trouble dealing with the complexity of state transition systems of this size. Sections 7.2 through 7.6 explore approaches that attempt to manage the complexity of large state transition systems.

7.2 SUBGRAPHS ARE FACTORED OUT OF STATE TRANSITION GRAPHS

Software designers have long subdivided complex programs into independent subprograms, each of which can be designed separately. Dialog designers can use a similar approach for dealing with large state transition graphs (Wasserman, 1985).

A large state transition graph can be partitioned into subgraphs. Let G be a state transition graph and S be a subgraph of G such that A is an arc from a node in G but not in S to a node in S. If S is replaced by a single node N, then A is modified to point to N.

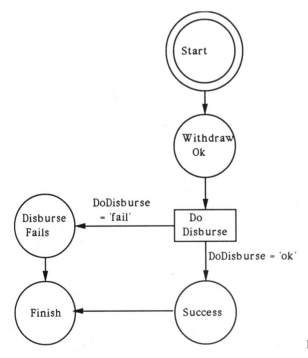

Figure 7.3 Subgraph.

Example 7.3

Suppose that the script designer decides that the WithdrawOk, DoDisburse, Success, and DisburseFails nodes of Figure 7.2 should be placed into a separate transition graph. These nodes are removed from the graph of Figure 7.2 and placed into a new subgraph, called Sub1, illustrated in Figure 7.3. A new node, a rectangle labeled sub1, replaces the deleted subgraph in Figure 7.2 resulting in the graph of Figure 7.4. ■

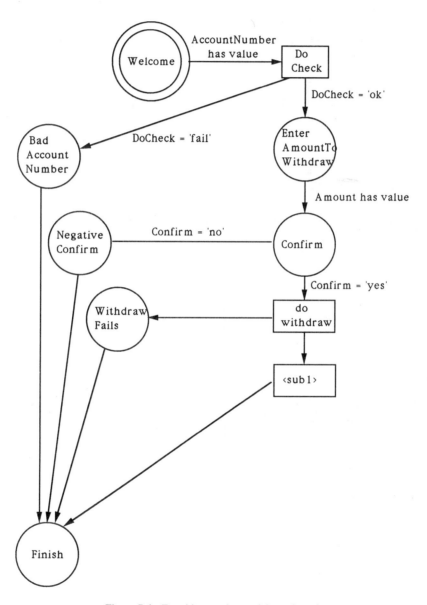

Figure 7.4 Transition graph containing subgraph.

The following guidelines can be used to partition a state transition graph into subgraphs. (These guidelines closely parallel the guidelines in Chapter 3 for partitioning the dialog design problem into separate classes.)

- *Sufficiency.* All nodes are part of the original graph or some subgraph.
- *Necessity.* The nodes and transitions in each subgraph describe a significant portion of a dialog.
- *Understandability.* The dialog represented by the subgraph should be easily understood by the human mind. Some script designers feel that each subgraph should contain no more than 18 to 20 states. This number of states, and the corresponding transitions, is also a convenient number to fit on a single sheet of paper.
- *Independence.* The number of arcs between subgraphs should be small. Changes made to one subgraph result in minimal changes to other subgraphs.
- *Reusability.* The subgraph has the potential of being used in other scripts.

7.3 REDUNDANT TRANSITIONS CAN BE FACTORED OUT OF A STATE TRANSITION DIAGRAM

Another approach for controlling the complexity of state transition systems is to convert state transition graphs into state trees. Figure 7.5 illustrates a state transition diagram in which the user can arbitrarily switch among the six states. Each arc has two arrows indicating that it represents two transitions, one for each arrow. Figure 7.6 illustrates the same states organized as leaves of a state tree. Nonleaf nodes of a state tree are used to organize and group similar states together. It is possible to transition between any two leaf nodes in Figure 7.5 by transitioning along the path of nodes between them in Figure 7.6.

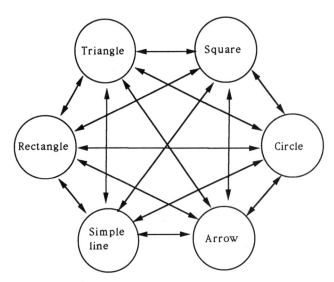

Figure 7.5 State transition graph.

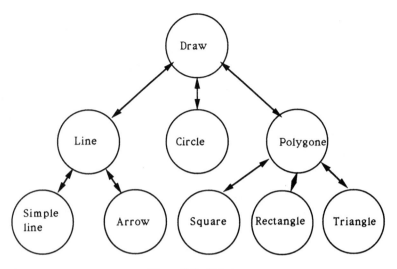

Figure 7.6 State tree.

From a representational point of view, the *state tree* (Rumbaugh, 1988) of Figure 7.6 may be more modularized and easier for user interface designers to work with than the state transition diagram of Figure 7.5. State trees may be considered less complex than the corresponding state transition system because they are more structured and contain fewer transitions. However, the execution engine for state trees is more complex, and the state tree has additional nodes (line, draw, polygon) which can be considered as "modes," which some designers feel make a user interface complex.

7.4 A MERGED STATE REPLACES MANY STATES

Nodes containing help messages may account for many of the large number of states which can exist in a state transition diagram representing a script. For each state in which the user enters commands or information, the user interface designer may design a corresponding help state. Figure 7.7(a) illustrates an example of a state transition graph with help nodes. The execution engine transitions to the appropriate help state whenever the user requests help by entering a help signal in some standard way, such as entering the keyword "help" or by pressing the question mark button. Inserting help states into a finite state transition system may nearly double the number of states. However, there are many similarities among help states in a state transition diagram.

- Users cause a transition to its help state by signaling help.
- Each help state displays a message.
- Each help state transitions back to the original state when the user signals resume in some standard way (such as pressing the return key) and the main dialog continues.

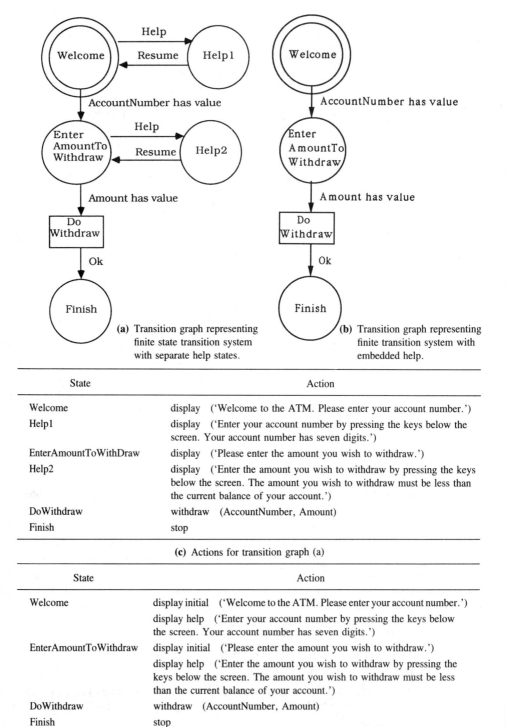

(a) Transition graph representing finite state transition system with separate help states.

(b) Transition graph representing finite transition system with embedded help.

State	Action
Welcome	display ('Welcome to the ATM. Please enter your account number.')
Help1	display ('Enter your account number by pressing the keys below the screen. Your account number has seven digits.')
EnterAmountToWithDraw	display ('Please enter the amount you wish to withdraw.')
Help2	display ('Enter the amount you wish to withdraw by pressing the keys below the screen. The amount you wish to withdraw must be less than the current balance of your account.')
DoWithdraw	withdraw (AccountNumber, Amount)
Finish	stop

(c) Actions for transition graph (a)

State	Action
Welcome	display initial ('Welcome to the ATM. Please enter your account number.')
	display help ('Enter your account number by pressing the keys below the screen. Your account number has seven digits.')
EnterAmountToWithdraw	display initial ('Please enter the amount you wish to withdraw.')
	display help ('Enter the amount you wish to withdraw by pressing the keys below the screen. The amount you wish to withdraw must be less than the current balance of your account.')
DoWithdraw	withdraw (AccountNumber, Amount)
Finish	stop

(d) Actions for transition graph (b)state

Figure 7.7   Simplifying complex transition graph.

Help states can be removed from a finite state transition system by placing help messages within the main script states as illustrated in Figure 7.7(b). The finite state transition system execution engine is extended so that it displays the help message whenever the user signals help. When the execution engine is processing any state and the user signals help, the help message associated with that state will be displayed. Regular execution engine processing resumes when the user indicates in the standard way that the main script should resume.

This approach can be extended in at least two ways.

1. *Help in depth.* An additional help message can be displayed each time the user signals help. When the user is finished viewing the help messages, the user signals that he or she is ready to resume normal processing and the main script should continue.

2. *Tailored help messages.* If the script is to be used by two or more classes of users, help messages can be tailored for each class. As an example, help messages can be expressed in English or in Spanish, depending on the preferred national language of the user.

Several states can be merged into a single state consisting of several parameters:

- A prompt message
- A default value
- A name of another state to be transitioned to if the user enters an ''escape'' request
- One or more help messages
- A name of a routine that performs semantic processing to verify that the value entered by the user is correct

A modified execution engine performs the following processing steps when the state transition system enters each new state (Benbasat & Wand, 1984):

1. *Prompt.* Display the predefined prompt to the user.
2. *Input.* Either accept input from the user or use the default value.
3. *Escape.* If the user requests escape, transition to the state identified as the escape state.
4. *Help.* If the user requests help, predefined help messages are displayed to the user and the processing of the node begins again.
5. *Check.* Semantic checking routines are invoked to verify that the information entered by the user is appropriate. If not, an error message is displayed to the user.
6. *Action.* Any actions to be performed in this state are done. The next state is selected.
7. *Flow control.* The execution engine transitions to the selected state, and this cycle begins again.

Other types of frequently appearing state transition diagram fragments can be replaced by inserting additional information into states and extending the finite state transition system execution engine, for example, a state transition which attempts to use a resource which is momentarily unavailable (such as send a mail message on a currently used telephone line) and presents the message ''abort or try again?'' This fragment can be replaced by inserting the error message into the main script state, extending the state transition system processor to display the error message when the error occurs, and prompting the user to choose between aborting or trying again.

Combining several nodes into a single node results in state transition diagrams with fewer nodes, but increases the complexity of the state transition system execution engine.

7.5 SUPERNODES ENCAPSULATE SUBGRAPHS

Supernodes encapsulate a subgraph, enabling designers to treat it as a single node in some situations and in other situations treat it as a graph. For example, consider the state transition graph of Figure 7.8(a). The subgraph consisting of the four ''Try'' nodes and the transitions among them are encapsulated into a supernode in Figure 7.8(b). The arc from the supernode to the Success node represents four transitions, from each of the nodes within the supernode to the Success node. The arc between the LastTry node and the GiveUp node in Figure 7.8(b) illustrates a transition from a single node within a supernode to a node outside of the supernode. Supernodes can be used to simplify the visual complexity of state transition graphs by reducing the number of arcs in the graph. State transition graphs containing supernodes are called state charts (Horel, 1987; Wellner, 1989).

An arc pointing to the edge of a supernode is somewhat like an ''exclusive or'' in that it can transition to exactly one of the nodes inside of the supernode. Sometimes this type of supernode is called an *exclusive or grouper* because only one node within the supernode can be active. Figure 7.8(b) shows a small arc with a ball at its tail leading to the FirstTry node. This arc is called a default arc. When an arc leads to the supernode [as illustrated by the arc leading to the left of the super node in Figure 7.8(b)], the default arc identifies the node inside of the supernode which the state transition execution engine executes when it transitions to the supernode.

Sometimes it is desirable to remember the node inside of a supernode so that the execution engine can return to it at a later time. For example, if the user uses a workstation to access a mainframe computer, communication errors may occur. As illustrated in Figure 7.8(c), an error processing node named FixError is transitioned to whenever a communication error occurs. After resolving the error, we desire to return to the state where the error occurred. This is denoted by the small H inside of the supernode of Figure 7.8(c). The H notation (which stands for ''History'') indicates that the most recently active node within the state transition system represented by the supernode is dynamically chosen to be the target of the transition into the supernode from the FixError node.[*]

[*]When the H notation is used, only nodes at the first level within the supernode can be selected. If the supernode itself contains a hierarchy of supernodes and we wish to transition to the most recently visited node anywhere within the hierarchy of supernodes, then the notation H* is used instead. Without an asterisk, only a subnode at the topmost level of the supernode is revisited; with the asterisk, the most recently visited state in any level of the supernode is revisited.

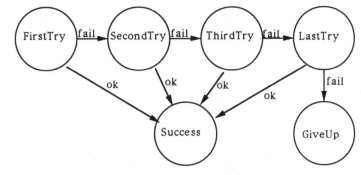

(a) Example state transition diagram for sign-on activity

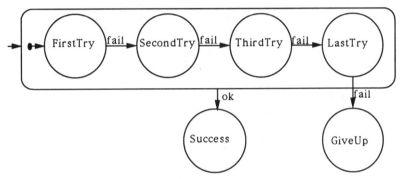

(b) Sign-on supernode with FirstTry as
default start node

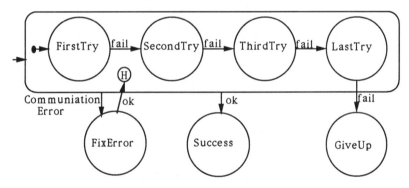

(c) Use of history to select node with supernode

Figure 7.8 Supernodes.

Changes to a supernode can often be isolated from changes to nodes outside of the supernode. For example, the ThirdTry node of Figure 7.8(c) has been removed from the supernode in Figure 7.8(d) without changing any of the transition to or from the supernode.

As illustrated in Figure 7.8(e), the arc to the supernode is again dynamically attached to one of the nodes inside of the supernode. The S notation indicates that a

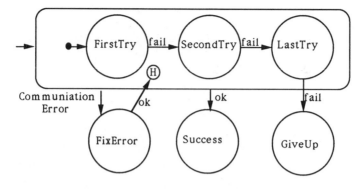

(d) Another supernode for the sign-on
activity with sign-on supernode

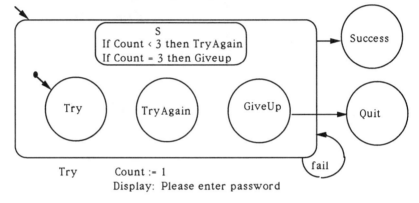

Try   Count := 1
           Display: Please enter password

TryAgain   Count := Count + 1
           Display: Please enter password again

Giveup   Display: Contact your supervisor. Goodbye.

(e) Using S to select a node within a sign-
on supernode

Figure 7.8 (continued)

condition determines which node within the supernode is dynamically chosen to be the target of the transition into the supernode. In Figure 7.8(e), the Try node is selected as the
default node for the first transition to the supernode. When executing the Try node, the
execution engine initializes the variable count to 1. The S notation indicates that as long
as Count is less than 3, transitions (other than the first transition) to the supernode will be
dynamically transitioned to the TryAgain node, which increments the value of Count by
1. When the Count is equal to three, transitions to the supernode will be dynamically
transitioned to the GiveUp node, which in turn transitions to the Quit node outside of the
supernode.

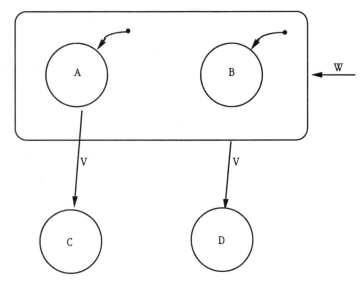

Figure 7.9 State chart with two nondeterministic transitions.

It is easy to create supernodes which are nondeterministic. Figure 7.9 illustrates a supernode in which transition "W" and transition "V" each result in two nodes being selected as the target of each transition. Nondeterministic transitions like these should be avoided.

Supernodes can be nested to arbitrary levels. This enables script designers to develop hierarchies of script fragments in a structured, modular manner. The use of supernodes also decreases the number of arcs explicitly represented when using the graph notation because arcs from supernodes may represent multiple transitions.

7.6 STATE CHARTS REPRESENT MULTITHREADED DIALOGS

Figure 7.10 illustrates another type of supernode which itself contains two state transition diagrams separated by a dotted line. One of these state transition diagrams is used for entering the AccountNumber; the other is used for entering the AmountToWithdraw. In this simple case, the user may either first enter the AccountNumber and then enter the AmountToWithdraw, or first enter the AmountToWithdraw and then enter the Acount-Number. Both these state transition diagrams must be completed before the user may continue to the Confirm state. The nodes labeled T in Figure 7.10 are nodes that perform no actions other than transition to another node.

Figure 7.11 illustrates a multithreaded dialog. In a multithreaded dialog, the user interacts with two or more scripts in an interleaved fashion, interchanging some information with first script, then switching to the second script, interchanging some information, and then switching back to the first again. The two scripts are represented as state transition graphs within a supernode and are separated by a dotted line. The dotted

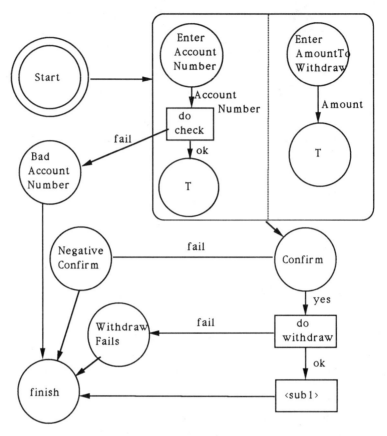

Figure 7.10 Transition graph containing supernode.

line indicates that users may switch between the two scripts represented by the two state transition graphs at any time, always returning to the most recently visited node in the target graph. In a *multithreaded dialog,* the user multiplexes among several scripts. In the multithreaded dialog illustrated in Figure 7.11, the user switches back and forth between reading electronic mail and withdrawing funds from a bank account.

The funds withdrawal dialog itself is a special case of a multithreaded dialog. It contains a supernode which contains two state transition diagrams. However, these two diagrams are so simple that once the user begins one of them, it is finished before the user can switch to the other dialog. This illustrates how order-independent tasks are a special case of multithreading.

An arc pointing to the edge of a supernode containing multiple scripts separated by dotted lines is somewhat like an ''and'' in that it transitions to all of the scripts inside of the supernode. (Sometimes this type of supernode is called an *and grouper.*) Users may switch between scripts within an and grouper at any time, resulting in multithreaded dialogs.

One of the major advantages of state charts is that they can be used to describe

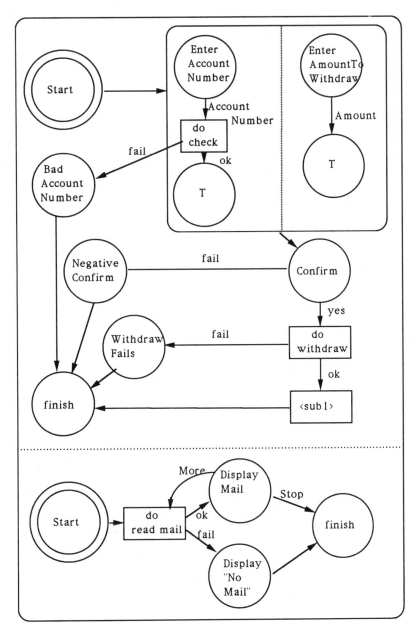

Figure 7.11 Multithreaded dialog.

multithreaded dialogs. Using traditional state transition graphs to describe all possible multithreaded dialogs involving two independent state transition graphs with *m* and *n* states requires *2mn* additional transitions. No additional transitions are required when these multithreaded dialogs are represented using state charts.

The execution engine must be extended to process multithreaded dialogs. The execution engine for state charts performs the following tasks:

- Detect when a switch between scripts should be performed. The execution engine detects this by detecting when the user signals a script change. There are several possible ways in which a user signals a script change, including moving the cursor to another window, selecting another window from a menu of active windows, and entering a command that can only be executed by another script. In effect, the execution engine examines each request and routes it to the appropriate script.
- Save the state of each suspended script, and be able to reactivate that script when the user switches back to it. The execution engine does this by saving the state and global variables in a buffer when the script is suspended and loading the state and global variables back when the script is reactivated.

7.7 TRANSFORMATIONS IMPROVE SCRIPTS

There are many types of transformations which can be performed on scripts. The previous sections suggest several "syntactic" transformations which help manage the combinatorial explosion of arcs and nodes in large scripts. These syntactic transformations change the notation used to represent the script, but do not change the dialogs which can be generated from the script.

Other useful transformations identify and factor out common script fragments embedded within a script. Two script transformations which change the set of dialogs which can be produced by a state transition graph may be useful:

1. *Folding.* Folding transformations remove ordering. Figure 7.12(a) illustrates a graph in which the order of two or more operations is prespecified. Figure 7.12(b) illustrates the transformed graph in which (a) the user determines the order between the two operations and (b) the user can perform any number of operations.
2. *Multithreading.* Figure 7.12(c) illustrates a graph in which the user can switch between the steps involved in the moving and copying operations.

7.8 DIALOG DESIGNERS USE MANY TECHNIQUES FOR SPECIFYING SCRIPTS

User interface designers differ in the methodology used to design state transition graphs. Some prefer a top-down approach consisting of first designing a high-level state transition graph and then expanding each node of the high-level graph into a subgraph. Some prefer a bottom-up approach in which state transition graphs are first designed for dialog fragments, followed by the design of a superstate transition graph that references these state transition graphs. Some designers use a combination of top-down and bottom-up approaches.

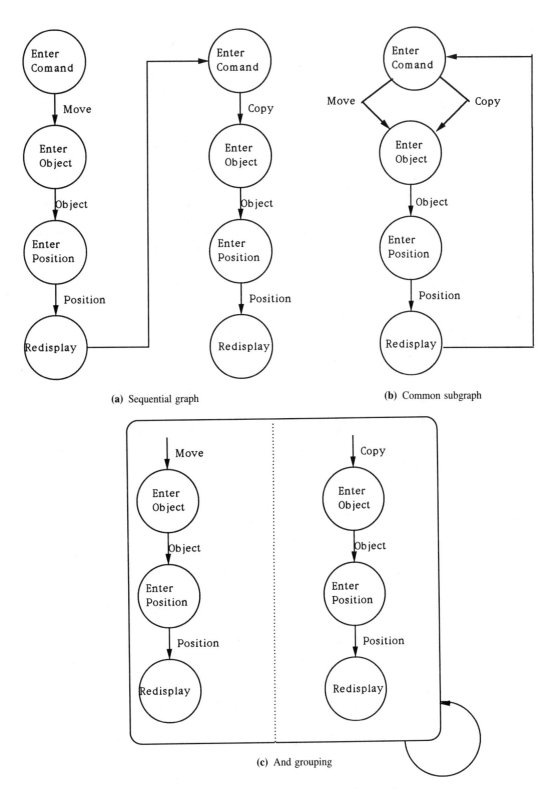

(a) Sequential graph

(b) Common subgraph

(c) And grouping

Figure 7.12 Transformations on state transition graphs.

Whatever the approach taken by the dialog designer, the state transition graphs must be eventually described to the user interface system. Several tools are available for this purpose, including the following:

- *Tables*. The dialog designer encodes a state transition graph into tables describing the nodes and arcs. BLOX®/TEMPLATE® (1986) is a dialog development environment in which dialog designers specify a table in which each row corresponds to a state with pairs of actions and new states.

- *Keyword languages*. The dialog designer encodes a state transition graph into a keyword-oriented language. For example, in RAPID™ (Rapid Prototyping of Interactive Dialogs) (Wasserman, 1985), an early tool for designing interactive question and answer style dialogs, the dialog designer describes dialogs using a state transition graph with four types of statements: diagram name statement, variable definition statement, node statements, and arc statements.

- *Graph editors*. Rather than describe each state and transition, a graph editor can be used to draw each node and arc. For example, RAPID has been extended (Mills & Wasserman, 1984) to support a state transition diagram editor in which users select node and arc icons and position them on a screen. Designers can enter additional information about each state and transition via pop-up dialog boxes.

- *Flowchart editor*. Flowcharts have long been used to describe the control flow of software. Flowcharts can also be used to represent state transition systems. Flowchart editors are used by dialog designers to create representations of scripts.

- *Hypertext systems*. Dialog designers often use hypertext systems to represent state transition systems. Each screen corresponds to a state, and links between screens correspond to a transition between two states. Hypercard (Goodman, 1987) on the Macintosh and similar products on PCs are frequently used to prototype scripts. Hypertext systems also enable dialog designers to simulate the user interface appearance associated with each state.

- *Programming languages*. Probably the most frequently used technique to represent state transition systems is by using traditional programming languages such as C or Pascal.

7.9 SUMMARY

State transition systems may be used to represent single-threaded dialogs among a user and several applications. The complexity of the large number of states of a state transition system can be controlled by partitioning the corresponding state transition graph into subgraphs. Fragments of state transition systems can also be collapsed into a single node provided that the execution engine is extended to process the resulting superstate. Dialog designers may use a variation of state transition diagrams called state charts to describe multithreaded dialogs. Several techniques are used by user interface designers to specify state-transition systems, including keyword languages, tables, graph editors, hypertext systems, and programming languages.

8

Grammars for Representing Dialogs

This chapter describes

> - How grammars are used to describe dialogs.
> - How to generate dialogs from grammers.
> - How grammars support automatic prompting, context messages, graphical rubout, and undo.

8.1 GRAMMARS REPRESENT MONOLOGS

Context-free grammars are often used to describe the vocabulary and word sequences of monologs such as command languages and programming languages. We will first review the use of grammars to describe monologs; and then we extend the use of grammars to describe dialogs.

Example 8.1

Figure 8.1 illustrates four monologs which correspond to the dialogs of Figure 4.2. In Figure 8.1, each monolog consists of semantic tokens which are presented to the script execution

```
monolog A (user cancels request):

2. USER to UI: $AccountNumber
4. check to UI:"Ok"
6. USER to UI: $Amount
8. USER to UI: "No"

monolog B (bad account number):

 2. USER to UI: $AccountNumber
10. check to UI:"Fail"

monolog C (insufficient funds):
 2. USER to UI: $AccountNumber
 4. check to UI:"Ok"
 6. USER to UI: $Amount
12. USER to UI: "Yes"
14. withdraw to UI: "Fail"

monolog D (successful withdrawal):

 2. USER to UI:      $AccountNumber
 4. check to UI:     "Ok"
 6. USER to UI:      $Amount
12. USER to UI:      "Yes"
16. withdraw to UI: $NewBalance
18. disburse to UI: "Ok"
```

Figure 8.1 Four monologs.

engine. The semantic tokens are either entered by the user or sent from an application program to the script execution engine. (Even though semantic tokens come from several sources, to the script execution engine, they appear as though they came from a single source and are hence considered as a monolog by the execution engine.) ∎

A *context-free grammar* for a set of monologs consists of the following:

- A finite set of symbols called *nonterminals,* each of which represents a portion of a monolog. There is a special nonterminal symbol called the *start symbol* which represents the set of all possible monologs acceptable to the script execution engine.
- A finite set of symbols called *terminals* which represent semantic tokens used in monologs.
- A set of production rules which define each nonterminal in terms of other nonterminal and terminals. A production rule has the form

```
label: nonterminal ::= sequence of one or more nonterminal
                       and/or terminal symbols
```

Each nonterminal is enclosed in triangular brackets "<" and ">." A space between two symbols indicates a sequence of the two symbols.

Example 8.2

The production labeled P16:

```
P16: <successful withdrawal> :=
                    <distribute funds> <goodbye>
```

indicates that the nonterminal on the left-hand side, <successful withdrawal>, can be replaced by the sequence of the two nonterminals on the right-hand side, <distributed funds>, and <goodbye>. ∎

A grammar is said to be *context free* if the nonterminal of the left-hand side can be replaced by the sequence of terminals and nonterminals on the right-hand side irrespective of in what context the nonterminal on the left-hand side appears; that is, there are no restrictions on when the replacement can be performed.

A grammar for the four monologs of Figure 8.1 is shown in Figure 8.2.

```
P1: <S>::= <number>
<interaction>
P2: <number> ::= USER to UI: $AccountNumber
P3: <interaction> ::= check to UI: "Fail"
P4: <interaction> ::= <ok>
                          <amount>
                          <confirmation>
P5: <ok> ::= check to UI: "Ok"
P6: <amount> ::= USER to UI: $Amount
P7: <confirmation> ::= USER to UI: "No"
P8: <confirmation> ::= <yes>
                          <withdrawal>
P9: <yes> ::= USER to UI: "Yes"
P10: <withdrawal> ::= withdraw to UI: "Fail"
P11: <withdrawal> ::= <newbalance>
                          <ok>
P12: <ok> ::= disburse to UI: "Ok"
P13: <newbalance> ::= withdraw to UI: $NewBalance
```

Figure 8.2 Context-free grammar for the monolog traces of Figure 8.1.

A monolog can be generated from a grammar by starting with the start symbol, <S>, replacing each nonterminal by the right-hand side of some production with that nonterminal on its left-hand side and stopping when there are no more nonterminals left to replace.

We will use context-free grammars to represent the monolog *received* by a script execution engine rather than the monolog entered by a user. A script execution engine may receive semantic tokens from several sources, so in the context-free grammar of Figure 8.2, we have labeled each terminal by the source that produces that terminal.

Example 8.3

The four monologs of Figure 8.1 can be derived from the context-free grammar of Figure 8.2 as illustrated in Figure 8.3. For example, monolog A is derived by starting with <S>,

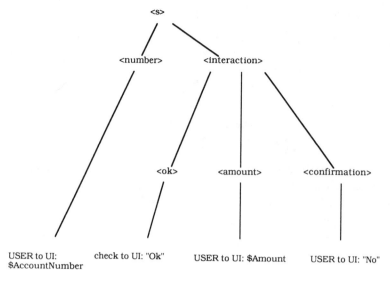

(a) Parse tree for monolog A of Figure 8.1.

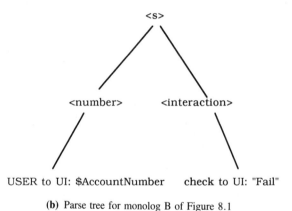

(b) Parse tree for monolog B of Figure 8.1

Figure 8.3 Parse trees.

replacing <S> with the right-hand side of P1, replacing <number> by the right-hand side of P2, replacing <interaction> by the right-hand side of P4, replacing <ok> by the right-hand side of P5, replacing <amount> by the right-hand side of P6, and then replacing <confirmation> by the right-hand side of P7. ∎

Figure 8.3 illustrates how the derivation of monologs from the start symbol can be represented in the form of trees called *derivation trees* or *parse trees*. The parse trees for each of the four monologs of Figure 8.1 are shown in Figure 8.3. Any valid monolog can be deduced from the grammar by building a parse tree with the following:

- The nonterminal symbol at the root
- The monolog as the leaves

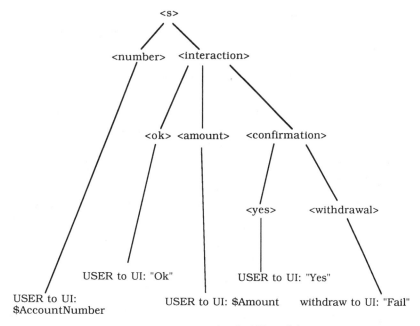

(c) Parse tree for monolog C of Figure 8.1

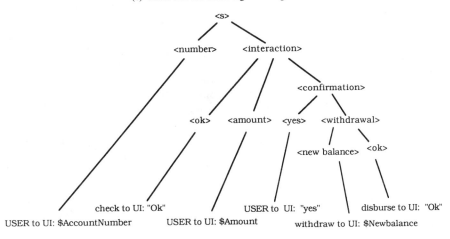

(d) Parse tree for monolog D of Figure 8.1

Figure 8.3 Continued

- Productions as internal branches of the parse tree with the nonterminal on the left-hand side of the production as a parent and symbols on the right-hand side as its children

If a parse tree cannot be constructed for a monolog, then the monolog is not valid. When a dialog designer defines a context-free grammar for a monolog, the dialog designer defines productions which can be used in the parse trees of several monologs. For example, production P4 is used in the parse trees for monologs A, C, and D.

8.2 GRAMMARS ARE EXTENDED TO REPRESENT DIALOGS

Context-free grammars can be extended to describe valid dialogs by appending an action to productions which describes what the user interface system should do after receiving the semantic token represented by terminal nodes of the derivation tree. The content-free grammar of Figure 8.2 has been extended in Figure 8.4 in this manner.

Example 8.4

The four dialogs of Figure 4.2 can be derived from the context-free grammar of Figure 8.4.
■

```
P1: <S> ::= <number>
              <interaction>
P2: <number> ::= USER to UI: $AccountNumber
                   action: (UI to check:
                                 check($AccountNumber))
P3: <interaction> ::= check to UI: "Fail"
                        action (UI to USER: 'The account
                               number', $AccountNumber, 'does
                               not exist. Your request has
                               been canceled. Goodbye'.)
P4: <interaction> ::= <ok>
                        <amount>
                        <confirmation>
P5: <ok> ::= check to UI: "Ok"
               action (UI to USER: 'How much do
                      you wish to withdraw?')

P6: <amount> ::= USER to UI: $Amount
                   action (UI to USER: 'Please confirm
                          that you wish to withdraw',
                          $Amount, 'from account',
                          $AccountNumber.)
P7: <confirmation> ::= USER to UI: "No"
                         action (UI to USER: 'Your request
                                has been canceled.
                                Goodbye.')
P8: <confirmation> ::= <yes>
                         <withdrawal>
p9: <yes> ::= USER to UI: "Yes"
                action (UI to withdraw: 'Withdraw
                       ($AccountNumber,$Amount).')
```

Figure 8.4 Context-free grammar for the dialogs of Figure 4.2.

```
P10: <withdrawal> ::= withdraw to UI: "Fail"
                                action (UI to USER: 'There are not
                                    sufficient funds in your
                                    account to withdraw',
                                    $Amount, 'Your request
                                    has been canceled.
                                    Goodbye.')
P11: <withdrawal> ::= <newbalance>
                          <ok>
P12: <ok> ::= disburse to UI: "Ok"
                            action (UI to USER: $Amount, 'has been
                                withdrawn from your account.
                                Your new balance is',
                                $NewBalance, 'The money will
                                appear in the slot to the
                                right of the screen. Thank
                                you. Goodbye.')
P13: <newbalance> ::= withdraw to UI: $NewBalance
                            action (UI to disburse: 'Disburse
                                ($Amount).')
```

Figure 8.4 Continued

The actions appended to productions are similiar to the actions performed within a state of a state transition system:

- present a semantic token to the user,
- transmit a semantic token to an application function,
- modify a variable.

In the grammar of Figure 8.4, each terminal is labeled by the component which generates or produces the corresponding semantic token. For example, "USER to UI" indicates that the user, via some interaction object, enters the semantic token which is accepted by the script execution engine (UI); "disburse to UI" indicates that the function disburse generates the semantic token to be accepted by the script execution engine; "UI to USER" indicates that the script execution engine generates the semantic token for delivery to the user via some interaction object.

The idea of labeling terminal symbols can be extended to labeling nonterminal symbols by the component (sometimes called party) producing all the semantic tokens associated with the nonterminal. For example, the following production:

```
USER to UI: <form> ::= <data-box-1> ... <data-box-n>
```

indicates that all the semantic tokens associated with each of the <data-box-i>'s are to be entered by the user for delivery to the script execution engine. A grammar containing this type of notation is called a *multiparty grammar* because the symbols in the grammar indicate the party or component which produces each semantic token.

Some additional symbols are used to combine several productions into a single production.

Alternation Notation.   Two productions with the same left-hand side can be combined by using the alteration symbol, (" | "). For example, the two productions

```
P3: <interaction> ::= check to UI: "Fail"
                      action: {UI to USER: 'The account
                              number', $AccountNumber, 'does
                              not exist. Your request has
                              been canceled. Goodbye.'}
P4: <interaction> ::= <ok>
                      <amount>
                      <confirmation>
```

can be written as

```
P3': <interaction|> ::= check to UI: "Fail"
                        action: {UI to USER: 'The account
                                number', $AccountNumber, 'does
                                not exist. Your request has
                                been canceled. Goodbye.'}
                    (<ok>
                  |     <amount>
                        <confirmation>)
```

Repeat Notation.   Curly braces, ({and}), are used to indicate a repeating phrase. For example,

```
<Command> ::= AVERAGE
              <value> {1,99}
```

specifies semantic token AVERAGE may be followed by between 1 and 99 values.

Order-Free Notation.   The && notation is useful when the order of the nonterminals is immaterial. For example,

```
<form> ::= <value-1> && <value-2>
```

is equivalent to

```
<form> ::= (<value-1>, <value-2>)
         | (<value-2>, <value-1>)
```

AND/OR trees represent scripts   Production rules are frequently used to represent scripts. However, many people find a graphical representation easier to use than lists of productions. One graphical form is an AND/OR tree with external (leaf) nodes representing terminal symbols and internal (nonleaf) nodes representing nonterminal symbols. A node labeled AND indicates that all its children nodes represent actions that must occur sequentially. A node labeled OR indicates that the actions associated with only one of its children need occur. Some nodes have only one nonterminal child. These nodes occur because of the use of a production with only one symbol on the right-hand side in the grammar. The actions associated with the child of this node are always processed. Figure 8.5 illustrates an AND/OR tree representation of the script represented by the grammar of Figure 8.4. If the grammar is recursive (a nonterminal can be derived from itself), then the AND/OR tree is cyclic. Cyclic AND/OR trees can be drawn in either of two ways: (1) as cycles (Figure 8.6) or (2) with nonterminal nodes at the leaves (Figure 8.7). Several rules can be used to modify AND/OR trees to make them shorter and more bushy, or taller and less busy. These rules are illustrated in Figure 8.8. Applications of these rules are illustrated in Figures 8.9 through 8.12.

Many find the AND/OR tree representation more convenient than the production rule representation of grammars because the relationships of productions are visible in the structure of the AND/OR tree while these relationships are implicit in the production rule

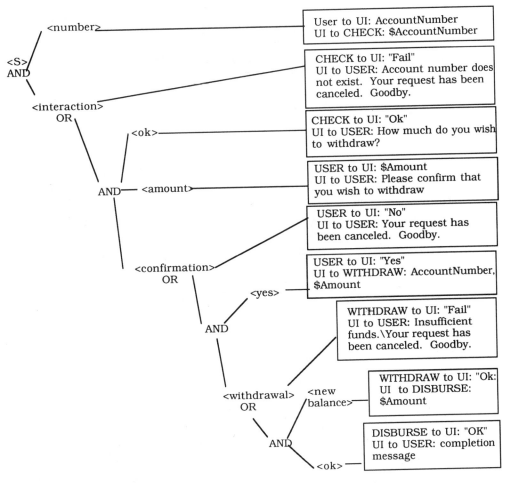

Figure 8.5 AND/OR tree representation of dialog of Figure 8.3.

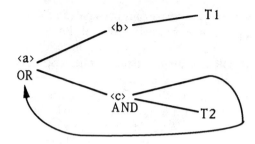

Figure 8.6 AND/OR tree with cycles.

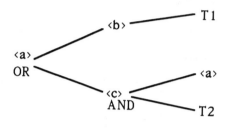

Figure 8.7 AND/OR tree with cycles represented by nonterminal node at the leaf of the tree.

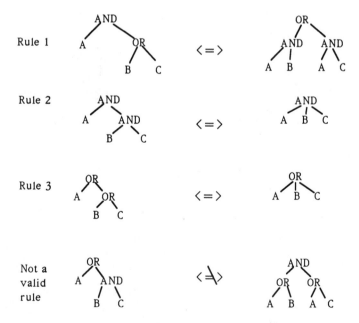

Figure 8.8 Rules for modifying AND/OR trees.

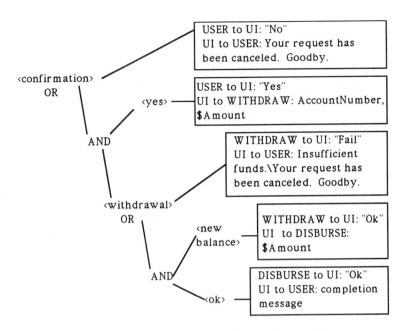

Figure 8.9 A portion of the AND/OR tree of Figure 8.5.

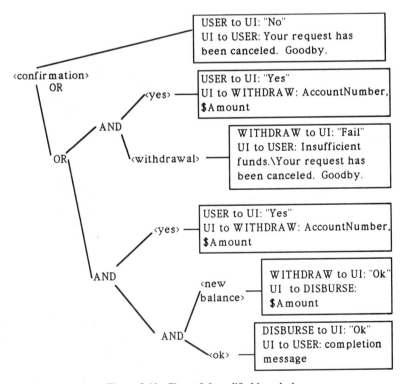

Figure 8.10 Figure 8.9 modified by rule 1.

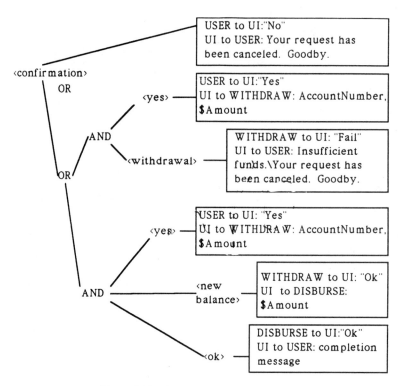

Figure 8.11 Figure 8.10 modified by rule 2.

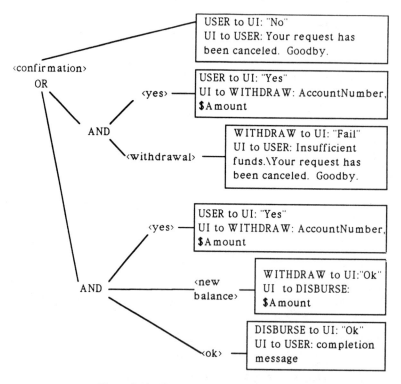

Figure 8.12 Figure 8.11 modified by rule 3.

representation. The EDGE user interface system (Chakravarty & Kleyn, 1989) uses this notation to describe dialogs.

8.3 TOP-DOWN PROCESSING USING A GRAMMAR

In the finite state transition system approach for dialog processing, semantic tokens obtained from the user or from application programs were used to select alternative transitions between states. In top-down processing using a context-free grammar, we will again use semantic tokens obtained from the user or from application programs, this time to select productions from the grammar. The semantic tokens will be used to build a parse tree with the terminals of the parse tree representing a monolog of semantic tokens. The actions associated with the terminals contain semantic tokens that, together with the monolog, constitute a valid dialog.

In general, the top-down approach works by processing, one at a time, semantic tokens obtained from either the user or application programs. The top-down processor uses the current semantic token to select productions for building a parse tree with terminals consisting of the sequence of semantic tokens already processed. After selecting one or more productions and extending the parse tree, the action associated with the current semantic token is executed, causing either information to be displayed to the user or an application to be invoked. The top-down processor then waits for the next semantic token to be supplied by either the user or an application program. The top-down processor continues in this fashion until there are no more semantic tokens from the user or from applications, or when there are no more productions that can be applied to the parse tree.

Example 8.5

Consider the derivation of a parse tree in Figure 8.13 for dialog B. Initially, the top-down processor has a parse tree which consists of a single node, <S>. When the user enters a value for $AccountNumber, the top-down processor examines the production rules for a production rule with <S> on its left-hand side. There is only one such production rule, P1. The top-down processor appends the right-hand side of production P1 to <S>, the current parse tree, as illustrated in Figure 8.13. The top-down processor now searches for a rule with <number> on the left-hand side, and selects production P2. It appends the right-hand side of production P2 to <number>. Having appended the $AccountNumber semantic token, the top-down processor executes the associated action

```
check ($AccountNumber)
```

The top-down parser now waits for the next semantic token. Suppose that when the check function is completed, it returns the semantic token

```
Fail
```

The top-down processor searches for a production which has <interaction> on the left-hand side. Two productions have <interaction> on the left-hand side: P2 and P3. Production P3

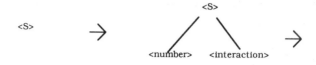

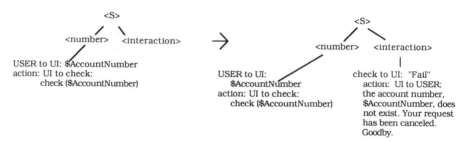

Figure 8.13 Top-down processing.

is selected because its right-hand side matches the semantic token "Fail." The action associated with P2 is executed, causing the following to be displayed to the user:

```
'The account number' $AccountNumber,'does not exist. Your
request has been canceled. Goodbye.'
```

Because there are no more productions which can be applied to the parse tree, the top-down processor stops. ∎

It is possible to generate parse trees for each of the dialogs of Figure 4.2 using the grammar of Figure 8.4 and the top-down processor described. In our example, given a single semantic token, the top-down processor is always able to select a single production for each nonterminal. If the grammar has a special property, then a top-down processor can always select the correct production.

Let FIRST be a function which can be applied to a production. The FIRST function calculates a set of all first terminal symbols in any dialog which can be generated from the production. Formally, let A ::= B be a production and let FIRST(A ::= B) be defined as follows:

If B is of the form "c D" where c is a terminal symbol, then

$$\text{FIRST}(A ::= B) \text{ contains } \{c\}.$$

If B is of the form "C D" where C is a nonterminal, and there is a production of the form C ::= F, then

$$\text{FIRST}(A ::= B) \text{ contains FIRST}(C ::= F).$$

If B is of the form B1 | B2 |... | B*n,* then

$$
\begin{aligned}
\text{FIRST(A ::= B) := FIRST(A ::= B1) UNION} \\
\text{FIRST(A ::= B2) UNION} \\
\cdots \\
\text{FIRST(A ::= Bn). } \blacksquare
\end{aligned}
$$

Example 8.6

The following is the complete set of values for FIRST applied to each production of Figure 8.4:

```
FIRST(P1)  = {$AccountNumber}
FIRST(P2)  = {$AccountNumber}
FIRST(P3)  = {Fail}
FIRST(P4)  = {Ok}
FIRST(P5)  = {Ok}
FIRST(P6)  = {$Amount}
FIRST(P7)  = {No}
FIRST(P8)  = Yes}
FIRST(P9)  = {Yes}
FIRST(P10) = {Fail}
FIRST(P11) = {$NewBalance}
FIRST(P12) = {Ok}
FIRST(P13) = {$NewBalance} ■
```

It turns out that if for each pair of productions with the same left-hand side, A ::= B and A::= C, and FIRST(B) INTERSECT FIRST(C) is always empty, then it is always possible for the top-down processor to select uniquely a set of production rules which match the current semantic token.

Example 8.7

Continuing with Example 8.6, we have

For <interaction>, FIRST(P3) INTERSECT FIRST(P4) = empty.

For <confirmation>, FIRST(P7) INTERSECT FIRST(P8) = empty.

For <withdrawal>, FIRST(P10) INTERSECT FIRST(P11) = empty.

Thus, it is always possible for the top-down processor to uniquely select a production from Figure 8.4 which matches the semantic token. ■

If there are two productions of the form A ::= B and A ::= C and FIRST(B) INTERSECT FIRST(C) is not empty, then it is possible for the top-down processor to choose a production which may not be the correct one. In the case of processing monologs, it is possible for the top-down processor to *backtrack,* that is, to remove a production from the partially constructed parse tree and replace it by another candidate production. In dialog processing, it may be impossible to backtrack because incorrect semantic tokens may already be sent to an application program or displayed to the user.

8.4 BOTTOM-UP PARSING USING A GRAMMAR

A bottom-up processor is a state transition system with a stack. The bottom-up processor accepts semantic tokens one at a time, examines the semantic token, and performs one or more of the following operations:

- *Shift*. The semantic token is placed on the stack.
- *Reduce*. The symbols on the stack match the right-hand side of a production rule. These symbols are removed from the stack and the nonterminal on the left-hand side of the production rule is placed onto the stack. Any action associated with the production rule is executed.
- *Accept*. The bottom-up processor accepts a special semantic token indicating that no more semantic tokens are forthcoming. The dialog is completed.
- *Error*. The bottom-up processor encounters a semantic token which does not conform to the production rules and can no longer continue processing.

After performing the one or more of these operations, the state transition system transitions to a new state.

Example 8.8

In this example, the bottom-up processor is driven by monolog B of Figure 8.1. The following series of steps occur:

1. The bottom-up processor receives the semantic token

```
User to UI: $AccountNumber
```

from the user via an interaction object. This semantic token is shifted onto the stack.

2. The semantic tokens on the stack match the right-hand side of production rule P2. A reduce operation is executed which removes $AccountNumber from the stack and places the nonterminal symbol <number> onto the stack. The action associated with P2 is executed

```
UI to check: check ($AcountNumber)
```

3. The check subroutine returns the following semantic token:

```
check to UI: Fail
```

This semantic token is shifted onto the stack.

4. The top symbol on the stack matches the right-hand side of production rule P3. A reduce operation is executed which removes Fail from the stack and places the nonterminal symbol <interaction> onto the stack. The action associated with production P3 is executed

```
UI to USER: 'The account number', $AccountNumber, 'does
            not exist. Your request has been
            canceled. Goodbye.'
```

5. The two symbols on the stack match the right-hand side of production rule P1. Both <interaction> and <number> are removed from the stack. The right-hand side of production rule P1, <S> is placed onto the stack.

6. The symbol on the top of the stack, <S> cannot be reduced further. No more semantic tokens can be accepted and processing stops. ■

The general algorithm for building the state transition system which drives the bottom-up processor is complex and will not be discussed here. Given a set of production rules and actions written in the proper form, commercially available compiler-generators can automatically generate the appropriate bottom-up parser. For example, Yacc, a compiler-compiler that runs under UNIX, produces a C program which can be used as a bottom-up processor.

8.5 SYNGRAPH IS A GRAMMAR-DRIVEN USER INTERFACE GENERATOR

SYNGRAPH (SYNtax-directed GRAPHics) is an early user interface generator for interactive system graphics developed by Dan R. Olsen, Jr. and Elizabeth P. Dempsey (Olsen & Dempsey, 1983). It produces Pascal source code for a top-down processor.

The application on which the user interface is built supplies a set of data types and a set of application procedures which manipulate those types. SYNGRAPH supports several interesting features, including automatic prompting, context messages, graphical rubout, and semantic recovery

Automatic Prompting. Most of the prompting for user input is performed automatically by SYNGRAPH. SYNGRAPH examines a set of input tokens that are acceptable for a given state and displays them in a menu. For example, given the two productions (SYNGRAPH used a slightly different notation than shown here),

```
<confirmation> ::= USER to UI: "No"

<confirmation> := USER to UI: "Yes"
                  <withdrawal>
```

SYNGRAPH generates a menu containing the two options "No" and "Yes," which is displayed to the user who selects one of the two options. (This idea of automatically generating interaction objects has been extended by Olsen in the Mike and Mickey user interface generators described in Appendix D.2.)

Context Messages. Context help messages can be added to the grammar as special productions. For example, the foregoing productions can be modified as follows:

```
<confirmation> ::= USER to UI: "No"
                  <help: "This option indicates that
                         you wish to cancel your
                         withdrawal request."
```

```
<confirmation> := USER to UI: "Yes"
                       <help: "This option indicates that
                               you wish to continue with
                               your request.">
                       <withdrawal>
```

These help messages are displayed to the user only when the user requests help. The idea of placing additional operations in production rules is similar to merging states in a state transition system.

Graphical Rubout. Sometimes users desire to change parameter values which they have entered but have not yet been used by application functions. Users use the *rubout* command to retract these parameter values. SYNGRAPH uses nonterminals in the grammar to identify whole commands. When the SYNGRAPH processor encounters a nonterminal marked "closure," it saves all the inputs it receives while it builds the parse tree. None of the application functions associated with the closure nonterminal are invoked until all the parse tree with the closure nonterminal as a root has been derived (and all the input parameters have been received). During the processing of the parse tree associated with the closure nonterminal, if the user enters a rubout request, the input is removed from the saved inputs and the parse is restored to the state it was in before the input was encountered. Prompting and feedback displays are also restored to the appropriate status for that state. However, rubout actions cannot be processed once the parse tree with the closure nonterminal as a root has been derived and the application functions associated with the closure nonterminal are invoked.

Example 8.10

Consider the following grammar:

```
<command> ::= MOVE <object> TO <location>
                  action: move (<object>, <location>)
<object> ::= HOUSE | WINDOW | DOOR (In SYNGRAPH, the user
                                    specifies a HOUSE,
                                    WINDOW, or DOOR by
                                    pointing to it, not by
                                    entering the object names
                                    via a keyboard.)
<location> ::= X, Y
```

The <command> nonterminal is considered a closure terminal because it invokes a function when values for <object> and <location> are available. Suppose that a house is initially at location (0,0) and the user wishes to move it to location (5,5). If the user enters

```
MOVE HOUSE rubout
```

the MOVE action has not yet been invoked, so the choice of HOUSE for <object> is removed from the set of inputs, and a message is displayed instructing the user to select a HOUSE, WINDOW, or DOOR. However, if the user enters

```
MOVE HOUSE TO 5,5 rubout
```

then a message will be displayed to the user stating that rubout cannot be carried out because the move operation has already been performed. Fortunately in this example, the move operation is its own inverse, and the user can move the HOUSE back to its original position (0,0) by entering

`MOVE HOUSE TO 0,0` ■

Undo.   Rubout can only be used to remove input parameters that have not yet been used by applications. Sometimes users invoke an application function after they gave it the wrong parameters, or invoked a wrong application. In SYNGRAPH there are two approaches for undoing the effects of executing an application function. Both approaches require that there exist an inverse function that can cancel the effects of the undesired function.

- *The user selects the inverse function.* The user realizes that an undesired function has been executed. The user selects the appropriate inverse function and gives it the parameters necessary to undo the effects of the undesired function.
- *The user enters an undo command.* Productions for closure nonterminals are extended to invoke the inverse function if the user should enter a undo command.

Example 8.11

Consider the following grammar:

```
<command> ::= MOVE <object> TO <location>
              action: MOVE (<object>, <location>)
              undo action: MOVE
                              (<object> <original location>)
<object> ::= HOUSE | WINDOW | DOOR
<location> ::= X, Y
```

If the user enters

`MOVE HOUSE TO 5,5 UNDO`

then the following cancel action is invoked:

`MOVE HOUSE TO 0,0` ■

It is theoretically possible for the user to enter several undo commands, each undoing the most recent command that has not yet been undone. In order to accomplish this, two criteria must be satisfied.

1. The processor must record (usually in a pushdown stack) all the original values of parameters which are modified during a command.
2. Each operation must have an inverse operation. If an operation does not have an inverse, then neither it nor operations executed prior to it can be automatically undone.

This approach is similar to creating an inverse state containing inverse operations as discussed in Section 7.1 on state transition systems. The other two approaches (implicit undo by stacking and implicit undo by spooling) can also be used if the top-down execution engine is extended to support parameter stacking or function spooling.

8.6 SUMMARY

Grammars have long been used to describe monologs and can be extended to describe dialogs. Two approaches for processing dialogs based on context-free grammars include top-down processing and bottom-up processing. SYNGRAPH, a grammar-driven user interface generator, pioneered the use of grammars for processing dialogs. Grammars are as descriptive as state transition diagrams, but may be more difficult for many dialog designers to use.

9

Rules and Constraints

This chapter describes

- How rules support user-driven dialogs.
- How rules support error correction.
- How to process rules.
- How constraints support dynamic interaction objects.
- How constraints enforce spatial relationships and appearance.

State transition systems and grammars are used to describe user interface dialogs in which the sequence of information entered by the end user is totally ordered or almost totally ordered. User interface designers often use rules and constraints to describe dialogs in which end users may enter information in arbitrary orders. Interaction object designers may also use rules and constraints to describe the appearance and behavior of interaction objects.

We will begin by describing how rules may be used to describe dialog scripts. We will then discuss how two-way constraints may be used to specify the layout of interaction objects within a composite interaction object.

9.1 RULES SUPPORT USER-DRIVEN DIALOGS

Dialog designers may use rule graphs to specify the relationship between information entered by the user and information displayed to the user. A *rule graph** is a graph consisting of two types of nodes.

1. *Slots*. A slot node contains a value entered or modified by the user or calculated by a rule node. In this chapter, slot nodes are represented by ovals.

2. *Rules*. A rule node contains a rule for calculating the value of a slot from the values of other slots. Rule nodes can be thought of as constraints on how values of slots are derived from other slots. In this chapter, rule nodes are represented by rectangular boxes.

Several types of rule nodes are possible.

1. *Rules enforcing constraints*. For example,

   a. *Upper and lower bounds on the range of values*. In Figure 9.1, for example, the age of a commercial truck driver must be greater than 17 and less than 95. The input parameter, Age, is compared to the upper and lower bounds, 17 and 95. If the value for Age falls within these bounds, then the value of Age is placed into the Age* slot.

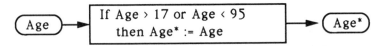

Figure 9.1 Rule involving upper and lower bounds.

   b. *Rules that enumerate the acceptable values*. In Figure 9.2, if the value of the Color slot is one of the values in the set {blue, green, yellow, orange, red, purple, violet}, then the value of Color is placed in the Color* slot.

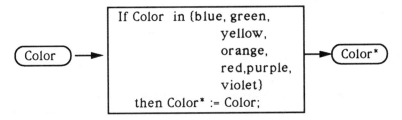

Figure 9.2 Rule involving enumeration of values.

   c. *Rules specified by a procedure*. For example, in Figure 9.3, if the value of AccountNumber is verified to be a valid account number by the check procedure, then the value of AcountNumber is placed in the AccountNumber* slot.

---

*Some readers will recognize a rule graph as a variation of a special type of network called a data flow diagram.

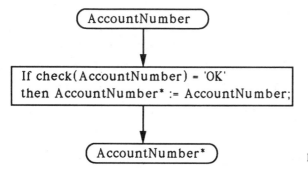

Figure 9.3 Rule involving a function.

d. *Rules involving multiple values of information.* For example, in Figure 9.4, if DateOfBirth is less than DateOfGraduation, then the value of DateOfGraduation is placed in the DateOfGraduation* slot.

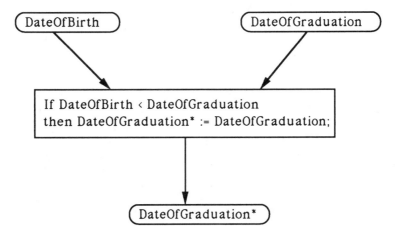

Figure 9.4 Rule involving multiple values.

2. *Functions that calculate new slot values.* For example, in Figure 9.5 the function convert generates a value for the WeightInKg slot, and the function calculate generates a value for the Cost slot.

Propagating Values Through Rule Graphs. A rule node is executed when one of its input slots is modified and all of its other input slots have values. If the rule fails, an appropriate message is displayed to the user and the output slot is not modified. If the rule succeeds, an appropriate message may be displayed to the user (often containing the derived value), and the derived value is placed in the output slot, possibly triggering the execution of other rule nodes.

Figure 9.6 illustrates the ATM script used in earlier chapters. The rule graph describes how information entered by the user is processed and results eventually returned to the user. There are two possible scenarios, depending on the order in which the user elects to enter values for AccountNumber and Amount.

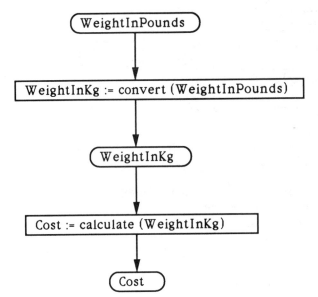

Figure 9.5 Functions that calculate new slot values.

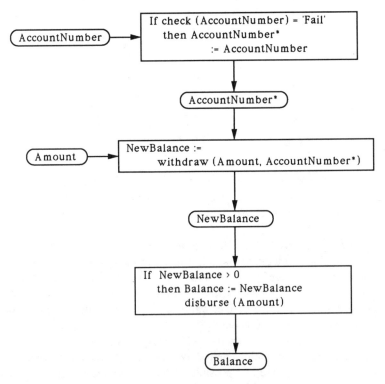

Figure 9.6 ATM withdrawal script.

In one scenario, the user first enters a value into the AccountNumber slot. This causes the check function to be invoked, which determines if the value in AccountNumber is valid. If the value for AccountNumber is acceptable, the AccountNumber* slot is updated. Next the user enters a value for the Amount slot. Because both AccountNumber* and Amount have values, the withdraw function is invoked. The slot NewBalance is modified. Finally, the disburse function is invoked which distributes the cash to the user. Appropriate feedback messages are displayed to the user at each step. If an operation node does not place a new value in its output slot, an error message is displayed to the user.

In the other scenario, the user first enters a value into the Amount slot. Because there is no value for the AccountNumber slot, the withdraw function is not yet invoked. Next the user enters a value into the AccountNumber slot. The check function determines if the value for AccountNumber is acceptable and updates the AccountNumber* slot. Because both Amount and AccountNumber* have values, the withdraw function is invoked, updating NewBalance. Finally, the disburse function is invoked. As in the first scenario, appropriate feedback messages are displayed to the user at each step.

Composite interaction object designers may use rule graph techniques to describe how to propagate values entered into interaction objects by users into other interaction objects of a composite interaction object. Recall from Chapter 5 that composite interaction objects consists of several individual interaction objects. A well-known example of a composite interaction object is a spreadsheet, which consists of several data boxes whose appearance is arranged as a two-dimensional array. Each data box may hold text (a label), a number (a value) or an expression involving constraints, operations, functions, and the values of other data boxes (a formula). The formula is used to calculate the value of that data box.

Example 9.1:

One major application of spreadsheets is budgeting in which a proposed budget for a collection of activities and time periods is represented as a table. As illustrated in Figure 9.7, rows 2, 3, 4, and 5 will represent the four quarters of a yearly budget and columns B, C, and D will represent the three major activities: personnel costs, material costs, and other expenses. The sum of the values in each quarter is listed in row 6, and the sum of the values in each column is listed in column E.

Figure 9.8 illustrates the rule graph for the spreadsheet illustrated in Figure 9.7. Whenever the user changes the value in the ith column and jth row, the sum of the values in the ith column, the sum of the values in the jth row, and the grand total are recalculated

	A	B	C	D	E
1		Personnel	Material	Other	Total
2	Quarter 1	14	15	3	32
3	Quarter 2	15	15	3	33
4	Quarter 3	16	15	2	33
5	Quarter 4	16	16	3	35
6	TOTAL	61	61	11	133

Figure 9.7 Example spreadsheet.

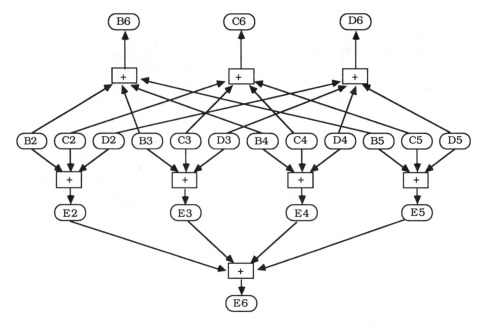

Figure 9.8 Rule graph for Figure 9.7.

and displayed. Suppose the user changes the estimate for first quarter materials from 15 to 17. The total for the material column will change from 61 to 63, the total for the first quarter row will change from 32 to 34, and the grand total will change from 133 to 135, as illustrated in Figure 9.9, where the modified values are shown in bold face.

In addition to entering values into data boxes, spreadsheet users may change formulas, insert or delete rows or columns, format the contents of data boxes, and save and load entire spreadsheets. Spreadsheets have become popular for two reasons: (1) users can observe the impact of changes in one value on the remaining values derived from it (as illustrated) and (2) the ease with which users can specify how derived values are calculated from other values.

The spreadsheet of Figures 9.7 and 9.8 can be modified by inserting a new column, called taxes. A new data flow graph must be declared: the total taxes value is the sum of the values in the taxes column. Several existing data flow rules must be modified: the total of the taxes column must be calculated. The ith quarter totals must include the tax value

	A	B	C	D	E
1		Personnel	Material	Other	Total
2	Quarter 1	14	**17**	3	**34**
3	Quarter 2	15	15	3	33
4	Quarter 3	16	15	2	33
5	Quarter 4	16	16	3	35
6	TOTAL	61	**63**	11	**135**

Example Spreadsheet

Figure 9.9 Example spreadsheet.

	A	B	C	D	E	F
1		Personnel	Material	Other	Taxes	Total
2	Quarter 1	14	15	3	2	34
3	Quarter 2	15	15	3	2	35
4	Quarter 3	16	15	2	1	34
5	Quarter 4	16	16	3	2	37
6	TOTAL	61	61	11	7	140

Figure 9.10 Spreadsheet of Figure 9.9 extended to contain a new column.

in the sum of the values in the ith row. Finally, the grand total calculation must be modified to include values of the new tax column. The result of these modifications is illustrated in Figures 9.10 and 9.11.

Some spreadsheet vendors have extended their products in two additional directions:

1. Application functions can be referenced within rule graphs. Spreadsheet users are thus able to invoke and display the results of application functions. The rule languages of some spreadsheet programs have also been extended to include if-then-else, do-while, and other programming control constructs so that users can write simple application functions using the spreadsheet rule language.

2. Spreadsheet programs have been extended to support a variety of interaction objects in addition to data boxes.

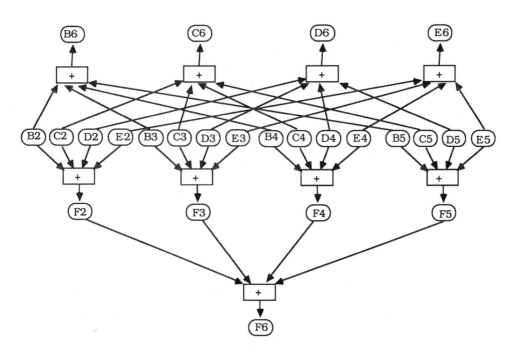

Figure 9.11 Rule graph for Figure 9.10.

Using these interaction objects, spreadsheet users construct a prototype of a user interface on top of the spreadsheet.

Spreadsheets provide a convenient mechanism to prototype some user interfaces and application functions. In effect, the spreadsheet is itself the script which controls the exchange of information between interaction objects and application functions.

9.2 LANGUAGES ARE USED TO SPECIFY RULES

Each rule consists of

- A precondition that must be satisfied before the actions associated with the rule are executed.
- Actions that are executed after all of the preconditions of the rule are satisfied.

The preconditions and actions of Figure 9.6 are summarized here:

Precondition	Actions
AccountNumber is modified	IF check (AccountNumber) = 'Ok' then AccountNumber* := AccountNumber;
AccountNumber* and amount are modified	NewBalance := withdraw(Amount, AccountNumber*);
NewBalance is modified	If NewBalance > 0 = then begin; Balance := NewBalance; disburse (Amount); end;

Rule-based techniques can be expressed using if-then syntax of most programming languages. We define the function *modified* as follows:

```
modified(x)  =  true, if x has recently been modified;
               false, otherwise.
```

We will use the notation

```
modified(x)  := true
```

to indicate that x has been recently modified and

```
modified(x)  := false
```

to indicate that x has not been recently modified. The constraints of Figure 9.6 can then be expressed as follows:

```
If modified(AccountNumber) and check (AccountNumber) = 'Ok'
then begin;
     AccountNumber* : = check(AccountNumber);
     modified(AccountNumber*) : = true;
     modified(AccountNumber) : = false;
     end;

If modified(Amount)
and modified(AccountNumber*)
     then begin;
          NewBalance : = withdraw
                    (Amount, AccountNumber);
          modified(NewBalance):= true;
          modified(AccountNumber*) = false;
          modified(Amount) = false;
          end;

If modified(NewBalance) and NewBalance > 0
     then begin;
     Balance : = NewBalance;
     disburse (Amount);
     modified(NewBalance) : = false;
     end;
```

In effect, the modified attribute of the slots encode a state transition diagram which specifies the sequence in which the functions are executed.

In addition to traditional programming languages, production systems can be used to express these rules: each precondition and action pair is expressed as a *production* or *rule* within a production system such as Prolog or Opps-5. A production system execution engine repeatedly examines preconditions and selects actions to execute.

9.3 RULES SUPPORT ERROR CORRECTION

In this section, we examine how a rule graph can be used to support error correction. First we define the concept of a reversible rule graph. Then we will examine two approaches for helping users back out of dialogs into which they have entered inappropriate semantic tokens.

A slot is said to be *derivable* if there is a rule which may modify its value. Otherwise a slot is nonderivable. A rule graph is *reversible* if, whenever one of its nonderivable slots is modified at time $t + 1$ and is reset to its original value at time $t + 2$, then all of the modified derivable slots are automatically reset to the values they had at time t.

Example 9.2

Figure 9.12 illustrates a reversible rule graph. Whenever the values in the TodaysDate or DateOfBirth slots are modified, the value of the Age slot is automatically modified. Suppose initially that TodaysDate slot has a value of 1990 and DateOfBirth slot has a value of 1960. The value of the Age slot is 30. If the user changes DateOfBirth to 1964, then the value of

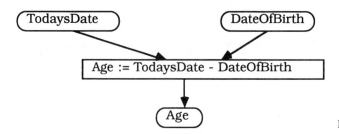

Figure 9.12 Reversible rule graph.

the Age slot is automatically changed to 26. If the user changes DateOfBirth back to 1960, then the Age slot is automatically changed back to 30. Similarly, if the user changes TodaysDate to 1991, then the Age is automatically changed to 31. When the user changes TodaysDate back to 1990, Age is automatically changed back to 30. ∎

Some rule graphs are not reversible. The following examples illustrate two such graphs.

Example 9.3

Figure 9.13 illustrates a rule graph which generates a value for NewSalary if the PerformanceReview is greater than 5. However, if the user changes the PerformanceReview to a value less than 5, the value of NewSalary is not modified. ∎

Example 9.4

The ATM script illustrated in Figure 9.6 is another example of a rule graph which is not reversible. Changing the value of Amount to zero cannot cause money withdrawn from the account and disbursed to the user to be taken back from the user and redeposited in the account. To do this, the user must invoke the deposit operation. ∎

Reversible rule graphs are desirable because users can retract an inappropriate value for a semantic token. The rule graph will automatically invoke the appropriate rules necessary to adjust all affected slots.

With reversible rule graphs, a user can retract multiple semantic tokens which he or she has entered or selected via interaction objects. One approach for accomplishing this is *chronological backtracking*. In this approach, the user resets the value of semantic

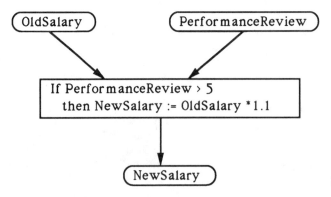

Figure 9.13 Nonreversible rule graph.

tokens in the reverse of the order in which values were entered or selected. Example 9.5 illustrates chronological backtracking.

Example 9.5

The following course enrollment choices are presented to a student, who selects up to four courses. The selected courses must not overlap in time.

Botany	8:10–9:00
Band	10:10–11:00
Computer Science	11:10–12:00
English	10:10–11:00
Physical Education	9:10–10:00
Sociology	9:10–10:00

Figure 9.14 illustrates the rule graph for this dialog. Suppose the student first chooses Botany, then Band, then Computer Science, and finally English. The rule graph detects a conflict in the variable ConflictTwoFour, which represents the overlapping time between Course2 (Band) and Course4 (English). The student can change the value of Course4 from English to either Physical Education or Sociology and remove the conflict.

However, suppose the student wishes to change Course2 from Band to Sociology. To accomplish this using the chronological backtracking approach, the student must change Course4 to blank, Course3 to blank, and Course2 to Sociology. The student then changes Course3 to Computer Science and Course4 to English. ■

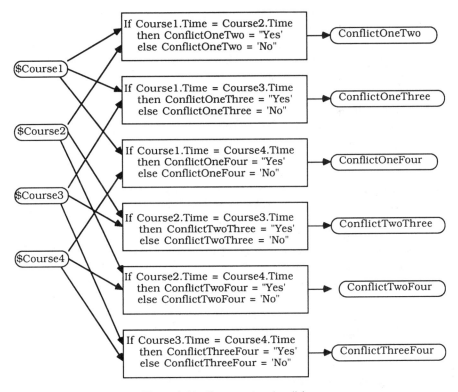

Figure 9.14 Course registration dialog.

The disadvantage with chronological backtracking is clear: many of the deselected choices have nothing to do with the rule violation. A better approach is to modify one of the choices which caused the rule violation. The procedure for identifying relevant choices which cause the conflict is called *dependency-directed backtracking* (Stallman & Sussman, 1977). To determine the slots which result in a conflict, merely examine all the arcs which lead to the rule node detecting the violation.

Example 9.6

In Example 9.5, the variable ConflictTwoFour detects the time conflict. Examining the rule graph of Figure 9.14, the semantic tokens Course2 and Course4 are sources of the conflict. When the rule ConlictTwoFour is violated, it generates a message to the user which displays the current values for Course2 and Course4 and asks the user to modify one of those values. The user is free to modify the value for either Course2 or Course4, and thus avoids the unnecessary steps required by chronological backtracking. ■

While state transition systems and grammars can support chronological backtracking, they cannot, in general, support dependency-driven backtracking as can rule based systems.

9.4 RULES CAN BE APPLIED EAGERLY OR LAZILY

One of the disadvantages of propagating values through rule graphs is the recalculation of each value for each derived slot which is directly or indirectly dependent on a modified slot. This is done irrespective of whether or not the derived slot contains an active value currently displayed in an interaction object. Such algorithms are called *eager evaluation* and keep all slots up to date. An alternative class of algorithms, called *lazy evaluation,* minimizes the number of slots which must be recomputed in order to update only those active values currently visible in interaction objects. The lazy evaluation technique postpones computations that cannot affect the currently displayed interaction object, thereby decreasing the time to modify the values of interaction objects visible to the user. However, lazy evaluation introduces extra bookkeeping in order to keep track of out-of-date slots. In addition, lazy evaluation can result in potential delays when the values of out-of-date slots need to be displayed. Lazy evaluation is most effective in situations where changes may occur to any slot, but the user is viewing only a limited number of them.

To illustrate the algorithm, Figure 9.15(a) shows an example rule graph in which the user has modified the value of the single slot with the dark border. The slot marked with an X is currently displayed in an interaction object. The interaction objects of the remaining slots are not currently visible on the screen.

The first step of the algorithm marks all slots that are reachable from the modified slot as "out of date." This is done by marking all the slots as out of date which have arcs from the modified slot and then recursively marking all slots as out of date which have arcs from a slot marked out of date. The out-of-date slots are shown as single-hashed nodes in Figure 9.15(b).

The second step of the algorithm marks as "recomputable" all out-of-date slots that reach any slot marked with an X. This is done by marking all the slots as recomputable

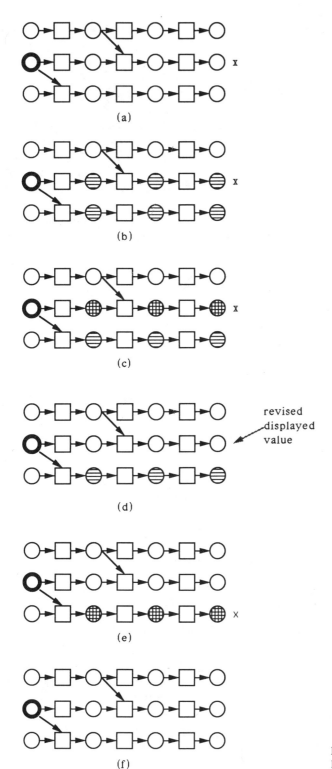

(a)

(b)

(c)

(d)

revised
displayed
value

(e)

(f)

Figure 9.15 Example application of the lazy value evaluation algorithm.

which are already marked as out of date and have arcs to a slot marked with an X and then recursively marking all slots as recomputable which are already marked as out of date and have arcs to a slot marked as recomputable. These slots are shown in Figure 9.15(c) as double-hashed nodes.

The third step of the algorithm is to recompute all the slots marked as recomputable. This is done by recomputing the recomputable nodes with arcs from the modified slot and then recursively recomputing the nodes marked as recomputable with arcs from nodes that were recomputed. Eventually the slots marked recomputable are recomputed. The result is shown in Figure 9.15(d), where all the recomputable slots from Figure 9.15(c) are now white indicating that they are up to date. Note that there are still some single-hashed slots which are marked as out of date, but they do not affect any of the values currently displayed in the interaction object.

Whenever an interaction object is made visible or enlarged so that it displays values marked as out of date, step 2 of the algorithm is invoked to mark additional slots that are recomputable. This is illustrated in Figure 9.15(e). A step similar to the third step is then executed to recompute the recomputable nodes in order to derive the value for the displayed value. The result of this is shown in Figure 9.15(f).

9.5 TWO-WAY CONSTRAINTS SUPPORT DYNAMIC INTERACTION OBJECTS

Rules describe how values are derived from other values. Rules are unidirectional. Two-way constraints are bidirectional. Two way constraints are written as equations. Two-way constraints can be used to indicate where icons *can* be placed, as the following two examples illustrate.

Example 9.7

Suppose we wish to draw an equilateral triangle with vertices a, b, and c. An equilateral triangle is a triangle such that the length of each of its three sides are equal:

$$\text{length } (a,b) = \text{length } (b,c)$$

$$\text{length } (a,b) = \text{length } (c,a)$$

Let (x_a, y_a), (x_b, y_b) and (x_c, y_c) be the coordinates of the vertices a, b, and c. Recalling that the distance between two points is the square root of the sum of the squares of the differences between their x coordinates and y coordinates. These two-way constraints can be expressed as

$$(x_a - x_b)^{**}2 + (y_a - y_b)^{**}2 = (x_b - x_c)^{**}2 + (y_b - y_c)^{**}2$$

$$(x_a - x_b)^{**}2 + (y_a - y_b)^{**}2 = (x_c - x_a)^{**}2 + (y_c - y_a)^{**}2$$

Given the coordinates for any two of the vertices, the coordinates for the third must satisfy the constraints given. Suppose the user indicates that an equilateral triangle is to be constructed, and indicates the positions for a and b to be (0,0) and (0,1), respectively. Substituting these coordinates into the foregoing equations yields

$$1 = (1 - x_c)^{**}2 + (-y_c)^{**}2$$

$$1 = (x_c)^{**}2 + (y_c)^{**}2$$

Solving two equations for two unknowns yields two possible answers

$$c = (x_c, y_c) = (0.5, 0.86)$$

$$c' = (x_c, y_c) = (0.5, -0.86)$$

The two possible equilateral triangles are shown in Figure 9.16. The user has two choices for placing vertex c, depending on the orientation of the equilateral triangle. Two approaches for helping the user position the c vertex are possible.

1. Highlight the two possible positions and have the user select the desired position.
2. After the user enters the approximate position of the third vertex, move the vertex to the closest possible position for the vertex. ■

Example 9.8

Snapping is the automatic movement of a point or object from the position that the user entered to the nearest permitted location. Usually the user drags the object or point to the approximate location; then it is redrawn or "snapped" into the nearest position which satisfies existing spatial constraints. Snapping is useful during the editing of geometric objects. This technique is used to align edges so that they are parallel, align objects so that some of their edges are parallel or congruent, and in general enforce spatial constraints among geometric objects. Many drawing programs support a "grid" of positions to which end points of lines and vertices of polygons are automatically snapped. ■

Two-dimensional constraints can also be used to generate warning messages.

Example 9.9

Semantic warning messages. When the user requests the execution of a critical or irreversible operation, a warning message may be displayed to the user informing the user of the potential effects of the operation and asking the user to confirm that the operation should be executed. Constraints can be used to display such warning messages *before* the user actually requests the operation in direct manipulation interfaces. For example, if the user drags a file icon within a prescribed distance from a garbage can icon, then a two-dimensional constraint would be violated. This triggers a warning message to be displayed to the user: "Warning, you are about to delete this file." The user may then either continue to move the file icon to the garbage can icon to delete the file, or move the icon away from the garbage can and not delete the file. ■

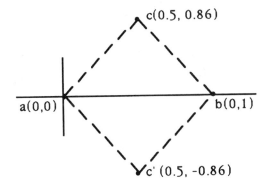

Figure 9.16 The two possible positions for the third vertex of an equilateral triangle.

The next section describes a general approach for using two-way constraints to constrain the layout of interaction objects.

9.6 CONSTRAINTS ENFORCE SPATIAL RELATIONSHIPS AND APPEARANCE

The *geometrical or spatial structure* of a composite interaction object describes the relative position of component interaction objects with respect to each other, and the degree that they may be repositioned. Two-way constraints may be used to describe the allowable geometric relationships among interaction objects within a composite interaction object.

Interviews, a graphical user interface tool kit developed at Stanford (Linton, Vlissides, & Calder, 1989), is a library of C++ classes that define interaction objects and composition strategies. Composite interaction objects which contain simple interaction objects such as menus, buttons, and data boxes are defined using boxes and glue. Each composite interaction object is represented by a box which contains subboxes. A subbox may either be a simple interaction object or another composite interaction box. The position of a subbox within a box is specified by geometric two-way constraints called *glue*. Glue describes how interaction objects may be repositioned relative to neighboring objects. Figure 9.17 illustrates the hierarchical relationship of the boxes and glue that define the composite interaction object illustrated in Figure 9.18. In Figure 9.18, glue is represented by double-headed arrows.

Two important types of boxes in Interviews are hboxes and vboxes:

1. Hbox arranges its subboxes horizontally. For example, box 5 is an hbox which arranges its two subboxes, each containing buttons, horizontally. Box 5 contains horizontal glue represented by arrows 10, 12, and 14, which indicate how the two buttons are horizontally spaced.

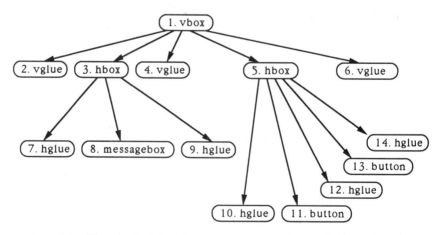

Figure 9.17 Hierarchical relationships among components of a complex interaction object.

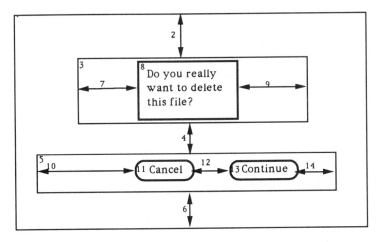

Figure 9.18 Composite interaction object.

2. Vbox arranges its subboxes vertically. For example, box 1 is a vbox which arranges its subboxes, hboxes 3 and 5, vertically. Box 1 contains vertical glue (represented by arrows 2, 4, and 6) which define how the two hboxes are vertically spaced.

Both boxes and glue have various natural sizes, shrinkabilities, and stretchabilities. If glue has a fixed size, then the size of the space between the two objects it connects cannot be changed. If glue is expandable to a prescribed limit, then the space between the two objects it connects can be enlarged up to the prescribed limit. Likewise, some glue is shrinkable to a prescribed limit. Boxes can be repositioned, enlarged, or shrunk subject to the constraints expressed by the glue. For example, Figure 9.19 illustrates the example composite interaction object of Figure 9.18 with Hboxes 3 and 5 enlarged. Because glue

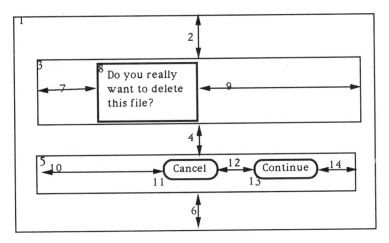

Figure 9.19 Enlarged version of Figure 9.18.

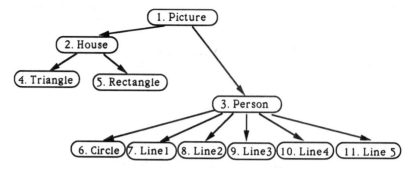

Figure 9.20 Hierarchical representation of graphical objects.

7 has a fixed size and glue 9 is stretchable, box 8 is repositioned to the left of its original position. Because glue 12 and 14 have fixed sizes and glue 10 is stretchable, the cancel and continue buttons are repositioned to the right of their original positions.

Interaction objects containing graphic figures are also composed by establishing a hierarchy of graphic objects. For example Figure 9.20 illustrates the hierarchical representation of graphical objects illustrated in Figure 9.21. Each object is glued to a fixed position with respect to its parent object. However, each object can be repositioned, rotated, enlarged, shrunk, or flipped within its parent. For example, Figure 9.22 illustrates the result of moving the person (object 3) inside the house (object 2).

Textual objects can also be arranged into a hierarchy. Figure 9.23 illustrates an example phrase consisting of

1. the name of a function, "Sort,"
2. a list of parameters to the function, "InputFile, OutputFile,"
3. the terminator of the function call, ");."

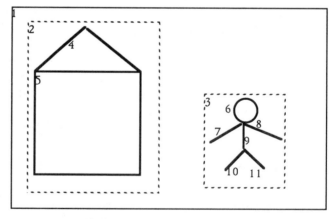

Figure 9.21 Graphical objects.

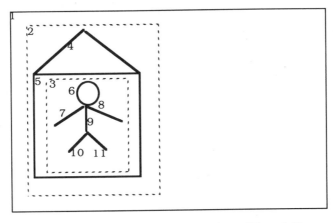

Figure 9.22 Modification of graphical objects of Figure 9.21

For textual objects, the geometrical structure is determined by a set of predefined algorithms which consider the amount of space available to display the textual object. The text can appear in one of several layouts, depending on the available space. In Figure 9.24(a), all the text can fit onto a single line. In Figure 9.24(b), the length of text box has been reduced so that the parameter list appears on a separate line. In Figure 9.24(c), the length of the text box has been further reduced, causing the parameter list to be displayed as a vertical list.

Geometry Managers. Some systems (such as interviews and the X Toolkit Intrinsics) automatically calculate the spatial structure of composite interaction objects. Two-way constraints are used to specify relationships among the component interaction objects. When a new component interaction object is inserted, an existing component interaction object is deleted, or an existing component interaction object changes size, the geometry manager makes the appropriate spatial adjustments.

Automatic geometry managers are desirable because they free the programmer from coding the algorithms to perform spatial layout. Instead, the programmer only specifies the geometric two-way constraints to be enforced by the geometry manager. Automatic

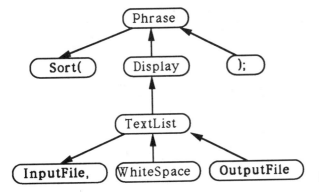

Figure 9.23 Structured text.

```
Sort (InputFile, OutputFile);
```

(a)

```
Sort (
      InputFile,OutputFile
);
```

(b)

```
Sort(
   InputFile,
   OutputFile
   );
```

(c)

Figure 9.24 Rule involving a function.

geometry managers may be quite complex, making assumptions when geometric constraints are underspecified and resolving conflicts when the constraints are overspecified.

9.7 SUMMARY

Rules may involve values of a single slot, values in multiple slots, and the sequencing of semantic tokens entered by the user and delivered to application functions. Rule systems are processed by an execution engine which produces a dialog controlled by rules and the semantic tokens entered into the slots. When a rule system is reversible, the user can undo previous requests by reentering original values. Chronological backtracking requires that operations be undone in the reverse of the order in which they were originally performed. Dependency-directed backtracking uses a rule graph to identify slots which violate rules. Both rule-based programming systems and traditional programming languages can be used to specify rule systems.

Two-way constraints may be used to specify the behavior and appearance of interaction objects. A spreadsheet is a composite interaction object containing multiple data boxes whose value are dependent on each other. Spreadsheet constraints can be specified by end users. Constraints can control the placement of interaction objects within the presentation of composite interaction objects. Constraints are used to specify the geometry structure of composite interaction objects and determine when warning messages should be presented to the user.

10

Multiagent Techniques

This chapter describes

> - How to control dialogs using shared memory.
> - How event handlers generate dialogs.
> - How event loops support multithreaded dialogs.
> - How to use object-oriented techniques to implement user interfaces.

An agent is an interaction object or application function which participates in a dialog. This chapter concentrates on various ways to model agents and the nature of the communications among them. Approaches for communications among agents can be categorized as either shared memory or message-passing techniques. In Section 10.1 we describe how shared memory can be used as a medium for information exchange among agents. In Section 10.2 we discuss special types of messages called events and how they are used to exchange information among agents. Section 10.3 discusses event handlers, agents which respond to events. Section 10.4 describes how each agent can be implemented as three objects (models, views, and controllers) and how these objects exchange information.

First we discuss shared memory techniques for representing scripts in which the user may enter information in arbitrary sequences. One way in which business employees often communicate with each other is by sharing information on paper reports and forms. For example, a traveling employee fills out a weekly travel expense form which describes his or her expenditures. An employee in the accounting department reviews this form and issues a travel reimbursement check to the employee.

A variation of a paper form can also be used for communication between user and application functions. A *shared memory* is a set of labeled slots, in which each may contain a semantic token. Semantic tokens in these slots are shared among the user (via interaction objects) and application functions. Using our example, the traveling employee enters values for each expenditure, advance, charge, and credit into slots in shared memory. Application functions then review the slot values, compute the amount to be reimbursed to the employee, place that value into another slot, and then generate a reimbursement check.

Slots in a shared memory contain semantic tokens which are shared by the user and application functions. The values of some slots are provided by the user and the values of other slots are provided by application functions. Some slots may be updated by both the user and application functions. Slots may also have default values.

The user interface may consist of an electronic form interaction object which presents the value of each slot in shared memory to the user. However, other interaction objects may be used in place of the electronic form. Information needed by the shared memory may be solicited from the user by displaying menus from which the user selects options, questions to which the user types responses, or almost any other type of interaction object. Shared memory describes what information needs to be communicated between the user and application functions. Interaction objects describe how information is entered by and displayed to the user.

Each shared memory contains several attributes, including a FormName which names the form template, and several slots. Associated with each slot are the following attributes and rules:

- SlotName
- Purpose, natural language description of the purpose of the semantic token in the slot
- ValueType, such as character, digit, and so on
- DefaultSource, indicates the normal source of the value for the slot (user, application function, or both)
- CurrentValue
- NotifyInteractionObject, rule indicating which interaction objects should be notified whenever CurrentValue is modified
- NotifyApplicationFunction, rule indicating which application functions should be notified whenever CurrentValue is modified
- EnumeratedValues, rule listing of all possible values which may be placed into the slot

Example 10.1

Figure 10.1 illustrates a shared memory used for the ATM application. The CurrentValue of each slot contains a semantic token entered by the user or supplied by an application function. Figure 10.2 illustrates the CurrentValues for each of the slots during several points in time during a successful automatic withdrawal dialog. At time t_1, all four slots are nil. The user enters a value of 137 into AccountNumber at time t_2. This causes the check function to be invoked, which returns a value of "ok" at time t_3. The user enters the value of 110 for Amount at time t_4. At time t_5, the value of NewBalance is calculated to be 90. ∎

```
FormName:  "Account Withdrawal Form"
Purpose:   "Used to withdraw funds from an account"

SlotName:                    AccountNumber
Purpose:                     "Identify account number"
ValueType:                   Digit
DefaultSource:               User
CurrentValue:                nil
NotifyInteractionObject:     —
NotifyApplicationFunction:   check
SlotName:                    Verify
Purpose:                     "Indicates if AccountNumber is
                             valid account"

ValueType:                   Character
DefaultSource:               check
EnumeratedValues:            "Ok", "Fail"
CurrentValue:                nil
NotifyInteractionObject:     Yes
NotifyApplicationFunction:   —

SlotName:                    Amount
Purpose:                     "Amount user wishes to withdraw"
ValueType:                   Digit
DefaultSource:               User
CurrentValue:                nil
NotifyInteractionObject:     nil
NotifyApplicationFunction:   withdraw

SlotName:                    NewBalance
Purpose:                     "Amount remaining in account
                             after withdrawal"
ValueType                    Digit
DefaultSource:               withdraw
CurrentValue:                nil
NotifyInteractionObject:     Yes
NotifyApplicationFunction    disburse
```

Figure 10.1 Forms template representation of the automatic banking withdrawal dialog.

Slot	Time				
	t_1	t_2	t_3	t_4	t_5
AccountNumber	nil	137	137	137	137
Verify	nil	nil	Ok	Ok	Ok
Amount	nil	nil	nil	110	110
NewBalance	nil	nil	nil	nil	90

Figure 10.2 Current values for each slot of the form template of Figure 10.1 during a successful automatic withdrawal dialog.

As illustrated in Figure 10.1, an application function may be invoked when the value of a slot changes. This limited form of control flow can be generalized to the use of rules. Rules are more general than simply invoking an application function whenever a slot value changes. In Serpent, a rule may involve several actions.

Serpent (Bass, Hardy, Little, & Seacord, 1990), developed at CMU's Software Engineering Institute, uses an interface definition language similar to a database schema to define the structure of data to be shared by the user interface and application functions. Data may be placed into the "shared data" at any time by either application functions or the user (via interaction objects). Scripts are specified using a rule language called SLANG which describes (1) a collection of active slots that await the arrival of values and (2) rules which specify actions performed by the Serpent execution engine when the values are available.

Figure 10.3 illustrates the shared data of the ATM example. The shared data consists of

- AccountNumber and Amount, which are supplied by the end user via interaction objects
- ResultCheck and ResultWithdraw, which are return codes supplied by the check and withdraw application functions
- NewBalance, which is calculated by the withdraw function

```
AccountInfo:  shared data

AccountInfoRecord: record

    AccountNumber:   integer;
    ResultCheck:     string (10);
    Amount:          integer;
    NewBalance:      integer (10);
    ResultWithdraw:  string;

    end record;
    end shared data;
```

Figure 10.3 Example shared data.

Figure 10.4 illustrates several view controllers. A *view controller* is one or more interaction objects which are to be displayed when the associated creation condition is satisfied. Rules called creation conditions associated with view controllers determine when to present interaction objects to users. Rules called methods specify when messages

```
OBJECTS

   Background:   form_widget

      {ATTRIBUTES:
         width: 200;
         height: 200;
      }

VC:  EnterAccountNumber

     Creation Condition (TRUE)

     OBJECTS:

     WelcomeMessage:                 label_widget

        {ATTRIBUTES:
           parent:                   Background;
           horiz_distance:           10;
           vertical_distance:        50;
           width:                    180;
           height:                   70;
           foreground_color:         white;
           label_text:               "Welcome to the ATM ",
                                     "Please ",
                                     "enter your account number.";
           justify:                  1;
           internal_width:           5;
           internal_height:          5;
        }

     AccountNumberDataBox:           text_widget

        {ATTRIBUTES:
           parent:                   Background;
           horiz_distance:           10;
           vertical_distance:        10;
           width:                    180;
           height:                   50;
           send_buffer:              1;
           foreground_color:         black;
           text_buffer:              " ";
```

Figure 10.4 Serpent dialog.

```
    METHODS:
       send {check (AccountNumber)}
    }

    end vc EnterAccountNumber

VC:   CheckNotOk

    Creation Condition (CheckResult = "Fail")

    OBJECTS:

    CheckNotOkMessage:              label_widget

    {ATTRIBUTES:
       parent:                 Background;
       horiz_distance:         10;
       vertical_distance:      50;
       width:                  180;
       height:                 70;
       foreground_color:       white;
       label_text:             "Account number is not valid",
                               "Goodbye";
       justify:                1;
       internal_width:         5;
       internal_height:        5;
    }

    end vc CheckNotOk;

VC:   EnterAmount

    Creation Condition (CheckResult = "Ok")

    OBJECTS:

    CheckOkMessage:                 label_widget

       {ATTRIBUTES:
          parent:              Background;
          horiz_distance:      10;
          vertical_distance:   50;
          width:               180;
          height:              70;
          foreground_color:    white;
          label_text:          "Please enter the amount ",
                               "you wish to withdraw";
          justify:             1;
```

Figure 10.4 (Continued)

```
                    internal_width:          5;
                    internal_height          5;

              AmountDataBox:                 text_widget

              {ATTRIBUTES:
                 parent:                     Background;
                 horiz_distance:             10;
                 vertical_distance:          10;
                 width:                      180;
                 height:                     50;
                 send_buffer:                1;
                 foreground_color:           black;
                 text_buffer:                " ";

              METHODS:
                 send {withdraw (AccountNumber, Amount)}
              }

end vc EnterAmount;

   VC:  WithdrawNotOk

        Creation Condition (WithdrawResult = "Fail")

OBJECTS:

   WithdrawNotOkMessage:                     label_widget

      {ATTRIBUTES:

            parent:                          Background;
            horiz_distance:                  10;
            vertical_distance:               50;
            width:                           180;
            height:                          70;
            foreground_color:                white;
            label_text:                      "You have insufficient ",
                                             "funds. Goodbye";
            justify:                         1;
            internal_width:                  5;
            internal_height:                 5;
      }

   end vc WithdrawNotOk;

VC:  DisplayNewBalance

     Creation Condition (WithdrawResult = "Ok")
```

Figure 10.4 (Continued)

Sec. 10.1   Shared Memory Controls Dialogs

```
OBJECTS:

    WithdrawOkMessage:          label_widget

      {ATTRIBUTES:
          parent:               Background;
          horiz_distance:       10;
          vertical_distance:    50;
          width:                180;
          height:               70;
          foreground_color:     white;

          label_text:           "Your new balance is",
                                NewBalance,
                                "Please remove the cash ",
                                "from the slot below the",
                                "screen";
          justify:              1;
          internal_width:       5;
          internal_height:      5;


    end vc DisplayNewBalance;
```

Figure 10.4 (Continued)

are sent to application functions. For example, the EnterAccountNumber view controller contains two interaction objects, WelcomeMessage and AccountNumberDataBox. The creation condition rule associated with the EnterAccountNumber view controller (TRUE) implies that these two interaction objects are automatically displayed when the application starts. The EnterAmount view controller contains two interaction objects, CheckOkMessage and AmountDataBox. According to the creation condition rule associated with the EnterAmount view controller, these two interaction objects are automatically displayed when the value of CheckResult is changed to ''OK.''

Serpent illustrates the use of the Seeheim model. The interaction objects describe the presentation of information to the user. The view controller rules and the shared data describe the script. The application functions describe the computation aspects.

Rules can be used to describe the conditions for invoking application functions and for displaying composite interaction objects to the user. The next section discusses the use of messages called events for exchanging semantic tokens among application functions and interaction objects.

10.2. EVENT HANDLERS RESPOND TO EVENTS

An *event* is a message generated by the user, by an application function, or by the script execution engine. Examples of events include

- Entry of information by a user
- Invocation of an application function by the script execution engine

- Generation of results by an application function
- Generation of results by the script execution engine for display to the user

We will represent an event as a structure which has a type and a value. For example, the EnterNumber event has a type (AccountNumber) and a value (the value of the AccountNumber).

An *event handler* is a process that waits for events which it can accept. When an event occurs, the event handler becomes active, services the event, and then waits for another event. When it is active, an event handler may perform computation, generate new events, call application functions, and display information to the user. Several event handlers can process the same event.

Example 10.2

Figure 10.5 illustrates an event handler for the ATM example. To start, the user signals that he or she is ready to begin the bank withdrawal action, possibly by turning on a switch, inserting a bank card into a slot, or some other action which can be interpreted by the ATM as a Start event. The withdraw handler M1 becomes active, and triggers a Display event (causes a Display event to occur) whose handler displays the message "Welcome to the automatic bank teller." (The display event is handled by another event handler not shown in Figure 10.5.) Event handler M1 then triggers another display event whose handler displays the message "What is your account number?"

Event handler M2 is triggered when the user enters a value for AccountNumber. First, event handler M2 invokes the check function to verify if the value for AccountNumber entered by the user is valid. If the value is valid, then event handler M2 triggers a Display event whose handler displays instructions to the user. If the value for AccountNumber is not valid, event handler M2 triggers a Display event whose handler displays a message informing the user that the account number does not exist, and then triggers the cancel event.

Event handler M5 is triggered when the user enters a value for Amount. Event handler M5 triggers a display event to display a message asking the user to confirm the values for Amount and AccountNumber.

Event handler M6 is triggered when the user enters a value for Confirmation. If the value for Confirmation is "No," then event handler M6 triggers the Cancel event. If the value for Confirmation is "Yes" then event handler M6 invokes the WITHDRAW function. If the return code from the WITHDRAW is "Fail" then event handler M6 triggers a Display event to display a message to the user indicating that there are not sufficient funds in the account, and then triggers the cancel event. If the return code from the withdraw function is "Ok," the disburse function is invoked, the Display event is triggered, and then the Goodbye event is triggered. ∎

```
event handler M1 triggered on event Start do; (* triggered
                                   at beginning of dialog *)
    signal Display ("Welcome to the automatic bank teller");
    signal Display ("What is your account number?");
    end event handler M1;

event handler M2 triggered on event Number (AccountNumber)
do;
```

Figure 10.5 Example event handler.

```
      (* triggered when user enters AccountNumber *)
      check := check(AccountNumber);
      if check = "Ok" then
         signal Display ("How much do you wish to withdraw?");
      if check = "Fail" then
         begin
         signal Display ("The account number", AccountNumber,
                                           "does not exist");
            signal Cancel;      (* triggers the cancel event *)
         end;
   end event handler M2;

event handler M3 triggered on event Cancel do;
 (* triggered by other events handled by withdraw handler *)
   signal Display ("Your request has been canceled");
   signal Goodbye;          (* triggers goodbye event *)
   end event handler M3;

event handler M4 triggered on event Goodbye do;
 (* triggered by other events handled by withdraw handler *)
   signal Display ("Goodbye");
   end event handler M4;

event handler M5 event AmountEvent (Amount) do;
   (* triggered when user enters amount *)
   signal Display ("Confirm that you wish to withdraw",
Amount, "from account number," AccountNumber
  end event handler M5;

event handler M6 event ConfirmationEvent (Confirmation) do;
   (* triggered when user enters confirmation *)
   if Confirmation = "No" then signal Cancel;
   if Confirmation = "Yes" then
         rtncode := withdraw (AccountNumber, Amount,
                                           NewBalance);
      if rtncode = "Fail" then
         begin
         signal Display ("There are not sufficient funds in",
                    "your account to withdraw", Amount);
         signal Cancel;
         end;
if rtncode = "Ok" then
   begin
   disburse (Amount);
   signal Display (Amount, "has been withdrawn from",
      "your account. Your new balance is", NewBalance,
      "The money will appear in the slot to the right"
      "of the screen. Thank you.");
   signal Goodbye;
   end;
end event handler M6;
```

Figure 10.5 (Continued)

An event loop processes events Events can be generated by several sources:

- Users manipulate hardware such as keyboards and mice to interact with interaction objects.
- Application functions may generate results which need to be presented to the user.
- Event handlers may trigger new events while processing the actions associated with an event currently being processed.

An *event loop* is an execution engine that receives events and activates event handlers. Event loops and event handlers have three interesting properties that make them useful for implementing scripts.

1. Individual event handlers may be enabled and disabled. The event loop can activate only enabled event handlers.
2. Several event handlers can be activated in response to a single event.
3. Some event handlers require that multiple events must occur before they can be activated.

Examples of event handlers exhibiting each of these properties follow.

Activation and deactivation of event handlers If an event handler has been disabled, it cannot process events. When an event handler is disabled, the event loop can not select it for activation. The event handler ignores all of the events to which it would otherwise respond.

Example 10.3

The event handler M3 illustrated in Figure 10.6 is responsible for generating help messages. Depending on which event handler is enabled, either terse or verbose help messages are generated. Whenever the event handler M3 is triggered, it triggers both TerseHelpMessage and VerboseHelpMessage events. Because only one of the corresponding event handlers is enabled, only one event handler is invoked so the user receives only one help message. ∎

```
event handler M1 triggered on event Start do;
  display ("Do you want terse or verbose explanations?);
  end event handler M1;

event handler M2 triggered on event SetMessageLevel (Answer)
do;
  if Answer = "terse" then begin;
                        disable M4;
                        enable M5;
                        end;
```

Figure 10.6 Enabling and disabling event handlers.

```
    if Answer = "verbose" then begin;
                              disable M5;
                              enable M4;
                              end;
    end SetMessageLevel;


event handler M3 triggered on event Help do;
  signal TerseHelpMessage;
  signal VerboseHelpMessage;
  end event handler M3;


event handler M4 triggered on event VerboseHelpMessage do;
  <generate and display verbose help message>
  end event handler M4;


event handler M5 triggered on event TerseHelpMessage do;
  <generate and display terse help message>
  end event handler M5;
```

Figure 10.6 (Continued)

Events triggering multiple event handlers Figure 10.7 illustrates how a single event, DisplayDataBoxes can trigger two event handlers. One event handler displays a data box into which the user enters a value for Amount and the other event

```
event handler M1 triggered on event Start do; (* triggered at
  beginning of script *)
  signal Display ('Welcome to the automatic bank teller');
  signal DisplayDataBoxes;
  end event handler M1;


event handler AccountNumberBox triggered on event
DisplayDataBoxes do;
    signal Display ('Enter your account number');
    end event handler AccountNumberBox;


event handler AmmountBox triggered on event DisplayDataBoxes
do;
  signal Display ('Enter amount to withdraw');
  end event handler AccountNumberBox;


event handler M2 triggered on event EnterAccountNumber
(AccountNumber) do; (* triggered when user enters
                                    AccountNumber *)
  check := check(AccountNumber);
  if check = "Ok" then
     signal NumberOk;
  if check = "Fail" then
```

Figure 10.7 Script in which the user may enter either values for AccountNumber or Amount first.

```
      begin
      signal Display ('The account number', AccountNumber,
                                  'does not exist');
      signal Cancel;      (* triggers the cancel event *)
      end;
   end event handler M2;


event handler M5 triggered on event EnterAmount (Amount) do;
        (* triggers when user enters value for Amount *)
   signal AmountOk;
   end event handler M5;


<other event handlers go here>
```

Figure 10.7 (Continued)

handler displays a data box into which the user enters a value for AccountNumber. By using the script illustrated in Figure 10.7, the user can enter either value first.

Nonsequential input (event handler triggered after multiple events)

In Figure 10.7, the user can enter values in any sequence into the data boxes in the form template. As illustrated in Figure 10.8, only after both of the events NumberOk and AccountOk have been triggered are the withdraw and disburse functions invoked.

The University of Alberta User Interface Management System (Green, 1985), ALGAE (Flecchia & Bergeron, 1987), and Sassafras (Hill, 1987a, 1987b) are three experimental user interface management systems which are based on the event model. In Sassafras, flags are associated with each event handler to indicate whether or not the corresponding events have occurred. When an event occurs, a flag corresponding to that

```
event handler M6 triggered on all (NumberOk, Amount) do;
    rtncode := withdraw (AccountNumber, Amount,
                            NewBalance);
    if rtncode = "Fail" then
       begin
       signal Display ('There are not sufficient funds in',
                       'your account to withdraw', Amount);
       signal Cancel;
       end;
    if rtncode = "Ok" then
       begin
       disburse (Amount);
       signal Display (Amount, 'has been withdrawn from',
          'your account. Your new balance is', NewBalance,
          'The money will appear in the slot to the right'
          'of the screen. Thank you.');
       signal Goodbye;
       end;
    end event handler M6;
```

Figure 10.8 Event handler triggered after two events occur.

event is turned on in each event handler that can respond to that event. The Sassafras execution engine selects only event handlers for execution with all of their flags turned on. When an event handler is activated, all of its flags are turned off. This handles the following situations:

- Each event handler will be activated after all of its required events occur. The flags associated with an event are turned on in each event handler which the event can trigger. The execution engine selects event handlers, one at a time, with all of their flags set to on.
- Some event handlers can be activated only when multiple events have been triggered. When one event is triggered, the flag associated with the event in the event handler is turned on. However, the event handler cannot be selected for activation by the execution engine until all of its flags are set to on.
- An event handler can be activated only once in response to an event. An event handler can only be activated if all of its flags are set to on. After activation, all of its flags are set to off. Because an event handler cannot be activated if any of its flags are set to off, an event handler can be activated at most once for each event. Note, however, that it is possible for an event to occur multiple times yet the event handler is activated only once.

10.3 EVENT LOOPS SUPPORT MULTITHREADED DIALOGS

Multiagent techniques are frequently used to describe multithreaded dialogs. A multithreaded dialog occurs when a user triggers several events that are processed by event handlers in different scripts.

Figure 10.9 illustrates a partial script for a direct manipulation interface for a text editor. Figure 10.10 illustrates a partial script for a direct manipulation interface for a spreadsheet. Figure 10.11 illustrates a typical multithreaded dialog in which the user switches between these two scripts. Initially the user begins by interacting with the TextEdit script, switches to the SpreadSheet script, switches back to the TextEdit script, and finally switches back to the SpreadSheet.

```
event handler GetDocument triggered on event Get do;
        (* triggered when the user enters the Get command *)

        < description of event handler for searching the
          database and retrieving the specified document >

event handler ModifyDocument triggered on event EnterText
do;
        (* triggered when user enters text into document *)

        < description of event handler for inserting and
          replacing text within the document >
```

Figure 10.9 Partial event-handler specification for text editing script.

```
event handler SaveDocument triggered on event Save do;
        (* triggered when user enters the save command *)

    < description of event handler for saving the
      document into the database >

event handler QuitTextEditing triggered on event Quit do;
        (* triggered when the user enters quit command *)

    <description of clean up tasks performed before
     terminating the text editing task >
```

Figure 10.9   (Continued)

```
event handler GetSpreadSheet triggered on event Get do;
        (* triggered when the user enters the Get command *)

    < description of event handler for searching the
      database and retrieving the specified spreadsheet >

event handler ModifySpreadSheet triggered on event EnterText
do;
        (* triggered when user enters value into
                                        spreadsheet *)

    < description of event handler for inserting and
      replacing text within the spreadsheet >

event handler SaveSpreadsheet triggered on event Save do;
        (* triggered when user enters the save command *)

    < description of event handler for saving the
      spreadsheet into the database >

event handler QuitSpreadSheet triggered on event Quit do;
        (* triggered when the user enters quit command *)

    <description of clean up tasks performed before
     terminating the spreadsheet task >
```

Figure 10.10   Partial event-handler specification for spreadsheet script.

Event handler specification techniques lend themselves very nicely to multithreaded dialogs. A multithreaded dialog is the union of the event handlers in the individual scripts making up the multithreaded dialog. The execution engine handles the switches between scripts in the same manner in which it selects event handlers to execute in a single-threaded dialog.

Generally, there is no communication among the individual scripts in a multi-threaded dialog. However, sometimes the applications may access the same database, and

Event Handler Invoked	Script Involved
GetDocument	TextEdit
ModifyDocument	TextEdit
ModifyDocument	TextEdit
GetSpreadSheet	SpreadSheet
ModifySpreadSheet	SpreadSheet
ModifySpreadSheet	SpreadSheet
SaveDocument	TextEdit
QuitTextEditing	TextEdit
GetSpreadSheet	SpreadSheet
ModifySpreadSheet	SpreadSheet
ModifySpreadSheet	SpreadSheet
QuitSpreadSheet	SpreadSheet

Figure 10.11 Example of a multithreaded dialog involving the scripts of Figures 10.9 and 10.10.

thus share information. More frequently, the user wishes to transfer information from one dialog to another dialog. For example, one window contains a dialog for a spreadsheet application, and another window controls a dialog for a text editing application. The user creates a spreadsheet in one window and wishes to include it in the text being edited in the second window. Most windowing systems permit users to "cut" or "copy" information from one dialog into a buffer called a clipboard. The user first copies the spreadsheet from the window containing the spreadsheet to the clipboard, activates the text editing window, and then "pastes" that information from the clipboard into the text being edited. Basically, the clipboard acts as a database which multiple dialogs may access.

Multithreading is similar, but not the same as multiprocessing. In multiprocessing, the CPU is multiplexed among several tasks, performing some computations for one script, switching to another script, performing some computations for that script, and then perhaps switching back to the first script. In multithreading, the *user* controls the switching, not the CPU. A *concurrent dialog* is a multithreaded dialog where more than one script can be executed simultaneously by the multiprocessing system.

Some windowing systems permit several windows for the same dialog. Often these windows display different views of the dialog. For example, in a three-dimensional editing application, each window displays the object being edited from a different viewpoint. Whenever the user changes something in one window, the corresponding change is reflected in the other windows. This is not considered multithreading because only one dialog is involved. It is only displaying multiple views of the same dialog.

10.4 MODEL, VIEW, AND CONTROLLER OBJECTS IMPLEMENT THE USER INTERFACE IN SMALLTALK

SmallTalk is an object-oriented programming environment which supports the model view controller (MVC) programming paradigm (Krasner & Pope, 1988). In this approach, each agent consists of three objects.

1. *Model* is the underlying application function. The model is responsible for the computational parts of the agent, such as solving equations, calculating correlations, accessing databases, and so on.
2. *View* controls the presentation of the model to the end user. Views display values from the model.
3. *Controller* manages the end user interactions with the model. A controller is the interface between input devices (keyboard, pointing device, time) and the other two components. Controllers accept various events (mouse movements, keyboard entry, and other input sensing) and routes them to the model and possibly to the view.

The following describes one possible set of activities of each of the controller, model, and view agents during the withdrawal of funds from an ATM.

1. The controller accepts a message from the keyboard handler indicating that the end user wishes to withdraw funds. The message also contains the number of the customer's account. The controller forwards the value of AccountNumber to the model.
2. The model receives the value of AccountNumber from the controller. The model attempts to retrieve the bank customer's account from the database. The model forwards information about the customer's account to the view.
3. If the model was able to validate the customer's account information, the view displays a prompt message to the end user asking how much the user wishes to withdraw. If the model was not able to validate the customer's account information, the view displays a message informing the end user that the account number does not exist and terminates the interaction.
4. The user responds to the prompt by entering the amount the user wishes to withdraw.
5. The controller receives the amount the user wishes to withdraw and forwards that amount to the model.
6. The model receives the amount the user wishes to withdraw and calculates the value of NewBalance. A message is sent to the view containing the value of NewBalance.
7. If the value of NewBalance is negative, the view informs the user that the transaction is canceled and terminates the dialog. If the value of NewBalance is positive, then the view displays a message prompting the user to confirm the transaction.
8. The user responds to the prompt for confirmation.
9. The controller examines the confirmation message. If the confirmation is affirmative, then the controller sends a message instructing the model to update the value of Balance with the value of NewBalance, causes the cash to be disbursed to the end user, instructs the end user to remove the cash from the delivery slot, and terminates the dialog. If the confirmation is negative, then the controller terminates the dialog.

Views can be tailored by modifying parameters associated with the display produced by views. This tailoring capability results in *pluggable views* and promotes the reuse of standard views.

10.5 OBJECT-ORIENTED TECHNIQUES ARE USED TO IMPLEMENT USER INTERFACES

SmallTalk is an example of an object-oriented programming environment. The very popular Hypercard® and similar systems such as ToolBook® are also object oriented. Hypercard consists of several objects which are arranged in the hierarchy of Figure 10.12.

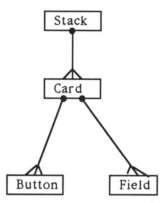

Figure 10.12 HyperCard objects.

In Hypercard, each agent, called an object, has an appearance and several event handlers. Briefly, these objects are

- *Button,* an interaction object which causes the current card to be removed from the screen and another card to be displayed on the screen.
- *Field,* an interaction object which can accept information from the user and echoes the information within the corresponding data box.
- *Card,* a composite interaction object containing static text, graphics, images, buttons, and fields.
- *Stack,* a collection of cards, one of which can be displayed to the user at a time.

A *Hyperstack author* is a user who creates a stack of cards. A *Hyperstack user* is a user who browses stacks of cards.

Object-oriented techniques are becoming popular in user interface programming because of their encapsulation, polymorphism, and inheritance capabilities.

Encapsulation of an object is the hiding of its data structure and algorithms from other objects. The data structures and algorithms of an object can be modified without affecting the implementation of other objects. Because objects are self-contained, objects can also be reused. Associated with each object may be one or more event handlers written in a special language called HyperTalk™ (discussed in section 11.2).

In Hypercard, each object is encapsulated. For example, the processing that occurs when the Hyperstack user enters a value into a field is completely hidden from other Hypercard objects.

Polymorphism means two different objects may respond to the same message with different operations because of encapsulation. For example, the single-message display can be sent to several objects and invoke a different algorithm encapsulated within each object to display itself to the user. In this way, new objects, each containing their own display algorithms, can be added to a system without having to add any new, object-specific display commands.

The actions when a Hyperstack user clicks a button are described by an event handler specified by the Hyperstack author. The actions performed by the event handler for two different buttons may be quite different. For example, when the user clicks one button, the current card disappears and a second card appears. When the user clicks another button, the current card disappears, an application function is invoked, and another card appears which contains the result of the application function.

Inheritance is the ability of one object to reuse data structures and algorithms of another object without reimplementing them.

In Hypercard, the "background" describes the appearance of all of the cards in a stack. For example, a Hyperstack author paints the background to resemble the appearance of a card in a Rolodex file, a page in a diary, or a page in an address book. All of the cards in the stack inherit the background appearance. When a Hyperstack author changes the background, the appearance of all the cards in the stack changes.

When developing new applications, programmers using traditional programming languages such as C or Pascal typically begin with a clean sheet of paper, develop a design, and then implement the code. Object-oriented programmers, on the other hand, typically search through existing objects looking for objects that perform functions similar to those in the new application, and then copy and modify those objects. For user interface designers and implementers, the potential for object reuse is especially desirable because applications which share commmon user interface objects have consistent user interfaces.

Multiagent approaches are currently receiving widespread attention because they support multithreaded dialogs. However, using a multiagent approach tends to obscure temporal relationships in high-level sequencing behavior. Some dialog designers suffer from the "lose sight of the forest for the trees" syndrome by concentrating on individual objects and losing sight of the overall dialog structure. Modifying and debugging dialogs can be difficult because of the "distributed" nature of the dialog: making a minor change to the interface to one object may affect other objects in unsuspected ways.

10.6 MULTIAGENT APPROACHES ARE USED FOR IMPLEMENTING DIRECT MANIPULATION USER INTERFACES

Multiagent approaches seem ideal for direct manipulation interfaces in which the total user interface is partitioned into multiple interaction objects which can be manipulated in a sequence-free manner. The end user can arbitrarily switch between interaction objects, resulting in a multithreaded dialog.

Each icon is the physical representation of an object. The icon may be managed by an event handler within an object [Figure 6.10(a)], a presentation object which is a companion to a computation object [Figure 6.10(b)], or a pair of objects, the controller and the view, which are companion to the model object [Figure 6.10(c)].

Some have claimed that direct manipulation user interfaces will make the Seeheim user interface model obsolete. An alternative opinion is that direct manipulation user interfaces have applied the Seeheim model at a lower level of granularity, at the level of objects rather than at the level of systems.

10.7 SUMMARY

Multiple agents may share information placed in a shared memory. Agents may examine shared memory and react to data found there. Events may be associated with changes to shared memory which trigger events handlers. Event loops act as execution engines that route events to the appropriate event handler. Event handlers may be enabled and disabled. Event handlers may be activated by one or more events. The model view controller paradigm of SmallTalk and the objects of HyperCard are examples of multiagent techniques. Multiagent techniques are widely used to implement direct manipulation user interfaces.

11

Other Dialog Specification Techniques

This chapter discusses

- How existing programming languages are extended to support user interfaces.
- How special programming languages are designed to support user interface specification.
- How knowledge bases can help to design scripts.
- What the advantages and disadvantages are of each approach for specifying scripts.

In addition to state transition diagrams, grammars, rules and constraints, and multiagent approaches, user interface designers use a variety of techniques for specifying scripts, including the following:

- Traditional programming languages. For example, the script is expressed using the syntax of Pascal, C, or Lisp. The availability of programming language compilers currently makes this the most popular technique for implementing scripts.

- Programming languages which have been extended to support special features. Section 11.1 addresses some possible extensions to programming languages which support the specification of user interface scripts.

- Specially designed keyword-oriented languages. Examples include the D language of the TeleUse UIMS and Hypertalk, used in HyperCard. Hypertalk is discussed in Section 11.2

- Graphics-oriented languages. For example, a graphics editor can be used to specify a state transition diagram representing a user interface script.

- Performing actions which are recorded by a user interface authoring tool. For example, the designer moves an icon along a path on the screen. The sequence of positions on the path and the speed which the designer moves the icon between the positions is recorded and constitute an animation script which can be later executed.

- Automatic generation of scripts from user interface knowledge bases. Section 11.3 discusses this approach.

11.1 EXISTING PROGRAMMING LANGUAGES ARE EXTENDED

Conventional programming languages such as C and Pascal do not support many features needed to build contemporary user interfaces. Extending traditional programming languages to support the implementation of user interfaces has several advantages, including the following (Dewan & Vasilik, 1989):

- The application programmer uses a single, familiar language for describing both the application and its user interface.

- Data structures shared between the application and the user interface are defined by a single type system, thus eliminating ''impedance mismatch'' between application data types and user interface data types.

- The user interface specification automatically inherits all of the features of the programming language and environment that aid the programming task.

The Suite UIMS project at Purdue (Dewan & Vasilik, 1989) extends traditional programming languages to support the following features:

- *Input/output of complex structures.* Traditional programming languages support input and output of only simple data types such as integers, strings, reals, and characters. Output values are displayed on a screen for review by users, and input values are entered by users via a keyboard (and echoed on the screen). Suite supports the input and output of complex data structures. In Suite, enumerations, records, variant records, and most other data types can be displayed to the user. The presentation of a pointer variable shows the value of the referent. The presentation of a nil pointer shows a place holder which indicates the type of its referent. As a result, recursive pointer-connected structures can also be displayed.

- *Structure-based commands.* Conventional programming languages do not support commands that understand and manipulate the structure of displayed data. Suite supports several such commands. Application users can use commands to hide/show the children of a variable. Commands are also provided to create/delete referents of pointers and elements of sequences. A menu is used to display the literals that users can assign to an enumeration variable.

- *Continuous display of data structures.* In Suite, variables displayed on the screen are redisplayed with revised values upon application request.
- *Editing.* Conventional programming languages separate the process of input and output. They do not allow editing of the display of a variable to input a new value for the variable. In Suite, a variable may be declared to have one of the following editing modes:

  - *Output.* The value a variable may be updated by the application but not by the user.
  - *Input.* The value of a variable may be updated by the user, but not updated by the application. Users may edit the current value or enter a new value.
  - *Input output.* The value of a variable may be updated by both the user and the application.

Suite makes a copy of application variables for display to the user. When the user commits changes, the display copies are communicated to the application. Thus the user may change display copy values several times before communicating them to the application. Changes to the application copy are communicated to the display copy when the application raises the appropriate event. Thus intermediate application results can be hidden from the user.

While other dialog description approaches attempt to separate the user interface from the application, Suite has the opposite effect. User interface and application components are intermixed.

11.2 SPECIAL PROGRAMMING LANGUAGES ARE DESIGNED

General-purpose programming languages can be difficult to learn and complex to use. For this reason, computer scientists develop special-purpose languages for use in restricted application domains. Because they are not used to do everything a general-purpose programming language can do, they are not as complex and not as difficult to use. Computer scientists design special-purpose languages so that they can be easily used to specify programs in the domain for which they are to be used.

There are many special-purpose languages. Most database management systems have special-purpose languages called query languages for accessing data in the database. Text editors have special editing languages consisting of direct manipulation operations on the text string or document being edited. Graphics packages support special-purpose graphics languages for specifying the position and order in which graphical figures are created on a screen. It should not be surprising that special-purpose languages have been developed for describing user interface dialogs.

The TeleUse UIMS supports a dialog language called D. QUICK, developed at the University of Oregon, supports a special-purpose dialog language for describing direct manipulation. We will briefly discuss HyperTalk (Goodman, 1987), probably the most widely available special-purpose dialog specification language. HyperTalk is part of the HyperCard system available on the Macintosh computer.

HyperCard can be thought of as a state transition system. Each state is represented as a card which is displayed on the screen. A card may contain text, graphics, and a collection of buttons. A button may be thought of as a transition to another card. When a user clicks a button within a card, that card disappears and the card linked to the button appears. Users are able to navigate through a "stack" (set) of cards in arbitrary sequences. An application consists of a stack of cards which the user may browse.

Direct manipulation authoring tools enable the user to create and delete stacks of cards, create and delete cards within stacks, modify the text and graphics within a card, and link cards together. However, in order to link a card to an underlying application, or perform other actions when navigating between cards, application developers use a very simple language called HyperTalk.

Some of the commands in the Hypertalk language are shown in Figure 11-1. Application developers specify user interface dialog scripts by specifying an "on" statement, a sequence of commands, and finishing with an "end" statement. An "on" statement specifies an event handler. For example, the following script

```
on mouseUp
   visual effect wipe left
   go to next card
end mouseUp
```

is invoked when the user releases the button on the mouse. This script causes a visual effect called "wipe left" to occur, and then causes the next card to be displayed to the user. HyperTalk was designed to be easy to use, and yet quite powerful in the scripts that the language can describe.

```
add <source> to <container>
answer <question> [with <reply> [or <reply> [or <reply>]]]
ask <question> [with <reply>]
beep [<number of beeps>]
choose <tool name> tool
click at <location> [with <modifier key>]
close file <file name>
close printing
convert <container> to <format>
delete <component>
dial <phone number> [with [modem] <modem parameters>]
divide <container> by <source>
do <source>
doMenu <menu item>
drag from <location> to <location> [with <modifier key>]
edit script of <target>
find [char[acter]s | work] <source> [in <field>]
```

Figure 11.1 Selected HyperTalk commands.

```
get <expression>
get <property> [of <target>]
global <variable list>
go [to] <destination>
help
hide menubar | <window> | <field or button>
multiply <container> by <source>
open [<document> with] <application>
open file <file name>
open printing [with dialog]
play <voice> [tempo <speed>] [<notes>] [# | b]
     [octave] [duration]
pop card [into <container>]
print <file name> with <application>
print [all <number> cards] | [this <card>]
push [this | recent ] card
put <source> [into | after | before <container>]
read from file <file name> until <delimiter char> | for
     <number of bytes>
send <message> to <target>
set <property> [of <target>] to <new setting>
show [<number> | all] cards
show menubar | <window> | <field or button>
     [at <location>]
sort [ascending | descending]
     [text | numeric | international | datetime]
     by <container>
subtract <source> from <container>
type <source>
visual [effect] <effect name> [<speed>] [to black | white]
wait [for] <time quantity> ticks | seconds
wait until <boolean>
wait while <boolean>
write <source> to file <file name>
```

Figure 11.1 (continued)

11.3 PETRI NETS DESCRIBE CONCURRENT DIALOGS

So far we have discussed scripts for single- and multithreaded dialogs. This section describes a technique for representing concurrent dialogs, dialogs in which the computer performs more than one activity at the same time. Concurrent dialogs are necessary when user interfaces support more than one stream of output for simultaneous presentation to the user. Multimedia applications in which multiple streams of temporal data such as video and audio are presented to the user require concurrent dialogs.

A concurrent dialog requires that some form of multitasking or parallel processing be used to produce the concurrent dialog threads. We require that the concurrent dialog specification technique to be able to

- start a new dialog thread that executes concurrently with existing threads,
- terminate an existing dialog thread that is executing concurrently with other existing dialog threads,
- synchronize two or more existing dialog threads so that one doesn't get ahead of the other.

One representation technique is a variation of Petri nets. An interactive Petri net consists of a set of places, transitions, and directed arcs.

Places are denoted by ovals and represent the presentation of information to the user or entry of information from a user. Associated with each place is a unit of time. If the activity is associated with input from the user, the time is determined by how long the user takes to enter the information. If the activity associated with the place is the presentation of information to the user, the time denotes the length of the presentation. This time may be fixed (as in the time for replaying a video or audio clip) or dependent upon other activities (such as the time it takes the user to select and enter an option from a menu presented by another place). *Transitions* are denoted as vertical bars and represent synchronization points among parallel dialogs. Directed arcs connect places and transitions.

It is convenient to think of control flow tokens which flow through the directed arcs connecting transitions and places. Transitions act as a type of "gate" which controls the starting of activities associated with places. After it has received a control flow token from each of its input places, the transaction places a control flow token on each of its output places. Places cause semantic tokens to be exchanged with the user and/or underlying application programs. After receiving a control flow token, a place does the following:

1. The place exchanges semantic tokens with the user and/or underlying application programs.
2. After the place has completed all of its activities, it places a control flow token on each transition.

Figure 11.2 illustrates part of an interactive Petri net which consists of four places and three transitions. Place p_1 denotes the display of a video clip to the user, place p_2 denotes the presentation of an audio clip to the user, place p_3 denotes the display of a menu of the user, and p_4 denotes the user's selection of one of the options presented on the menu. The transition t_1 denotes the simultaneous beginning of p_1 and p_2. The

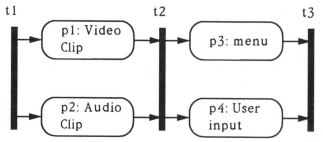

Figure 11.2 Petri net.

Chap. 11   Other Dialog Specification

transition t_2 denotes the ending of both p_1 and p_2 and the simultaneous beginning of p_3 and p_4. The transition t_3 denotes the ending of both p_3 and p_4.

Initially, transition t_1 places control flow tokens in places p_1 and p_2. Both p_1 and p_2 fire at the same time, with p_1 displaying a video clip and p_2 replaying an audio clip. When p_1 completes the display of its video clip, it places its control flow token in transition t_2. When p_2 completes its audio clip replay, it also places its control flow token in t_2. When transition t_2 has received control flow tokens from p_1 and p_2 it places control flow tokens on p_3 and p_4. Place p_3 displays a menu of options to the user and places a control flow token on t_3. After the user selects a menu choice, it places its control flow token on t_3. When both of the control flow tokens from places p_3 and p_4 have been placed on t_3 the concurrent dialog stops.

11.4 A KNOWLEDGE BASE HELPS SCRIPT DESIGN

An end users' conceptual model knowledge base (Foley, Gibbs, Kim, & Kovacevic, 1988; Foley, Kim, Kovacevic, & Murray, 1989) can be used for a variety of purposes, including the following:

- Repository for the end users' conceptual model during the user interface design and implementation phases. The knowledge base can be checked for user interface consistency and completeness.
- Basis for a user interface management system. The knowledge base supplies information for run-time help messages for the user.
- Generation of a different but functionally equivalent user interface. Each user interface can be evaluated with respect to speed of use and ease of learning. Example transformations converting an end users' conceptual model to a different yet functionally equivalent conceptual model are presented in Appendix B.

Figure 11.3 illustrates a hypothetical script-generation system. A *knowledge base* is used to guide a script generator in the generation of alternative scripts. This knowledge base contains alternative sets of rules, a set for each of the major dialog styles (command, question answer, menu and form fill in, and direct manipulation). One set of rules will be used to generate each different dialog style. It is also possible to use rules from several rule sets to generate mixed-style dialogs.

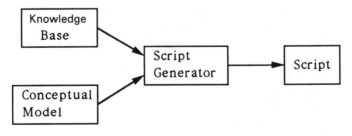

Figure 11.3 Hypothetical script generation system.

Depending on the dialog style, a knowledge base should contain rules which, given an end users' conceptual model, enable a script generator to make the following script design decisions (taken from Section 4.4):

1. For each task, determine the orderings among the functions.
2. For each function, determine which function parameters should be supplied by and displayed to the user.
3. For each function, determine the partial or total ordering in which parameter values should be supplied by and displayed to the user.

A dialog designer might use a script generator to generate several alternative scripts, and then implement one of them. The dialog designer may elect to modify the script produced by a script generator. The script generator may need to be interactive, seeking advice from the dialog designer if the knowledge base does not contain sufficient rules to infer complete decisions for each of the issues listed. Although a script generator did not exist when this book was written, script generation is an area of active research.

11.5 EVALUATION

There does not appear to be a "best" technique to describe all user interface script. Some techniques are better for user interface behavioral aspects, while other techniques are better for appearance aspects.

We will use the criteria from Section 4.7 to evaluate each of the dialog specification techniques discussed in Chapters 7 through 10.

Sequencing, multithreading, and concurrency *State transition systems* are useful for describing scripts in which user-entered information tokens are ordered. Multiple alternative orderings of information tokens can be represented by (1) explicitly describing each information token order as a separate path or (2) using OR grouping state charts to represent multithreading of separate sequences. Approach 1 leads to large, complex, state transition systems containing many nearly redundant states. Approach 2 leads to fewer states which are grouped in complicated ways.

Like state transition systems, *grammars* are useful for scripts in which user-entered information tokens are ordered. Multiple, alternative orderings of information tokens can be described in two ways: (1) multiple productions with alternative sequences of the same symbols on the right-hand side or (2) use of the "A && B" notation on the right-hand side of a production to indicate that either "A" or "B" may be entered first.

Rules and constraints are frequently used to describe scripts in which users may enter information tokens in arbitrary orders. If users must enter information tokens in a predefined order, then the script designer must explicitly specify a rule for the ordering.

Similar to rule- and constraint-based approaches, *multiagent techniques* are frequently used to describe scripts in which users may enter information tokens in arbitrary orders. Ordering on the entry of information tokens can be imposed by encoding the ordering as part of multiple event handlers. Because most direct manipulation user interfaces do not require, and even avoid sequencing, multiagent techniques are frequently used for direct manipulation user interfaces.

Understandability   *State transition systems* are easy to understand and comprehend by most designers. Large state transition systems, however, may be intractable for many humans. Approaches for dealing with the potentially large number of states and transitions include (1) replacing segments of a state transition diagram by subdiagrams, as discussed in Section 7.2, (2) clustering closely related states into branches of a state tree, as discussed in Section 7.3, (3) merging states, as discussed in Section 7.4, and (4) using supernodes, as discussed in Section 7.5. The problem of state explosion is especially severe when there is a partial ordering among the information tokens entered by the user. It may be easier to describe such dialogs using rule- and constraint-based or multiagent approaches.

The notation of *grammars* is more concise and tighter (in the sense of taking up less space) than state transition systems. While this avoids large state transition systems which are difficult for a human to comprehend quickly, the compactness of grammar notation requires cognitive processing for human understanding. In grammars, the distributed nature of productions make it difficult for some user interface designers to visualize valid dialogs.

Script designers generally like the nonprocedurality of *rule- and constraint-based approaches* once they become familiar with the notation for specifying rules. However, some user interface designers may have trouble determining the effect of several rules and how they interact.

In the *multiagent techniques,* a script's specification is distributed among several separate event handlers. It may be difficult for the dialog designer mentally to fit these event handlers together into a complete script making it difficult for them to debug and modify scripts.

Sound formal basis   *State transition systems* have a solid theoretical basis. State transition systems have been extensively used in lexical analyzers and various types of control systems.

Grammars have a solid theoretical basis from compiler theory.

Rule- and constraint-based approaches are frequently based on well-founded logic systems.

Multiagent techniques have some formal basis in the areas of structured programming (and concept hiding), abstract data types (where the implementation of the data types is encapsulated and hidden from users of the data type), and object-oriented programming. However, a general methodology for constructing multiple agents is still a research issue.

Reusability   *State transition systems* can be partitioned into subsystems, which can be reused in other dialogs. For example, systems representing scripts for sign-on, help request processing, collecting a list of parameters, and navigating through a hierarchy of menus can be frequently reused.

In *grammars,* sets of productions used in one script can be reused in another script. Script designers must take care when reusing productions to verify that the names of variables modified by actions are consistent with the new script and that there is no conflict in the names of symbols used in the productions.

Rule- and constraint-based approaches are, in general, fairly reusable, provided that clashing variable name classes are resolved.

Reusability is one of the strong points for the *multiagent approach*. Event handlers can be easily extracted from one script and reused in another. The dialog designer should examine each message which can be sent by the object and verify that those messages can be responded to in the system to which the object is ported.

Executable Both *state transition systems* and *grammars* can be interpreted. This is especially desirable during script development and debugging. State transition systems and grammars can also be compiled and optimized for faster execution. This may be desirable for scripts which will be frequently used. Techniques from compiler construction are useful for compiling grammars.

For *rule- and constraint-based approaches* complex execution engines may be necessary to execute specifications. Execution engines must respond to information tokens by selecting and executing one or more rules. The process of selecting the appropriate rule to execute may be both complex and time consuming. Often the software does not completely conform with the underlying logic system, sometimes leading to surprising and frustrating results. If the rules are interpreted rather than compiled to optimized procedural code, the response time of the script execution engine may be slow.

A few experimental *multiagent* execution engines exist (Hill, 1987a, 1987b; Flecchia & Bergeron, 1987). There are several object-oriented execution engines that may be used to implement multiagent scripts. As with any new technology in computer science, there is some concern about efficiency. Optimizing multiagent scripts is an open research problem.

Familiarity Many dialog designers sketch screen appearances on sheets of paper and then sequence the sketches. This "story board" approach is similar to specifying *state transition systems*. Of the various dialog representation techniques, state transition systems are probably the easiest for dialog designers to learn and use.

Grammars may be difficult for many user interface designers, who will need additional training to design and manipulate scripts described using grammars.

Unfortunately, not many script designers have the necessary background to take full advantage of the formal basis of *rule- and constraint-based approaches* or understand the shortcomings of the various logic systems which underlie these approaches. While the nonprocedurality of rule- and constraint-based approaches enables designers to specify rules quickly, understanding how the rules interact can be quite time consuming.

While some dialog designers are very enthusiastic about *multiagent approaches* others may find these approaches fundamentally different from traditional programming techniques with which they are more familiar. In general, object-oriented approaches are becoming popular in the user interface community, especially for direct manipulation user interfaces.

Perspicuity Because of the graphical nature of state transition systems, it may be possible for dialog designers to identify subsystems common to several scripts, leading to the identification of common script fragments. It may also be possible to recognize dialog styles using this specification technique. These ideas require additional research.

For *grammars*, transformations on AND/OR trees can be used to place dialogs into a canonical form, making it easy to identify common script fragments.

Analysis of *rule- and constraint-based* systems and *multiagent* systems is a current research topic.

Inconsistent and incomplete specification detection   For *state transition systems*, there exist algorithms to detect some types of incompleteness. It is possible to detect some states that can never be reached. It is also possible to detect some states that can never be exited.

For *grammars*, utilities can be built which analyze grammars to detect inconsistent and incomplete specifications.

Software based on the underlying logic systems can be used to detect some inconsistencies and incompleteness of *rule- and constraint-based systems* as well as *multiagent specifications*. In general, detecting inconsistencies is an undecidable problem. This means that it may not be possible to specify an algorithm which will detect all inconsistencies within an arbitrary script specification.

The big drawback of *multiagent* is that inconsistent and incomplete specifications may exist. Without actually executing all possible scenarios, these incomplete specifications may not be discovered.

Measurability   It may be possible to measure the complexity of a script by counting the number of states in its *state transition system* which must be executed to allow for the user to accomplish a task.

For *grammars* (Reisner, 1984) has suggested that the number of productions is proportional to the complexity of the dialog. Because many different sets of productions can describe the same dialog, it will be necessary to adopt a standard form for productions before using this approach to compare two alternative scripts. It is conceivable that the type of production (if the production contains alternation, repeating lists, etc.) may also be indicative of the complexity of the dialog.

Since they are similar to grammar productions, the number of rules might be used to measure the complexity of rule- and constraint-based systems. The number of event handlers might serve as a complexity measure for multiagent models. However, these approaches may only approximate the complexity. Measurability is an open research problem in the *rule- and constraint-based approach* and in the *multiagent approach*.

Backup and recovery   With *state transition systems*, a state may have an explicit transition to a previous state which reverses the actions of the current state. In this situation, users must explicitly enter the command which is the inverse of the most recently executed command. Some state transition execution engine maintain a pushdown stack of recently visited states with both the unmodified and modified values of variables changed. Users may enter successive undo commands to reverse the actions of states. Some states are specified to be commit states; the actions of these states cannot be undone, nor can the execution engine automatically undo states visited prior to a commit state.

Some execution engines based on *grammars* also maintain a pushdown stack of recently executed productions with the unmodifed and modified values of variables changed by those productions. Users may enter successive undo commands to reverse the actions of these productions. Some productions are marked "closure," which is like a commit state. The actions performed when executing this production, and the productions executed prior to this production cannot be undone.

Some *rule- and constraint-based* systems are reversible. To return to a previous state, the user reenters the values of independent variables to be the same as in the previous state, and the system recalculates all of the dependent variables. Some rule- and constraint-based systems maintain a stack of rules and the values of variables changed by those rules so that the user can undo actions via chronological backtracking. Dependency-directed backtracking is also useful for isolating rules to be reinvoked in reversible rule-based systems.

In theory, *multiagent* systems can be designed to be reversible. Multiagent execution engines can be designed to maintain a pushdown stack so that users can enter successive undo commands. In practice, this is seldom done.

Scalability   While *state transition systems* are easily used to describe small and simple scripts, they become unwieldly for large scripts because of the large number of states and transitions. Even with the techniques for dealing with large number of states and transitions described in Chapter 7, state transition systems are seldom used for large and complicated user interface scripts. While script representations using *grammars* are more compact than state transition systems, they seldom used to describe large scripts. *Constraint-based* techniques are becoming popular for describing scripts for interaction objects. *Rule-based* techniques appear promising for describing large, order-independent dialogs. Currently the most popular approaches for describing large, order-independent dialogs are *multiagent*. Using multiagent approaches, dialog designers can concentrate on individual portions of the dialog. However, extensive testing may be necessary to verify that the various dialog portions integrate appropriately.

11.6 SUMMARY

Dialog designers often use traditional programming languages to express scripts. Traditional programming languages are being extended to support additional user interface features. User interface designers also use special purpose languages for expressing scripts. A knowledge base may be used to represent the end users' conceptual model and form the basis for automatic user interface generation.

In general, state transition systems or grammars are used to describe scripts in which the information tokens to be entered by the user are ordered or nearly ordered. Dialog designers frequently prefer state transition systems because of their similarity to storyboards and flip charts widely used to prototype user interfaces. State transition systems are also used to describe device handlers and the behavior aspects of interaction objects.

Multiagent techniques are used to describe scripts in which the user enters information tokens in arbitrary orders. Multiagent and constraint-based techniques are frequently used to describe the appearance of interaction objects. Multiagent and constraint-based techniques are often used for direct manipulation dialogs.

12

User Interface Development Environment

This chapter discusses

> - What tools are useful for designing user interfaces.
> - What guidelines, conventions, and standards are important and why.
> - Whether interaction object libraries should be open or closed.
> - How scripts can be used to predict ease of use.
> - How logs can be used to improve user interfaces.
> - What tools are needed to develop multimedia user interfaces.

An interactive software development environment contains both a UIDE (user interface development environment) and an ADE (application development environment). Both environments contain common tools including programming language compilers, linkers, loaders, debuggers, code analyzers, configuration and version control managers, and documentation tools. This chapter concentrates on the tools and facilities that are unique to the UIDE. The last section of this chapter summarizes some of the special tools needed in user interface development environment for multimedia applications.

12.1 A USER INTERFACE DESIGN ENVIRONMENT CONTAINS USEFUL TOOLS AND FACILITIES

The tools and facilities in an ideal UIDE include the following:

- Guidelines and advisors
- Libraries of reusable software
- Tools for specifying user interfaces
- Tools for evaluating user interfaces

Each of these components is briefly described in this section. Some of the components will be described in greater detail in the following sections.

Guidelines and advisors   The use of guidelines, standards, and conventions leads to user interfaces which are both consistent and easy to use. Various types of on-line assistance are desirable, ranging from the ability to access on-line guidelines, to expert systems which act as user interface advisors. Guidelines and on-line advisors are described in Section 12.2.

Libraries of reusable software   Fully tested, evaluated, and documented user interface libraries are very useful. It is often more economical to locate and reuse an existing user interface or combine existing user interface fragments than to build a new user interface from scratch. Also, when the same user interface is reused in multiple applications, applications have a common look and feel, making it easier for users to switch among applications. Libraries of reusable software are discussed in Section 12.3.

Tools for specifying user interfaces   Tools for specifying user interfaces fall into two categories: interaction object appearance editors or script editors.

Designers may specify interaction objects by using any of three general approaches: (1) textual specifications as in Open Domain from Hewlett-Packard; (2) direct manipulation and form fill-in as in UMIX, TAE+, Interface Builder, and other user interface generators; and (3) automatic generation of default appearance, as in the Mickey and Petoud/Pigner systems. Example interaction object specification tools are described in Appendix D.

Some scripts describe the behavior aspects of interaction objects. Other scripts describe the exchange of information tokens among interaction objects and application functions. Script notations include state transition diagrams, grammars, rules and constraints, and multiagent techniques, each of which is discussed in Chapters 7 through 11. Some UIDEs support code generators which convert high-level script specifications into executable code. Scripts are also implemented as part of the computational portion of application programs, and thus represented using traditional programming languages.

Tools for evaluating user interfaces   Various types of tools are used to evaluate user interfaces:

1. Script simulators. Script simulators enable dialog designers to step through a script, one information token exchange at a time. Script simulators enable dialog designers to examine each semantic token received or transmitted by the script execution engine and determine its correctness. Potentially, a script simulator can proceed either forward or backward in time, enabling the dialog designer to home in on trouble spots quickly. In addition to seeing the semantic tokens exchanged during each step in the script, the dialog designer may also be able to view the interaction objects as they would appear to the end user. The user interface designer evaluates artistic and aesthetic aspects of the user interface appearance.

2. Consistency and completeness checkers. Various types of consistency and completeness checking tools are helpful to user interface designers. Such tools can verify, for example, that each interaction object is indeed used by a script and that the script only references existing interaction objects. Completeness tools examine scripts to verify that each part of the script can be reached (i.e., that there exist situations under which each part of the script will be executed) and that there are no missing parts of the script (i.e., that there exists a target state for each transition).

3. Analyzers. Designers use analyzers to examine interaction objects and/or scripts to determine how well they adhere to conventions and standards. Two types of analyzers are used to evaluate user interfaces. One type of analyzer examines user interface specification and generates ease of use scores. This type of analyzer is discussed in Section 12.4. Another type of analyzer examines previously executed dialogs stored on a log. This type of analyzer is discussed in Section 12.5.

4. Test management tools. Every piece of software must be tested to determine if it satisfies its requirements. User interface software is no exception. The following are useful in testing user interfaces:

- A formal representation for interaction objects and scripts
- A tool for generating interesting test sets of user input and the corresponding output to the user
- A tool for applying test sets and capturing the resulting output
- A tool for comparing the test results with the desired results

Unfortunately, little work has been done in the last three areas. A usable user interface test management system does not yet exist.

12.2 GUIDELINES AND ADVISORS HELP DESIGNERS

Criteria for judging user interfaces include standards, guidelines, and conventions.

Guidelines consist of general recommendations to be used with judgment and adapted to the specifics of the application. Guidelines are developed from current theory of computer-human interfaces and experimental results in evaluating various aspects of user interfaces. Acceptance and use of guidelines is normally voluntary.

Conventions are often defined by a vendor to make guidelines more specific in order to provide a vendor "look and feel" to the vendor's products. User interface conventions have been published for Apple® (Apple Computer, 1987) and Motif (Open Software Foundation, 1990).

Standards are developed by official standards organizations. Usually they are based on established guidelines. After community review and approval, standards are considered to be mandatory. Many customers may refuse to purchase products that do not conform to these standards. A number of user interface standardization efforts are currently underway.

A great deal of research and experimentation has been undertaken by psychologists and behavioral scientists to determine what constitutes a friendly interface. A new discipline of computer-human interfaces has emerged which has produced results that are applicable in designing interaction objects.

The results of this research have been compiled and are available in written form (Smith & Mosier, 1986). Applying guidelines during the user interface design may entail extra work, but should help produce better interaction objects and thus a better user interface.

The Smith and Mosier guidelines have been placed on line and can be browsed and examined interactively. This provides a convenient mechanism for designers to refer to guidelines as they enter design specifications.

It is conceivable that many of these guidelines can be represented as rules of an expert system. If the user interface design is represented formally, expert systems could examine the design and detect design decisions that violate the guidelines. The expert system could be invoked in one of the two following ways:

1. After the user interface designer has completed the design. (This is like using a compiler to detect syntax errors in a program.) The designer analyzes all error messages and makes any necessary adjustments to the user interface design.

2. As the user interface designer makes each design decision. (This is like using a syntax-directed editor to specify the language statements in a program.) An error message is generated whenever the user interface designer makes a decision that violates a guideline.

As a variation of the second approach, the user interface designer consults with the expert system prior to making each design decision. The expert system presents options, alternatives, and recommendations to the user interface designer.

Designing and building such user interface design aids is an open research problem. At least one expert system for designing user interfaces exists. ACE (Meier, 1988) is a color expert system which embodies color rules and applies them to user interface design.

Probably the most effective way of enforcing guidelines is to provide reusable code which adheres to the guidelines. It is more economical for developers to incorporate this reusable code into their user interfaces than it is to develop new code from scratch.

Issues in managing guidelines include the following:

- Writing the guidelines in a form which is useful to user interface designers.
- Enforcing the adherence to guidelines.

- Determining when to violate the guidelines. (Sometimes breaking the rules produces excellent user interfaces.)
- Determining when and how to modify and extend the guidelines.

12.3 INTERACTION OBJECT LIBRARIES MAY BE OPEN OR CLOSED

Libraries of interaction objects are used to provide consistent look and feel across multiple user interfaces and to minimize implementation effort by reusing existing interaction objects. Potential problems with the use of libraries include (1) mechanisms to help designers locate the desired interaction object and (2) useful documentation about each interaction object in the library.

The Macintosh user interface tool box is a library of software programs which manipulate interaction objects on Apple's Macintosh computers. Designers of applications to run on the Macintosh are encouraged to use this library when implementing user interfaces and discouraged from creating new interaction objects. This library is an example of a closed library of interaction objects which discourages new interaction objects. This has two advantages.

1. Closed libraries encourage consistent user interfaces. Once users learn how to use the interaction objects they are able to interact with any application which uses these interaction objects. This is one reason why experienced Macintosh users can often use a new application after reading only an overview of the applications capabilities. Experienced Macintosh users already know how to use the Macintosh interaction objects. By constraining the library to contain a small, fixed number of interaction objects, all applications using that library will have a common interface.
2. Closed libraries encourage efficient and error-free user interfaces. Because interaction objects are well used, they tend to be error free. Also, extra effort can be made to optimize the performance of these interaction objects because they will be widely used.

RAPID (*rap*id *p*rototyper for *i*nterface *d*esign), developed at Honeywell (Metz, 1987), is a software-based design environment for the rapid prototyping of small control panel interfaces. It supports a large and growing library of interaction objects. Designers can easily create new interaction objects and insert them into the library. Designers are encouraged to develop new interaction objects in order to evaluate new and novel user interfaces. New interaction objects can be

- created from scratch,
- created by copying and modifying an existing interaction object,
- created by copying and combining several existing interaction objects.

RAPID is an example of an open library of interaction objects which encourages new and creative interaction objects.

12.4 DESIGNERS USE SCRIPTS TO PREDICT EASE OF USE

Section 12.2 described how software tools can inform the user interface designer of guidelines, standards, and conventions. This section discusses software tools which evaluate a user interface from its specifications.

Shneiderman (1982) has suggested that the complexity of a user interface is proportional to the complexity of its script, as measured by the number of production rules used to define the script. Reisner (1981) showed that a formal grammar can be used to describe the user interface in terms of physical actions, including key presses and cursor motions which can be examined for ease of use and possible user errors. In Reisner (1984), these grammars are extended to include the user's cognitive actions in addition to the user's physical actions.

Researchers at George Washington University have developed the KAT (Keystroke Analysis Tool) (Senay et al., 1988) based on the Key Stroke Level Model of User Performance (Card, Moran, & Newell, 1980, 1983). KAT predicts the amount of time for an expert user to perform tasks using a user interface. KAT accepts the following parameters:

- User interface description
- Estimates of motor skill parameters of the end user
- System response time parameters
- User response time parameters
- Script consisting of sequences of actions which users perform to accomplish high-level tasks

KAT decomposes each input task of a script into a sequence of operators in a *key operator set,* a set of abstract operators that covers the set of activities performed by users and computers during a dialog. The larger the key operator set, the more accurate the resulting estimate, but the more overhead and complexity to compute the estimates. The designers of KAT have selected the key operator set to contain the following operators:

- K represents a keystroke, the pressing of a button on a keyboard.
- P represents pointing, the positioning of a pointing device onto an object on the video screen.
- H represents homing, the shifting between input devices, for example, moving the hand from a keyboard to a mouse.
- D represents drawing a line.
- M represents mental preparation, the cognitive process of choosing the next operation to perform.
- R represents response time, the time needed by application functions to produce the desired results.

KAT estimates the predicted time to execute each task in a script by summing all the estimated times to perform each of the individual key operators involved with the task.

For example, consider a simple script consisting of one action, rotating a triangle 45 degrees. The user types the command *rotate,* selects the triangle to be rotated by pointing to it, and finally types in the angle of rotation. The following key operators are assigned:

- *MHKKKKKKK.* The M represents the end user's mental preparation to enter the rotate command. H represents moving the user's hands to the keyboard, and the seven Ks represent the six characters in the rotate command followed by a carriage return.
- *MHPK.* The M represents the mental preparation to select the desired triangle. The H represents the user moving his or her hand to a mouse. The P represents manipulating the mouse to point to the desired triangle on the screen, and the K represents a mouse click which actually selects the desired triangle.
- *MHKKK.* Again, the M represents the user's mental preparation, and H represents moving the user's hand from the mouse to the keyboard. The three Ks represent keys 4 and 5 and the carriage return.

The sum of the times associated with 3 Ms, 3 Hs, a P, and 11 Ks results in the estimated total time.

Dialog designers may generate scripts in either of two ways: (1) by using a text editor or (2) by example using the actual user interface to record actions. KAT automatically inserts an H between the use of two different input devices and places M in front of each information unit to be entered by the user. KAT replaces each action by abstract operators. KAT currently assumes that the user is an expert that makes no errors.

KAT can be used to evaluate an entire script, or an individual task within a script. Designers may evaluate alternative interaction objects to determine which is most appropriate for the script. Designers may also incorporate new interaction objects by specifying how they map to the key operations.

12.5 DESIGNERS ITERATIVELY REVISE USER INTERFACE PROTOTYPES

Guidelines by themselves are not enough to guarantee a good user interface. Similarly, the analysis of scripts is not enough to guarantee a good user interface. Even the most carefully designed user interface requires testing by its intended users in order to confirm the value of good features and discover what bad features may have been overlooked. Often several prototypes need to be designed and tested before the final interface is chosen.

The iterative process of evaluating and modifying user interface prototypes is necessary to develop useful and efficient user interfaces. For example, the KAT analysis described in the previous section does not address errors, how frequently they are made, what causes them, and how the user interface should be modified so users make fewer of them. Only by exercising prototypes of the user interface can designers observe and measure aspects of the user interface which cannot be predicted by modeling and simulation.

Evolutionary and exploratory prototypes   Two types of user interface prototypes are possible, evolutionary and exploratory. An *evolutionary* user interface prototype is refined and modified until it satisfies the needs of the user, and then it is fielded and placed into production. Evolutionary user interface prototypes do not require reimplementation in order to be fielded.

An *exploratory* user interface prototype is refined and modified until it satisfies the needs of the users, but then must be reimplemented before it is fielded and placed into production. Exploratory user interface prototypes are often easier to modify and refine during the prototyping stage, but may not provide the efficiency needed by applications in use. For example, the Macintosh Hypercard software can be used to simulate a user interface and demonstrate that interface to potential users.When the user identifies a problem with the user interface, the user interface designer is often able to correct the problem immediately and demonstrate the revised user interface. While a user interface prototyped using Hypercard is easy to modify, it currently cannot be ported to non-Macintosh hardware, and thus may need to be reimplemented.

Test data for analysis   Often the user interface designer is constrained by time or resources, and must stop the user interface evaluation iteration prematurely. The number of iterations can be increased if the user interface execution engine itself can aid in the evaluation of the user interface by collecting and analyzing data which measures various aspects of a user interface. Useful data can be captured by a user interface execution engine while perspective users actually use the prototype user interface. This data includes the following:

- *Sum of the distances the cursor is moved between mouse clicks.* If this value is large, the screen layout should be reorganized to decrease cursor movement.
- *Command frequency.* If a command is seldom or never used, it becomes a candidate for removal from the user interface. Frequently executed commands are candidates for optimization.
- *Command pair frequency.* Pairs of frequently executed commands may be combined into a single, supercommand. Alternatively, the user interface may be modified so that they are easy to invoke together.
- *Number of physical input events required to select or specify a command or argument value.* If the number is excessively high, especially for frequently executed commands, then the user interface should be modified to minimize the number of physical input events.
- *Number of rubout, cancel, and undo operations.* These operations are indicative of confusion in the user's mind. The set of operations performed prior to a rubout, cancel, or undo operation can be compared to the set of operations performed after the rubout, cancel, or undo in order to understand the user's confusion.
- *The number of times the user switches between physical devices, such as keyboard and mouse.* If this occurs frequently, the user interface should be modified to minimize this switching.
- *Changes in the user's focus of attention on the screen.* Divide the screen into a rectangular grid of buckets. Record (1) the *output size,* the number of buckets

actually used to display the output of a command, (2) the *output extent,* the number of buckets in the smallest rectangle which contains all of the buckets actually used to display the output of the command; and (3) *dispersement ratio* which is the ratio of output size to output extent. Commands with a low dispersement ratio use widely separated portions of the screen to do relatively little work. A rearrangement of the screen layout may resolve this problem. A high output extent with a dispersement ratio close to one indicates nearly complete changes in the visual context of the command. If this occurs frequently, there is likely a major flaw in how contexts are used in the user interface.

MIKE, a user interface management system built by Dan Olsen, Jr., at Brigham Young University (Olsen and Halversen, 1988) generates a log containing the types of data discussed above. Each command and argument entered by the user is captured in the log. After the log is created by users performing typical tasks using the user interface, the log is sorted by command within each type of data so that there are several sorted lists, one for each type of data. The worst commands for each type of data are placed at the top of that metric's list. These lists can then be analyzed by user interface designers, who modify the user interface if necessary.

Trouble logs   A ''trouble log'' is useful for recording complaints, comments, suggestions, and recommendations from users as they experiment with the user interface. Although these comments cannot be automatically analyzed, designers can learn much about the usefulness of the user interface, especially its problem areas, from analyzing users' comments.

12.6 MULTIMEDIA USER INTERFACES REQUIRE TOOLS[*]

One great revolution in user interfaces occurred when character-based user interfaces were replaced by graphical user interfaces. Another major revolution to user interfaces may be coming. This revolution promises more natural user interfaces by providing image, audio, and video output.

Multimedia user interfaces involve more than the traditional data types of text and tabular information. Multimedia user interfaces include these data types and at least one of the graphics, image, audio, and video data types. Developers of multimedia applications are often called *authors* and the applications themselves are sometimes called *titles.* A *multimedia development environment* is an integrated collection of tools used by authors to create multimedia user interfaces and applications. A multimedia development environment contains tools from four different disciplines.

- *Desktop publication.* Many of the tools developed for desktop publishing can be used to create multimedia applications. These tools include text, graphics, and document editors. Multimedia authors use these tools to build the textual and graphical aspects of multimedia applications.

---

[*]This section is coauthored by Rune Skarbo and James A. Larson.

- *Film and sound editing*. Multimedia authors use videotape editors, audio editors, sound samplers (used to capture sounds), music sequencers (used to construct sequences of music), and synthesizers to construct the audio and video portions of multimedia applications.

- *Animation tools*. One of the great advantages of multimedia applications is their dynamic rather than static nature. In addition to videotape editors, multimedia authors use animation tools to give life to figures. Processes that appear as several figures in a textbook can be animated in multimedia applications.

- *Script tools program development*. Tools for generating interactive objects such as menus, dialog boxes, and fill-in forms are used to create objects with which users of interactive applications interact. Control flow editors such as flowchart builders, time line editors, and decision table builders are used to specify and rehearse mulitmedia scripts.

Tools from each of these four disciplines need to be integrated into a multimedia development environment. A multimedia development environment should satisfy several goals, including the following:

- *Openess*. New tools can be integrated as they become available.

- *Common user interface*. The author interacts with each tool using similar commands and techniques.

- *Common data structures*. The data produced by one tool can be used by another tool. Data used by more than one tool is placed into a shared database.

- *Direct manipulation*. Multimedia authors should be able to see and hear the results of what they specify immediately. Authors may make small incremental changes and observe the results of those changes immediately.

- *Edit in context*. To reduce the amount of guesswork and trial and error, multimedia authors should be able to edit any media in the context that it will appear together with other media. In other words, playback and record can take place simultaneously if necessary.

- *Ease of learning*. Tools available in the multimedia development encironment should support metaphors and paradigms familiar to multimedia authors.

Figure 12.1 illustrates one multimedia development environment consisting of four major levels or sets of tools: capture, clip, scene, and programming tools. The tools at each level are used to accomplish different objectives. Low-level tools, that is capture and clip tools, are used to record and edit "raw" data. Scene tools are used for combining clip data. Programming tools, in turn, are used for combining scenes, and for specifying control flow and user interaction.

In Figure 12.1, each tool is illustrated as a box. Each interface between tool levels is subject to standardization. By standardizing these interfaces, the author could pick and choose which tools to place in his or her workbench with a certainty that the tools would work together. We call this the *Lego* approach to constructing a workbench, after the popular building toys marketed under the name of Lego^{TM}.

In the remainder of this section, we describe tools in each of the four levels.

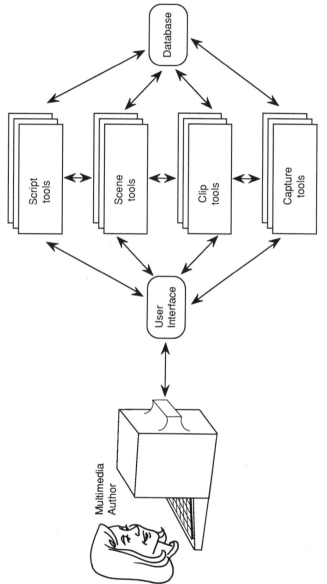

Figure 12.1 Multimedia authoring tools.

12.6.1 Capture Tools

Authors use a variety of tools to capture images, audio, and video. Scanners are used to capture and digitize images from paper. Digitizing cameras capture and digitize still images. Microphones and audio recorders are used to capture sound clips. Video and motion picture cameras are used to capture video clips.

12.6.2 Clip Tools

Clips are the basic building blocks of a multimedia application. Multimedia authors use tools at this level to edit individual audio clips, video clips, animation clips, and textual and graphical images (displayed for a period of time). Examples of individual clip tools include text editors, graphics editors, animation editors, audio editors, and video editors. These tools are briefly described in Appendix D1. Some of these editors already exist in desktop publishing systems. Other editors already exist in film and sound postproduction systems.

12.6.3 Scene Tools

Multimedia authors use tools at this level to arrange clips in space and time. A scene typically consists of multiple clips of different media types. Scene editors are used to arranged clips in several dimensions:

- Layout of clips in two-space dimensions and one-time dimension. The author can specify where on the screen a clip should be positioned and played back. The author can specify when a clip should be displayed. The display time can be absolute or relative to other clips.
- Layout of clips in three-space dimensions and one-time dimension. In addition to the capabilities mentioned, another spatial dimension can be specified. Objects in one plane obscure the view of objects on other planes, giving a three-dimensional effect to the viewer.

An example of a scene tool is Score from MacroMind Director™ editor. See Figure 12.2. This editor uses the multitrack tape recorder or musical score metaphor. There are 24 channels for animation in addition to separate channels for sound, tempo changes, visual effects, and labels. Typical text editing operations, such as cut, copy, and paste are performed on the action codes in the Score window.

Scenes, as we have defined them, do not contain any user interaction. Even without user interaction, useful applications can be created with scene editors including TV commercials, business presentations, and timed slide shows. For interactive applications, we must add user interaction and control flow which, in our model, are specified at the program level.

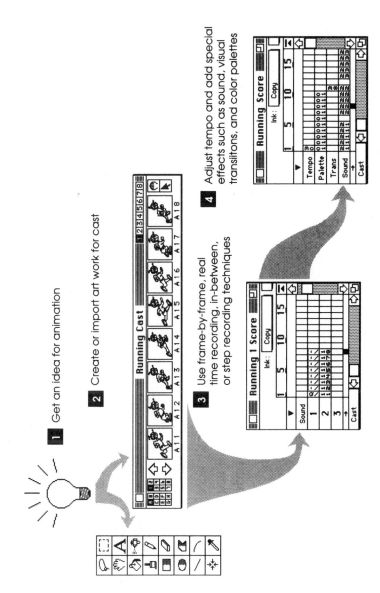

1 Get an idea for animation

2 Create or import art work for cast

3 Use frame-by-frame, real time recording, in-between, or step recording techniques

4 Adjust tempo and add special effects such as sound, visual translitons, and color palettes

Figure 12.2 MacroMind's Score editor. (Reprinted with permission of MacroMind, Inc.)

12.6.4 Script Tools

This tool set is used primarily to *glue* scenes together and to create interactive applications. Multimedia authors may use tools at this level to specify how users enter information and how entered information affects what is displayed to the user.

Two important aspects of user interaction are *timing* and *control flow*. Timing aspects include when to start a scene, when to end a scene, when to increase the tempo, and so on. Timing specifications are typically event driven. Control flow is used to specify what scene to present next and when to invoke application functions. These specifications are typically data driven.

In theory, any of the dialog specification techniques discussed in Chapters 6 through 11 can be used to describe scripts for multimedia applications. In practice, tools for specifying the exchange of information between user and application functions include the following:

- A time-line editor which authors use to control when scenes are presented to the user. A time-line editor is used to specify points in time when actions should occur. This tool is useful for constructing slide shows and video presentations with some simple form of user interaction, for example, "click OK when ready to move on to the next scene" or "back to previous scene."
- A flowchart editor can be used to specify simple data-driven interactions. Multimedia authors use the flow chart editor to specify alternative branches of the presentation which are executed depending on information entered by the user. This tool is useful for building tutorials, training applications, and Hypertext-like applications. A time-line editor can be thought of as a flowchart editor without branches.
- Script editors are used to specify complex user interaction activities (often event driven in nature), initialization and updating of variables, and control flow.

In Table 12.1, the three specification tools are related to user interaction aspects of timing and control flow. The methods also vary in simplicity. A plus (+) in Table 12.1 indicates a strength of the tool while a minus (−) indicates a weakness. For example, the time-line editor does not require knowledge of programming and it is quite intuitive, so it has a plus for simplicity. A script language, on the other hand, requires knowledge of both programming concepts and language syntax. It has a minus for simplicity.

The time-line editor and flowchart editor are examples of schematic editors. Appendix F describes an approach for generating schematic editors from a limited amount of information about the structure and appearance of nodes and links in a graph.

TABLE 12.1. Program specification tools and how they relate to user interaction aspects and simplicity of specification.

	Timing	Control Flow	Simplicity
Time line	+	−	+
Flowchart	−	+	+
Script	+	+	−

12.7 SUMMARY

Guidelines, standards, and conventions form the criteria for evaluating user interfaces. They also form the basis for rules which drive interactive expert systems to aid designers in designing user interfaces. Dialog designers analyze scripts to predict ease of use of user interfaces. Logs of activities performed by users may also be analyzed to determine the strong and weak points of the user interface.

User interface prototypes are necessary to analyze user interfaces in context of their use. To develop prototypes quickly, user interface designers need a variety of high-level languages and code generators, simulators, consistency and completeness checkers, and log analyzers.

Useful interaction objects and scripts are stored in a library and may be reused. A closed library promotes consistent, reliable user interfaces, while an open library promotes new and innovative user interfaces.

Four levels of tools are needed to develop user interfaces for multimedia applications. Capture tools include cameras and microphones and the associated recording facilities. Clip tools include bit-map editors, graphics editors, animation editors, audio editors, and video editors. Scene tools are used to arrange clips in space and time. A variety of script tools are used to glue scenes and application functions to form interactive, multimedia applications.

Appendix A

Relationships Between Objects in the Same Class

This appendix describes properties of relationships between conceptual objects in the same class. Relationships between conceptual objects in the same object class deserve special consideration because they are often represented by special interaction objects. Some of these special interaction objects are discussed in the second part of Appendix C. In addition to the two general properties of relationships between objects in different classes, relationships between objects in the same class have the following properties:

p6. The relationship is either reflexive or not reflexive.

p7. The relationship is either irreflexive or not irreflexive.

p8. The relationship is symmetric, antisymmetric, or neither symmetric nor antisymmetric.

p9. The relationship is either transitive or nontransitive.

We will examine each of these properties in greater detail. The relationship classes IsSameAgeAs, HasSameParentsAs, IsOlderThan, IsAncestorOf, IsParentOf, and Likes each contain relationships relating individuals belonging to the Person class. The IsA, IsPartOf, and IsMemberOf relates individual objects in a Thing object class. IsGreaterThanOrEqual and IsGreaterThan apply to the Integer class.

The following table summarizes the properties of these relationship classes.

	Reflexive	Irreflexive	Symmetric	Anti symmetric	Transitive	Non transitive
IsSameAgeAs	Y	N	Y	N	Y	N
HasSame ParentsAs	Y	N	Y	N	Y	N
IsOlderThan	N	Y	N	N	Y	N
IsAncestorOf	N	Y	N	N	Y	N
IsParentOf	N	Y	N	N	N	Y
Likes	N	N	N	N	N	Y
SameSocial Security NumberAs	Y	N	Y	Y	Y	N
IsA	N	Y	N	N	Y	N
IsPartOf	N	Y	N	Y	Y	N
IsMemberOf	N	Y	N	N	N	Y
IsGreaterThan OrEqualTo	Y	N	N	Y	Y	N
IsGreaterThan	N	Y	N	N	Y	N
NotEqualTo	N	Y	Y	N	N	Y

Reflexive and irreflexive   If each object in the class is related to itself, then the relationship is said to be *reflexive*. If no object in the class is related to itself, then the relationship is said to be *irreflexive*. No relationship can be both reflexive and irreflexive.

Example A.1:

Because each Person has only one age, the relationship class IsSameAgeAs is reflexive. Clearly, no person is his or her own parent. Thus, the relationship IsParentOf is irreflexive. Because some Persons like themselves and other Persons do not like themselves, the relationship Likes is neither reflexive nor irreflexive. ∎

Symmetric and antisymmetric   A relationship is *symmetric* when object a_i is related to object a_j implies that object a_j is also related to object a_i. A relationship is *antisymmetric* when object a_i is related to object a_j and object a_j is related to object a_i imply that $a_i = a_j$. A relationship may be both symmetric and antisymmetric.

Example A.2:

If both Joe and Sally are persons such that Joe has the same parent as Sally, then Sally has the same parent as Joe. Thus, SameParentAs is symmetric. IsGreaterThanOrEqualTo is antisymmetric, because A IsGreaterThanOrEqualTo B and B IsGreaterThanOrEqualTo A imply A = B. SameSocialSecurityNumberAs is both symmetric and antisymmetric. ∎

Transitive and nontransitive   If a_i, a_j and a_k are objects, a_i is related to a_j, and a_j is related to a_k, all imply that a_i is related to a_k, then the relationship is said to be *transitive*. If there exist objects a_i, a_j, and a_k such that a_i is related to a_j, a_j is related to a_k, but a_i is not related to a_k, then the relationship is said to be *nontransitive*. No relationship can be both transitive and nontransitive.

Example A.3:

The relationship class IsAncestorOf is transitive. Sally IsAncestorOf Fred and Fred IsAncestorOf George imply that Sally IsAncestorOf George. The relationship class IsParentOf is nontransitive. Sally IsParentOf Fred and Fred IsParentOf George does not imply that Sally IsParentOf George. ■

Partial Order   A relationship class R is said to have a *partial order* if it is reflexive, antisymmetric, and transitive.

Example A.4:

IsGreaterThanOrEqualTo is a partial ordering. ■

Total Order   A relationship class R is said to have a *total order* if it has a partial ordering and for every pair of objects a_i and a_j in the object class, either a_i R a_j or a_j R a_i.

Example A.5:

The relationship IsGreaterThanOrEqualTo applied to the class of objects consisting of the integers is a total ordering. ■

Appendix B

Conceptual Model Refinements

An end users' conceptual model can be transformed into an equivalent conceptual model which may be easier for users to learn and use. This appendix describes transformations for refining a conceptual model. It also describes transformations involving the insertion or deletion of each of three types of relationship classes. These transformations are illustrated in Figure B.1.

- Transformations involving insertion and deletion of IsA relationships (merging, horizontal partitioning). Two object classes can be merged together, and an existing object class can be horizontally partitioned into two classes.
- Transformations involving the insertion and deletion of IsMemberOf relationships (aggregation, factoring, join). A single-object class can be transformed to form two object classes, one of which IsMemberOf the other. Two object classes related by IsMemberOf can be joined to form a single-object class.
- Transformations involving interchanging IsPartOf relationships and IsMemberOf relationships (vertical partitioning, cross-product). The vertical partitioning transformation transforms IsPartOf to IsMemberOf, and the cross-product transformation transforms IsMemberOf to IsPartOf.
- Other transformations include cluster, collapse set, atomitize, concatenate, insert transitive closure, delete transitive closure, and inversion.

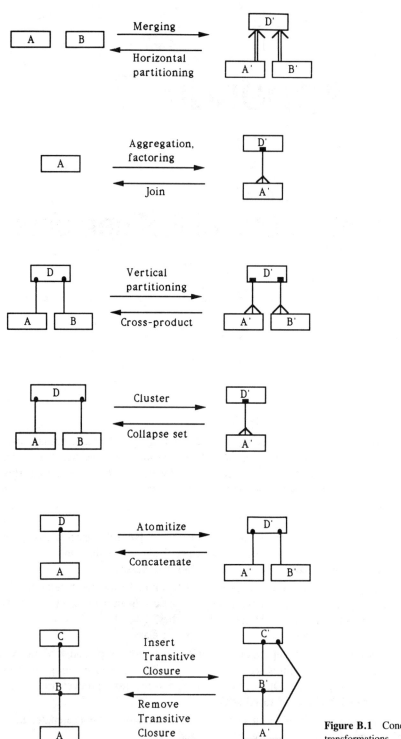

Figure B.1 Conceptual model transformations.

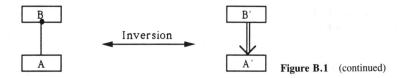

Figure B.1 (continued)

There are numerous variations and combinations of these transformations, as well as other transformations not discussed in this appendix.

To define the various transformations formally, we will use the following notation: RELATEDOBJECTS(X) denotes the set of object classes which are related to the object class X. OBJECTS (X), FUNCTIONS(X), and CONSTRAINTS(X) denote, respectively, the objects, functions, and constraints associated with object class X.

B.1 MERGING OBJECT CLASSES

If two separate object classes have similar relationship classes, functions, and constraints, then the two object classes may be merged into a single-object class. This is done if the designer feels that both classes contain the same type of objects. The merging transformation merges the objects in two different classes into a single-object class. The merging transformation is a generalization of the union operation from set theory. The merging transformation is formally defined as follows:

Definition: Merging transformation   The result of the merging transformation on object classes A and B are the new object classes D′, A′, and B′ which replace object classes A and B. There are also two additional IsA relationship classes, from A′ to D′ and from B′ to D′. The related object classes, functions, and constraints of the new object classes are defined as follows:

```
RELATEDOBJECTS(D') := 
     RELATEDOBJECTS(A) intersect RELATEDOBJECTS(B)
RELATEDOBJECTS(A') := 
     RELATEDOBJECTS(A) minus RELATEDOBJECTS(D')
RELATEDOBJECTS(B') := 
     RELATEDOBJECTS(B) minus RELATEDOBJECTS(D')

FUNCTIONS(D') := FUNCTIONS(A) intersect FUNCTIONS(B)
FUNCTIONS(A') := FUNCTIONS(A) minus FUNCTIONS(D')
FUNCTIONS(B') := FUNCTIONS(B) minus FUNCTIONS(D')

CONSTRAINTS(D') := CONSTRAINTS(A) intersect CONSTRAINTS(B)
CONSTRAINTS(A') := CONSTRAINTS(A) minus CONSTRAINTS(D')
CONSTRAINTS(B') := CONSTRAINTS(B) minus CONSTRAINTS(D')

OBJECTS(A') := OBJECTS(A)
OBJECTS(B') := OBJECTS(B)
OBJECTS(D') := OBJECTS(A') union OBJECTS(B')
```

If A′ has no relationships, constraints, or functions, it is eliminated. If B′ has no relationships, constraints, or functions, it is eliminated. ∎

The following examples illustrate the merging transformation.

Example B.1

Figure B.2 illustrates that Secretary object class is related to the following object classes:

```
Name
Salary
TypingSpeed
SocialSecurityNumber
```

and supports the following functions:

```
hireSecretary ($Name, $TypingSpeed, $Salary,
                                $SocialSecurityNumber)
generatePaycheck ($Name, $SocialSecurityNumber, $Salary)
```

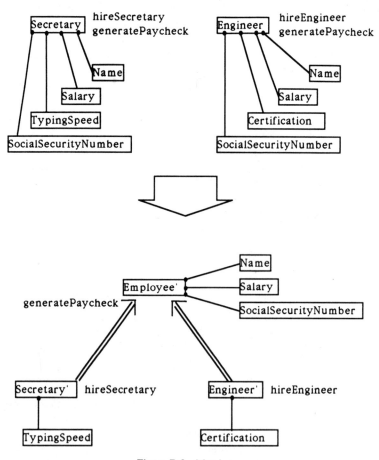

Figure B.2 Merging

The Engineer object class is related to the following object classes:

```
Name
Salary
Certification
SocialSecurityNumber
```

and supports the following functions:

```
hireEngineer ($Name, $Certification, $Salary,
                        $SocialSecurityNumber)
generatePaycheck ($Name, $SocialSecurityNumber, $Salary)
```

The Secretary and Engineer object classes have three common relationship classes and a common function. If the designer feels that both Secretary and Engineer object classes contain the same type of objects, then the two classes should be merged. The merging transformation creates a new object class, Employee', with the common relationship classes involving Name, Salary, SocialSecurityNumber, and the common function, generatePay-

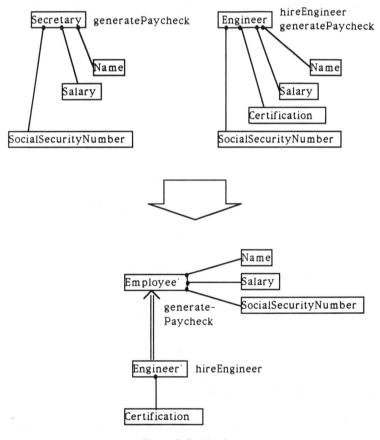

Figure B.3 Merging

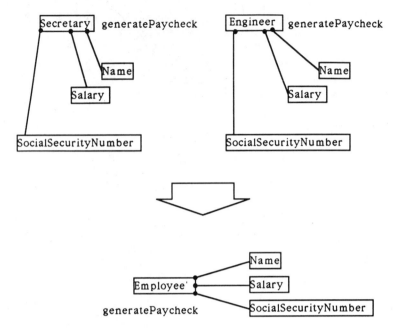

Figure B.4 Merging.

check. The Secretary' class will have a single relationship class, TypingSpeed, and the function, hireSecretary. The Engineer' class will have a single relationship class, Certification, and the function, hireEngineer. Two new relationship classes are created: Secretary' IsA Employee' and Engineer' IsA Employee'. ∎

Example B.2

Example B.2 is modified so that the Secretary class no longer has the relationship classes involving TypingSpeed and no longer supports the function hireSecretary. This is illustrated in Figure B.3. After merging the Secretary and Engineer object classes, Secretary' has no relationship classes, functions, or constraints. Because the user cannot perform functions on this object, it is not needed in the conceptual model, and is thus eliminated. This leaves the Employee' and Engineer' object classes with Engineer' IsA Employee'. ∎

Example B.3

Example B.3 is modified so that the Engineer class no longer is related to Certification and no longer supports the function hireEngineer. This is illustrated in Figure B.4. After merging the Secretary and Engineer object classes, Secretary' and Engineer' have no relationship classes, functions, or constraints; thus both are eliminated. The result is a single-object class, Employee', with all of the functions, relationships, and constraints from the original Secretary and Engineer classes. ∎

B.2 HORIZONTAL PARTITIONING

Horizontal partitioning of an object class is similar to the operation of horizontal partitioning of a file in distributed database design (Ceri & Pelegatti, 1984) in which the rows of a database table are separated to form multiple tables. When used in conceptual models, horizontal partitioning generates multiple-object classes, each containing objects from the original object class. Its formal definition follows.

Definition: Horizontal partitioning transformation   When the object class D and two of its subclasses are horizontally partitioned, two new object classes, A' and B', replace object class D. The relationships, functions, and constraints of the new object classes are defined as follows:

```
RELATEDOBJECTS(A') := RELATEDOBJECTS(D)
          union RELATEDOBJECTS(A)

RELATEDOBJECTS(B') := RELATEDOBJECTS(D)
          union RELATEDOBJECTS(B')

FUNCTIONS(A') := FUNCTIONS(D) union FUNCTIONS(A)

FUNCTIONS(B') := FUNCTIONS(D) union FUNCTIONS (B)

CONSTRAINTS(A') := CONSTRAINTS(D) union CONSTRAINTS(A)

CONSTRAINTS(B') := CONSTRAINTS(D) union CONSTRAINTS(B)   ■
```

This transformation is often applied whenever there are two or more types of objects in a single object class. This transformation may also be applied if there are functions which apply to different subsets of objects in the object class.

Example B.4

Figure B.5(a) illustrates three object classes:

- Employee' object class with relationships to the following object classes:

```
Name
Salary
Skill
```

and the function

```
printSkill ($Name, $Skill)
```

- BostonEmployee' object class with a relationship to the BostonAddress object class and the function

```
printBostonCheck ($Name, $Salary, $BostonAddress)
```

- NonBostonEmployee' object class with a relationship to the NonBostonAddress object and the function

```
printNonBostonCheck ($Name, $Salary, $BostonAddress).
```

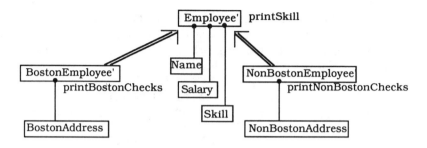

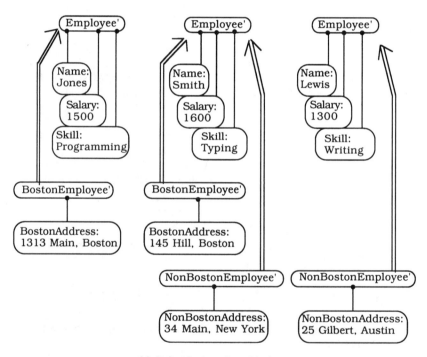

(a) Before horizontal partitioning

Figure B.5 Horizontal partitioning.

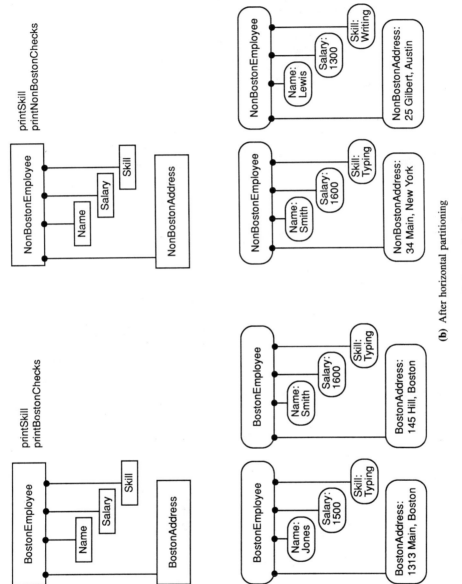

(b) After horizontal partitioning

Figure B.5 (continued)

There are two new IsA relationships, from NonBostonEmployee' to Employee' and from BostonEmployee' to Employee'.

The result of applying the transformation, illustrated in Figure B.5, is two object classes:
- The BostonEmployee object class with relationship classes to the following object classes:

```
Name
Salary
Skill
BostonAddress
```

and the functions

```
printSkill
printBostonChecks
```

- The nonBostonEmployee object class with relationship classes to the following object classes:

```
Name
Salary
Skill
NonBostonAddress
```

and the functions

```
printSkill
printBostonChecks  ■
```

A variation of horizontal partitioning is called *specialization* (Foley, 1987). In specialization, a function applied to general object is specialized for objects in each subclass. Figure B.6 illustrates an example of specialization:

Example B.5

As illustrated in Figure B.6(a), originally the Transaction object is related to the following object classes:

```
TransactionAmount
Date
AccountIdentifier
TransactionType
```

and supports the function

```
apply($TransactionAmount, $Date, $AccountIdentifier,
                          $TransactionType).
```

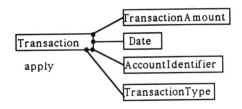

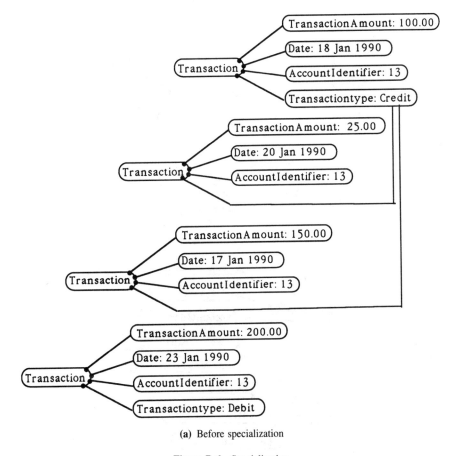

(a) Before specialization

Figure B.6 Specialization.

After specialization (Figure B.6(b)) the Transaction object is related to the following object classes:

```
TransactionAmount
Date
AccountIdentifier
```

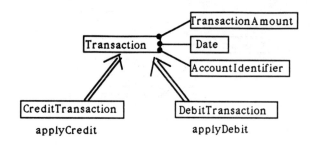

applyCredit   applyDebit

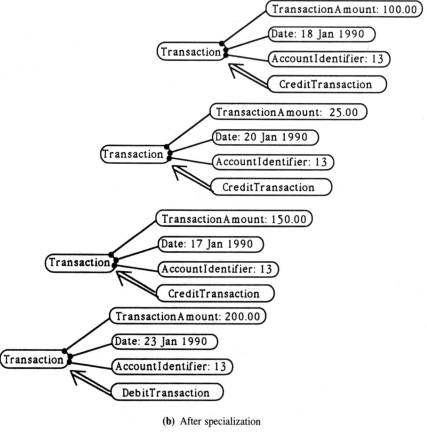

(b) After specialization

Figure B.6   (continued)

Two new object classes are generated: CreditTransaction and DebitTransaction where CreditTransaction IsA Transaction and DebitTransaction IsA Transaction. The Apply function has been specialized into two functions:

```
applyCredit ($TransactionAmount, $Date,
                        $AccountIdentifier)
```

which can be executed to create a new CreditTransaction object, and

```
applyDebit ($TransactionAmount, $Date,
                              $AccountIdentifier)
```

which can be executed to create a new DebitTransaction object. The new CreditTransaction and DebitTransaction object classes inherit all relationships from the Transaction object class. In effect, the Transaction class is horizontally partitioned so that a new function can be applied, one to each new subobject class. Note that the parameter $TransactionType is not present in either applyCredit and applyDebit. Specialized functions generally have fewer parameters than their parent functions. ∎

The horizontal partitioning transformation is the inverse of the merging transformation. Figure B.1 illustrates how the merging transformation transforms two object classes, A and B, into a new object class, D'. The new object classes A' and B' are specializations of D' and may not be present. Figure B.1 also illustrates how the horizontal partitioning function transforms object class D' into object classes A and B. Recall that A' and B' are specializations of D' and either may not be present. It is important to observe that horizontal partitioning transforms a single-object class into two classes and that merging transforms two classes into a single class. The two operations are the inverse of each other, after making adjustments for specializations.

B.3 AGGREGATION AND NORMALIZATION

The aggregation transformation partitions objects in a composite object class into sets with the same value for one or more simple objects called *grouping objects*. It may also perform aggregate functions such as Count, Sum, Max, Min, or Average on the objects in each set. A new object is created which is related to the grouping object(s). The original object class is related to the new object class by IsMemberOf. A simple object is created for each aggregate function applied during the transformation. The aggregation transformation is formally defined as follows:

Definition: Aggregation transformation   Let A be a composite object class to which the aggregation transformation is applied. Let GROUP be the set of objects related to A whose values are used to partition objects in A into sets. Let AGGREGATE-FUNCTIONS be the set of aggregate functions which are applied to objects in each set. The resulting object classes, A' and D', are defined as follows,

```
RELATEDOBJECTS(D') := GROUP union AGGRETATE-FUNCTION-RESULTS union A
where AGGREGATE-FUNCTION-RESULTS are new object classes,
each containing the result of applying an AGGREGATE-FUNCTION
to each GROUP. If no AGGREGATE-FUNCTIONS are applied, then
AGGREGATE-FUNCTION-RESULTS are nil.
```

(continued)

```
CONSTRAINTS(D') := {AGGREGATE-FUNCTION-CONSTRAINT, a
constraint enforced by applying AGGREGATE-FUNCTION to the
objects in each group, deriving the value for
AGGREGATE-FUNCTION-RESULT}.

FUNCTIONS(D') = null. (However, the designer will probably
define some functions, especially some that retrieve and
display the values in the AGGREGATE-FUNCTION-RESULTS.)

OBJECTS(D') := {objects such that each object has a
different value for GROUP}

RELATEDOBJECTS(A') := RELATEDOBJECTS(A)-RELATEDOBJECTS(D')
CONSTRAINTS(A') := CONSTRAINTS(A) - CONSTRAINTS(D')
FUNCTIONS(A') := FUNCTIONS(A)
OBJECTS(A') := OBJECTS(A)   ∎
```

Example B.6

The Employee object class is related to the following object classes (Figure B.7):

```
SocialSecurityNumber
EmployeeName
Salary
```

Let GROUP = {Salary} and AGGREGATE-FUNCTIONS = {count}. The result of applying the aggregation transformation using the function count applied to Salary is the new object class EmployeeGroup which is related to the object classes:

```
Salary
CountOfSalary
Employee
```

For each value for the Salary, the value of CountOfSalary indicates how many Employee objects have that value for Salary. Employee IsMemberOf EmployeeGroup. ∎

Aggregation is used to capture summary information in the end users' conceptual model. Summary information is important in spreadsheet applications and general-purpose reporting applications which present aggregate information to end users.

A variation of aggregation, called *factoring*, migrates one or more parameters required to carry out a function to a new object class. The parameter is then specified by a separate command and is automatically available for use whenever the original function is applied. To motivate the factoring transformation, consider the Employee object class [Figure B8(a)] which supports the function

```
hireEmployee ($Name, $Salary, $SocialSecurityNumber)
```

The user must supply a value for each parameter each time the function is invoked. Suppose that several new employees are being hired, all with the same value for $Salary.

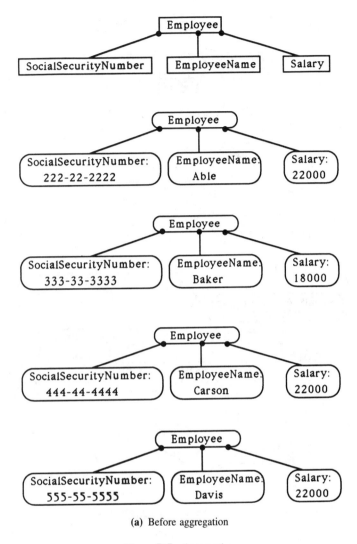

(a) Before aggregation

Figure B.7 Aggregation.

If there were a special function, setDefaultSalary ($Salary), then the user could use it to specify the value of the Salary once and have that value used for all the individual invocations of the hireEmployee function. In effect, the user would be able to set a default value for Salary by invoking the setDefaultSalary function.

    With what object class should the new command be associated? The new command should be associated with the object class which contains all the objects which are affected by the new command. This is the SelectedSet object class in Figure B.8(b).

    To establish a SelectedSet, the functions are needed to insert an object into the selected set, to remove an object from the selected set, and to clear the selected set (remove all objects). Each new Employee object that is created is automatically inserted

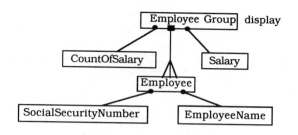

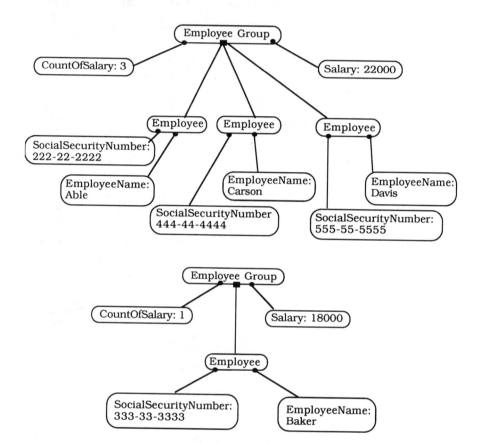

(b) After aggregation

Figure B.7 (continued)

into the selected set. The salary of any Employee object in the selected set is automatically set to the value of DefaultSalary.

Normalization is a process identifying composite object classes which represent two or more different types of object classes. It is based on a well-developed theory from the study of database design (Ullman, 1980; Elmasri & Navathe, 1989). These composite object classes should be partitioned into two or more object classes that each represent

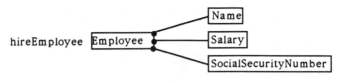

(a) Before factoring

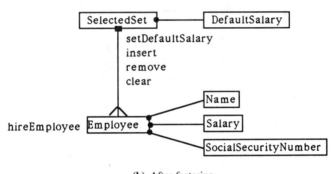

(b) After factoring

Figure B.8 Factoring.

represent objects of a single type. During normalization, the systems analyst examines each composite object class to verify that it represents exactly one type of concept, event, idea, object, or thing. Database designers have developed normalization theory for this purpose.

Example B.7

Consider the composite Warehouse objects illustrated in Figure B.9(a). A pair of redundant values can be observed: two objects have the same value for both WarehouseName (B) and WarehouseLocation (Seattle). Redundant values are a symptom of two or more object classes represented as a single-object class. In this case, the object classes PartInfo and WarehouseInfo are represented as the single-object class, Warehouse.

Several update anomalies occur when we try to update the values of simple objects related to Warehouse:

1. If all 300 of part number 13 are sold and we delete the corresponding Warehouse object, we lose the fact that warehouse A is in Chicago. Instead, we must set the values of PartNumber and Quantity to null and leave the values of WarehouseName and WarehouseLocation

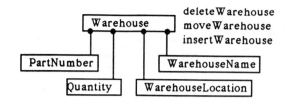

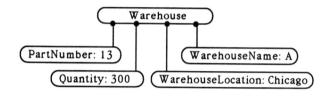

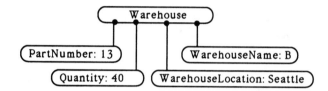

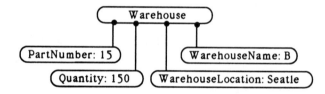

(a) Unnormalized warehouse conceptual object

Figure B.9 Normalization.

unchanged. Yet if all 40 of part number 13 are sold, we could delete the second Warehouse object and not lose the fact that Warehouse B is in Seattle because that information is in the third Warehouse object.

2. If the Seattle warehouse is moved to Minneapolis and we change the value of WarehouseLocation from Seattle to Minneapolis in the second object in Figure B.9(a) only, then the second object is inconsistent with the third object. Instead, we must update each and every object whose WarehouseLocation is Seattle.

3. Suppose we open a new warehouse in Portland, but we don't have anything to store there yet. We must create a new object with values for WarehouseName and WarehouseLocation, but null values for PartNumber and Quantity. We must remember not to include this object when counting parts.

These update anomalies can be avoided by breaking the Warehouse object class into two object classes, PartInfo and WarehouseInfo, as illustrated in Figure B.9(b). Let's reexamine the update anomalies with this revised conceptual model:

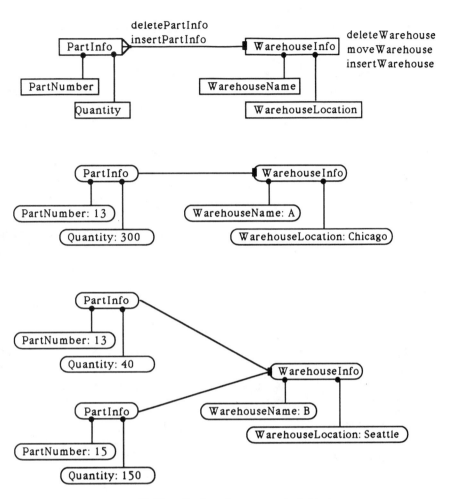

(b) Normalized warehouse conceptual object

Figure B.9 (continued)

1. If all 300 of part number 13 are sold, we delete the first PartInfo object. No change is made to the first Warehouse object, thus we do not lose the fact that warehouse A is located in Chicago.
2. If the Seattle warehouse is moved to Minneapolis, then we change the value of WarehouseLocation from Seattle to Minneapolis in the second WarehouseInfo object. With only one change, everything is consistent.
3. Suppose we open a new warehouse in Portland, but we don't have anything to store there yet. We create a new WarehouseInfo object with values for WarehouseName and Warehouse-Location slots. We do not create a new PartInfo object. ■

The theory of normalization gives us a criterion for breaking an object class into two or more object classes. This criterion is more precise than observing redundant values of slots of objects. This criterion involves the notions of functional dependencies

Definition of Functional Dependencies: Let A1 and A2 be two object classes which are both IsPartOf a third object class We use the notation A1 → A2 to indicate that for each value of A1 there can be at most one value for A2. The notation A1 → A2 can be read as "A1 functionally determines A2" or "A2 is functionally dependent on A1." ■

Examples of functional dependencies include

```
SocialSecurityNumber → Name
SocialSecurityNumber → BirthDate
```

because no two individuals should have the same SocialSecurityNumber. However,

```
BirthDate not → Name
```

is not a functional dependency because it is possible for two people to be born on the same date.

Guideline 1. If A1 and A2 are simple object classes which are both IsPartOf object class D, and there exists a functional dependency of the form A1 → A2, then A1 must be a unique identifier of object class D. If A1 is not a unique identifier of object class D, then partition object class D into two object classes D′ and D″ such that A1 is a unique identifier of D′, A1 IsPartOf D′ and A2 IsPartOf D′, and A′ IsMemberOf D″.

Example B.8

After understanding the meaning and intended use of WarehouseInfo, the conceptual model designer specifies the following functional dependencies:

```
PartNumber, WarehouseName → Quantity
WarehouseName → WarehouseLocation
```

The first functional dependency specifies that a value for PartNumber and a value for WarehouseName together implies single value for quantity. We cannot have two different values for quantity for the same pair of PartNumbers and Warehouses. The second functional dependency represents the semantic constraint that a Warehouse can have only one Location.

The second functional dependency,

```
WarehouseName → WarehouseLocation
```

does not satisfy guideline 1 because the WarehouseName, by itself, is not a unique identifier of the WarehouseInfo object class. Thus, the object class can be partitioned as shown in Figure B.9(b).

The two object classes of Figure B.9(b) both satisfy guideline 1. Consider all of the functional dependencies involving slots of the PartInfo object class:

```
PartNumber, WarehouseName → Quantity
```

Because PartInfo IsMemberOf Warehouse, PartInfo inherits the relationship involving WarehouseName. The combination of PartNumber and the inherited WarehouseName constitute the unique identifier of PartInfo. Thus, the left hand side of the functional dependency is the unique identifier. Hence, the PartInfo object class satisfies guideline 1 because the unique identifier of the PartInfo object class of Figure B.9(b) contains PartNumber and WarehouseName.

Now consider all the functional dependencies involving the WarehouseInfo object set:

$$\text{WarehouseName} \rightarrow \text{WarehouseLocation}$$

The WarehouseInfo object class satisfies guideline 1 because the unique identifier of the WarehouseInfo object class of Figure B.9(b) consists of the single object class, Warehouse-Name. ∎

B.4 JOIN

The join operation combines two object classes related by IsMemberOf into a single object class. During the join operation, the grouping objects may be replicated and attached to nongrouping objects.

Definition: Join transformation If A and B are two object classes such that A IsMemberOf B, then A and B are replaced by the new object class B' with relationships, constraints, and functions defined by the following:

```
RELATEDOBJECTS(B') := RELATEDOBJECTS(A) union
RELATEDOBJECTS(B)

CONSTRAINTS(B') := CONSTRAINTS(A) union CONSTRAINTS(B)

FUNCTIONS(B') := FUNCTIONS(A) union FUNCTIONS(B)
```

For every a in OBJECT(A) and for every b in OBJECT(B), a^b is in OBJECT(B'), where a^b denotes an object that is a constructed from pairs of objects from object classes A and B.

Example B.9

The object class Department is related to these object classes (Figure B.10) :

```
DepartmentName
DepartmentNumber
Budget
```

The object class Employee is related to the object classes

```
SocialSecurityNumber
EmployeeName
Salary
```

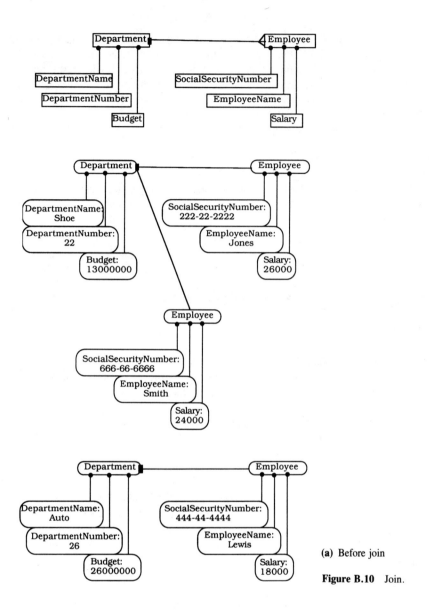

(a) Before join

Figure B.10 Join.

Employee IsMemberOf Department. The result of the join transformation is a new object class, Employee', which is related to each of the following object classes:

```
DepartmentName
DepartmentNumber
Budget
SocialSecurityNumber
EmployeeName
Salary ■
```

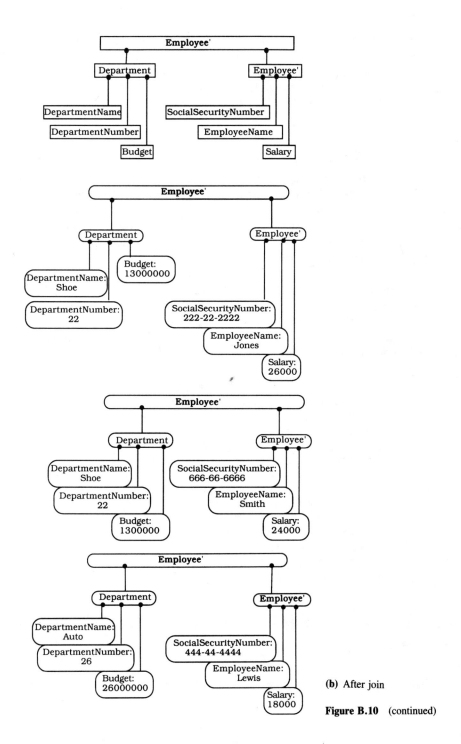

(b) After join

Figure B.10 (continued)

The aggregation and join transformations are inverses of each other in the following sense. An existing object class becomes related to a new object class by the IsMemberOf relationship under aggregation. Under join, two existing object classes related by IsMemberOf become a single object class.

B.5 CROSS-PRODUCT

This transformation replaces pairs of IsMemberOf relationship classes by pairs of IsPartOf relationship classes. Suppose both A and B are IsMemberOf D. This transformation will generate a new object D' for each pair of objects in, respectively, A and B, that are related to the same object in object class D. This transformation is a generalization of the set operation cross-product of two sets, A and B, which results in a new set having a member corresponding to each possible pair of members from A and B.

Definition: Cross-product transformation   Three-object classes, A, B, and D, where A IsMemberOf D and B IsMemberOf D are transformed into three object classes, A', B', and D', where A' IsPartOf D' and B' IsPartOf D'. The object classes A', B', and D' replace object classes A, B, and D. The relationships, constraints, and functions are defined by the following:

```
RELATEDOBJECTS(A')  :=  RELATEDOBJECTS(A)
RELATEDOBJECTS(B')  :=  RELATEDOBJECTS(B)
RELATEDOBJECTS(D')  :=  RELATEDOBJECTS(D)

CONSTRAINTS(A')  :=  CONSTRAINTS(A)
CONSTRAINTS(B')  :=  CONSTRAINTS(B)
CONSTRAINTS(D')  :=  CONSTRAINTS(D)

FUNCTIONS(D')  :=  FUNCTIONS(D)
FUNCTIONS(A')  :=  FUNCTIONS(A)
FUNCTIONS(B')  :=  FUNCTIONS(B)

OBJECTS(D')  =  {a^b}
OBJECTS(A')  =  {a portion of a^b}
OBJECTS(B')  =  {b portion of a^b}
```

where a^b denotes an object that is constructed from pairs of objects from object classes A and B. ∎

Example B.10

Figure B.11 illustrates that Supplier is an object class which is related to the following object classes

```
SupplierName
Address
```

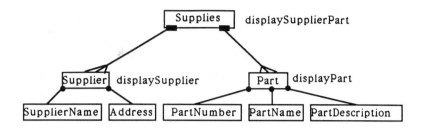

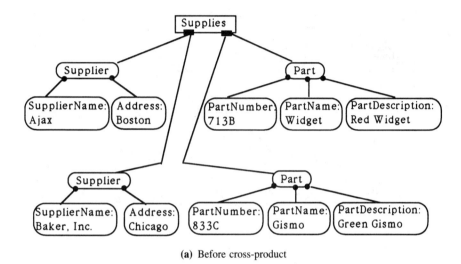

(a) Before cross-product

Figure B.11 Cross-product.

and supports the function

```
displaySupplier ($SupplierName, $Address)
```

Part is an object class related to these object classes

```
PartNumber
PartName
PartDescription
```

and supports the function

```
displayPart ($PartNumber, $PartName, $PartDescription)
```

Both Supplier and Part are IsMemberOf Supplies. The Supplies object class supports the function

```
displaySupplierPart $(SupplierName, $PartNumber)
```

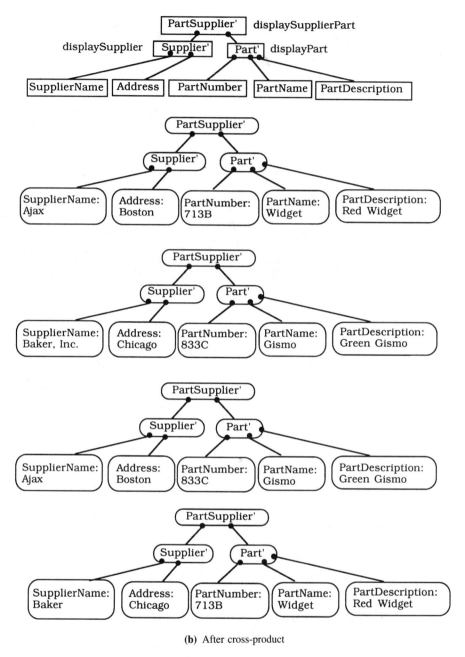

(b) After cross-product

Figure B.11 (continued)

After applying the cross-product transformation, the two IsMemberOf relationships are replaced by two IsPartOf relationships. Note that the number of D' objects is equal to the product of the number of A objects and the number of B objects. ∎

B.6 Vertical Partitioning

Vertical partitioning is the inverse of cross-product. It replaces two IsPartOf relationships by two IsMemberOf relationships. The term vertical partitioning comes from distributed database theory in which an object class is represented as a table with each object represented by a row in the table. Vertical partitioning partitions the table into two tables each containing some of the columns from the original table (Ceri & Pelagatti, 1984). The vertical partitioning is also related to the divide operation from relational database theory.

Definition: Vertical partitioning transformation   Object classes A, B, and D with A IsMemberOf D and B IsMemberOf D are replaced by three object classes, A', B', and D' with A' IsPartOf D' and B' IsPartOf D'. The relationships, functions, and constraints are defined as follows:

```
RELATEDOBJECTS(A') := RELATEDOBJECTS(A)
RELATEDOBJECTS(B') := RELATEDOBJECTS(B)
RELATEDOBJECTS(D') := RELATEDOBJECTS(D)

CONSTRAINTS(A') := CONSTRAINTS(A)
CONSTRAINTS(B') := CONSTRAINTS(B)
CONSTRAINTS(D') := CONSTRAINTS(D)

FUNCTIONS(D') := FUNCTIONS(D)
FUNCTIONS(A') := FUNCTIONS(A)
FUNCTIONS(B') := FUNCTIONS(B)

OBJECTS(D') = {d in OBJECTS(D) with duplicates removed}
OBJECTS(A') = {a in OBJECTS(A) with duplicates removed}
OBJECTS(B') = {b in OBJECTS(B) with duplicates removed}
```

Example B.11

Figure B.12 illustrates the three objects:

- EmployeePaycheck object class which is related to SocialSecurityNumber, EmployeeName, EmployeeAddress, and Telephone. The EmployeePaycheck object class supports the basic function:

```
printTelephoneListing ($EmployeeName, $EmployeeAddress, $Telephone)
```

- EmployeePosition object class, which is related to Salary, Title, and Department, and supports the basic function

```
displayPosition ($Title, $Department, $Salary)
```

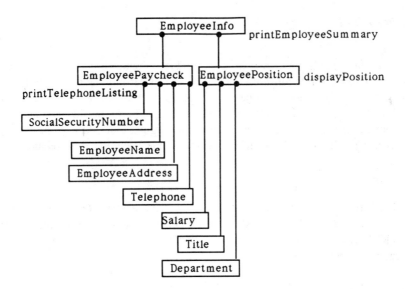

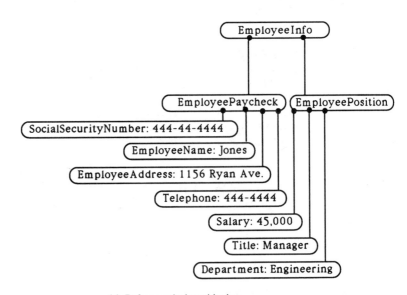

(a) Before vertical partitioning

Figure B.12 Vertical partitioning.

- EmployeeInfo object class, which is related to EmployeePosition, and EmployeePaycheck and supports the following basic function:

```
printEmployeeSummary ($SocialSecurityNumber,
    $EmployeeName, $EmployeeAddress, $Salary, $Title)
```

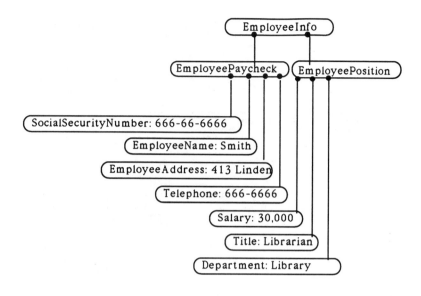

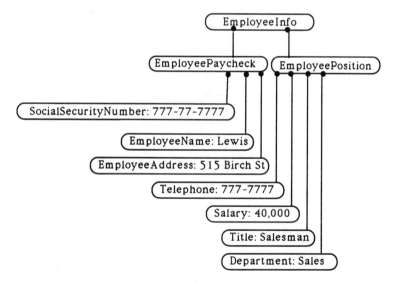

Figure B.12a (continued)

The result of vertical partitioning transformation replaces the two IsPartOf relationships

```
EmployeePosition IsPartOf EmployeeInfo
EmployeePaycheck IsPartOf EmployeeInfo
```

by the two IsMemberOf relationships

```
EmployeePosition' IsMemberOf EmployeeInfo'
EmployeePaycheck' IsMemberOf EmployeeInfo'
```

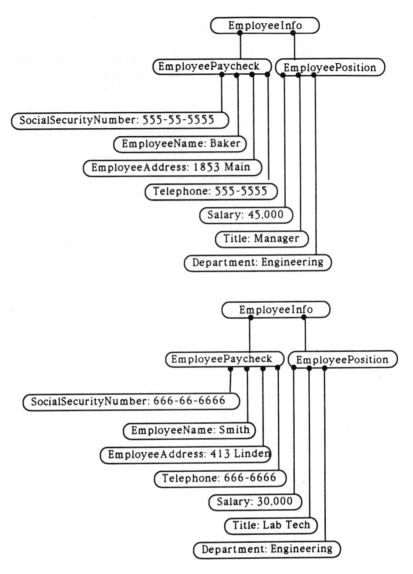

Figure B.12a (continued)

Note, however, how both the number of EmployeeInfo' objects and the number of EmployeePosition' have decreased. ■

In Section B.3 we used functional dependencies to avoid pairs of redundant values from appearing in objects in an object class and to tease apart object classes that really belong to two different object classes. The concept of multivalued dependency is also useful for this purpose.

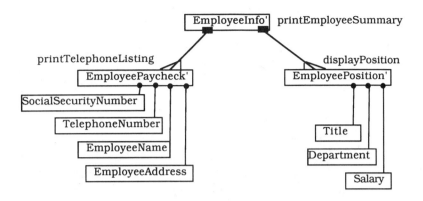

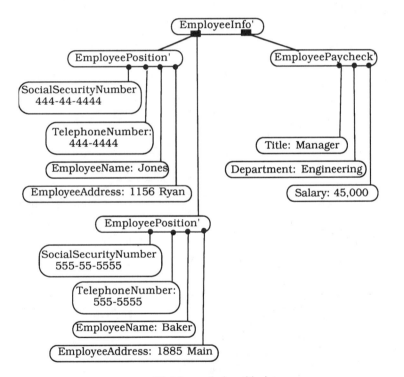

(b) After vertical partitioning

Figure B.12 (continued)

Definition of Multivalued Dependencies: Let A1 and A2 be two-object classes which both are IsPartOf a third object class We use the notation A1 $\twoheadrightarrow$ A2 to indicate that for each value of A1 there may be a set of values for A2. The notation A1 $\twoheadrightarrow$ A2 can be read as "A1 multidetermines A2" or "A2 is multivalued dependent upon A1." ∎

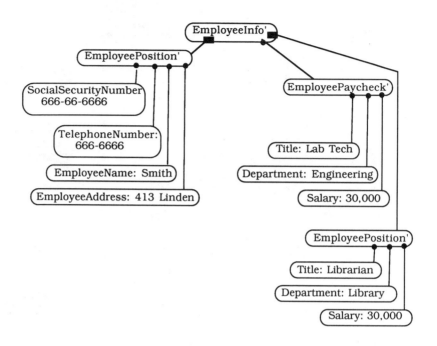

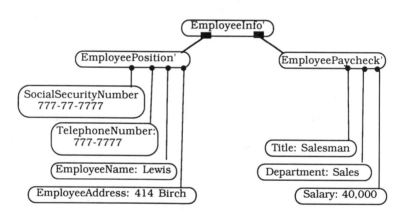

Figure B.12b (continued)

Guideline 2. If A1, A2, and A3 are object classes which are each IsPartOf complex object class D, and there are two multivalued dependencies of the form A1 →→ A3 and A1 →→ A2, then the values for A2 and A3 must be dependent. If the values for A2 and A3 are independent, then replace A1 IsPartOf D and A2 IsPartOf D by A1 IsMemberOf D and A2 IsMemberOf D.

Example B.12

Suppose that the conceptual model designer determines that the following multivalued dependencies hold for the Customer object class shown in Figure B.13.

$$\text{SocialSecurityNumber} \twoheadrightarrow \text{AccountNumber}$$
$$\text{SocialSecurityNumber} \twoheadrightarrow \text{Address}$$

The first multivalued dependency captures the semantics that a customer (identified by a SocialSecurityNumber) may have several accounts (each identified by an AccountNumber). The second multivalued dependency captures the semantics that a Customer may have several Addresses.

In Figure B.13(a), the bank customer with SocialSecurityNumber 222-22-2222 has two Accounts (numbered 13 and 22) and has two Addresses (Portland and Seattle). The fact that the customer has two Addresses is independent of the fact that the customer has two Accounts. Thus, the Customer object class violates guideline 2.

Here we really have three object classes represented as a single object class. One object class represents customer information, another object class represents account information,

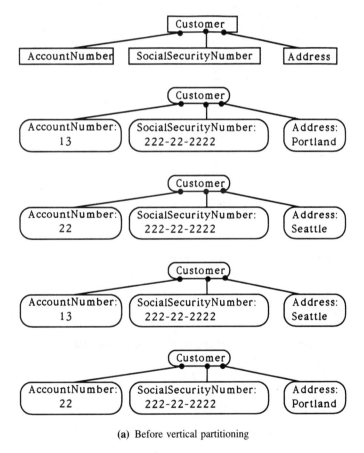

(a) Before vertical partitioning

Figure B.13 Another vertical partitioning example.

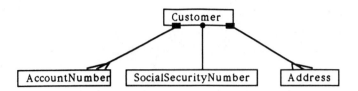

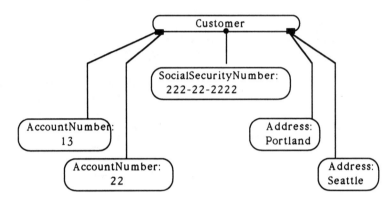

(b) After vertical partitioning

Figure B.13 (continued)

and the third object class represents address information. These three object classes and the relationships among them are illustrated in Figure B.13(b). We use the multivalued dependencies to separate these object classes from each other. ∎

B.7 ATOMITIZE AND CONCATENATION

The *concatenation* operation converts several IsPartOf Relationships to a single IsPartOf Relationship.

Definition of Concatenation Transformation: If A1, A2, . . . , An are all object classes which are all IsPartOf object class B, then they are replaced by a single-object class A′ which IsPartOf B′

```
RELATEDOBJECTS(A') := RELATEDOBJECTS(A1) union
    RELATEDOBJECTS(A2) union ... union RELATEDOBJECTS(An)
RELATEDOBJECTS(B') := RELATEDOBJECTS(B)
```

(continued)

```
CONSTRAINTS(A') := CONSTRAINTS(A1) union CONSTRAINTS(A2)
    union ... union CONSTRAINTS(An)
CONSTRAINTS(B') := CONSTRAINTS(B)

FUNCTIONS(A') := FUNCTIONS(A1) union FUNCTIONS(A2)
    union ... union FUNCTIONS(An)
FUNCTIONS(B') := FUNCTIONS(B)

OBJECTS(B') := OBJECTS(B)
OBJECTS(A') := {a1^a2^...^an
```

where a1 is in OBJECTS(A1), a2 is in OBJECTS(a2), . . ., an is in OBJECTS(an) and ai^aj denotes the concatenation of the values of ai and aj. ∎

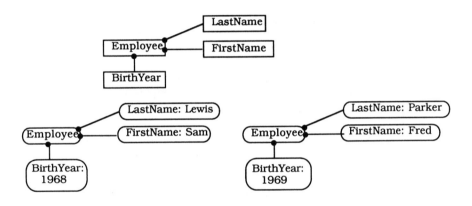

(a) Before concatenation

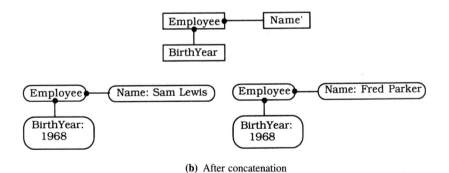

(b) After concatenation

Figure B.14 Concatenation.

Example B.13

Consider the two simple object classes, LastName and FirstName, as illustrated in Figure B.14. Each simple object takes on a character string of length 15. LastName IsPartOf EmployeeInfo and FirstName IsPartOf EmployeeInfo. These two simple-object classes may be merged to form a new simple object class, Name′ which takes on a character string of length 30. ∎

The atomitize transformation is the inverse of the concatenation operation. It replaces a single IsPartOf relationship by multiple IsPartOf relationships.

The end users' conceptual model property (p2) requires that each simple object contain a single value. The atomitize transformation converts a simple conceptual object with multiple values into several conceptual objects, each with a single value.

It is conceivable to perform the atomitize transformation several times until we are left with objects that contain character strings of only length 1. This is rarely done because users prefer to think at the abstraction levels higher than individual letters.

B.8 CLUSTER AND COLLAPSE SET

Definition of Cluster Transformation: The cluster transformation replaces the several IsPartOf relationships by a single IsMemberOf relationship Suppose A1, A2, . . ., An are each IsPartOf B. A1, A2, . . ., An and B are replaced by A′ and B′, where A′ IsMemberOf B′.

```
RELATEDOBJECTS(A') : = RELATEDOBJECTS(A1) union
    RELATEDOBJECTS(A2) union ... union RELATEDOBJECTS(An)
RELATEDOBJECTS(B') : = RELATEDOBJECTS(B)

CONSTRAINTS(A') : = CONSTRAINTS(A1) intersect CONSTRAINTS(A2)
    intersect ... intersect CONSTRAINTS(An)
CONSTRAINTS(B') : = CONSTRAINTS(B)

FUNCTIONS(A') : = FUNCTIONS(A1) union FUNCTIONS(A2)
    union ... union FUNCTIONS(An)
FUNCTIONS(B') : = FUNCTIONS(B)

OBJECTS(B') : = OBJECTS(B)
OBJECTS(A') : = OBJECTS(A) union OBJECTS(A2)
        union ... union OBJECTS(An)   ∎
```

Example B.14

Figure B.15 illustrates two object classes, Skill1 and Skill2, each of which are IsPartOf EmployeeInfo. The cluster operation forms a new object class, Skill, which is the union of the objects in Skill1 and Skill2. Skill IsMemberOf Employee. ∎

The *collapse set* transformation is inverse of the cluster transformation, replacing an IsMemberOf relationship by several IsPartOf relationships.

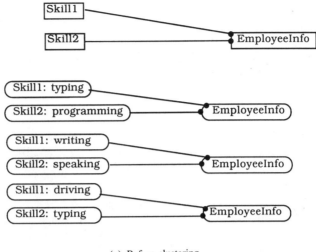

(a) Before clustering

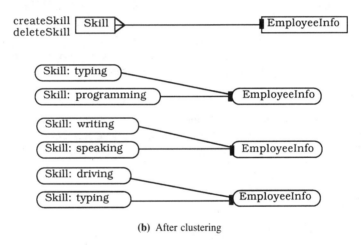

(b) After clustering

Figure B.15   Clustering objects.

B.9 OTHER TRANSFORMATIONS

Other possible transformations can be defined, including the following:

- Insert the transitive closure: If A IsA B and B IsA C, then insert the relationship A IsA C.
- Remove the transitive closure: If A IsA B, B IsA C, and A IsA C, then remove the relationship A IsA C.

Figure B.16 Inversion

- Identify object classes which are equivalent by virtue of combinations of relationships: If A IsA B and B IsA A, then A and B are equivalent and should be merged.
- Inversion. Replace B IsPartOf A by A IsA B. Conversely, A IsA B is replaced by B IsPartOf A. Figure B.16 illustrates the inversion of Frame IsPartOf Bicycle and Wheel IsPartOf Bicycle to Bicycle IsA Wheel and Bicycle IsA Frame. Bicycle is a specialization of Wheel (specifically, it is a wheel with a frame). Bicycle can also be considered a specialization of frame (it is a frame with two wheels). If there are multiple B objects which all are IsPartOf A, then inversion results in A being IsA to multiple B objects, with A inheriting all of the functions associated with each of the B objects. This is called multiple inheritance. Multiple inheritance leads to ambiguity if two or more B objects have different functions with the same name.
- Relationship creation and distribution. Establish a relation between two existing objects or remove an existing relationship between two objects. Adding or removing relationships in an end users' conceptual model extends rather than transforms the conceptual model.

An open research problem involves identifying and classifying other end users' conceptual model transformations which may lead to a better conceptual model.

Appendix C

Guidelines for Choosing Interaction Objects

Specifying rules for selecting simple interaction objects is an ongoing research problem. I have found the following incomplete set of guidelines useful for choosing interaction objects to represent conceptual objects.

A *nominal object* contains an identifier. Examples of nominal objects include names, identifiers, abbreviations, and so on. Nominal objects may be represented by interaction objects which contain character strings or integer values that denote the identifier of the object. Use a signal interaction object if the user may not change the value of the nominal object. Use an exclusive setting menu if the user may change the value, and there are only a few possible values for the object. Use a data box if the user may enter one of a large number of values.

A *magnitude object* provides a value which represents an approximate position on a continuous scale. Use a valuator to represent magnitude objects.

A *discrete value object* provides a value from among a discrete set of values. Use a signal whenever the user may not change the object value. Use exclusive setting menus and data boxes if the user may change the value. Use a toggle if there are only two possible values for a discrete object.

A *message interaction object* enables users to exchange messages with the script execution engine or applications. Use output signals (message boxes, audio messages, lights, and/or buzzers) if messages are to be presented to the user. Use an input signal if

	Output	Input and Output	
	Only	--	-------------
		Few	Many
		Values	Values
Nominative	Signal	Exclusive setting menu	Data box
Magnitude	Valuator	Valuator	Valuator
Discrete value	Signal	Exclusive setting menu, toggle	Data box
Message	Output signal	Input signal, toggle, exclusive setting menu	Command box

users may enter only a prescribed signal. If only a few messages can be entered by the end user, then use a toggle or exclusive setting menu containing either command names or the corresponding icons. Use a command box if many commands or parameters may be entered.

After choosing appropriate interaction object for each simple conceptual object, the interaction object designer then constructs a composite interaction object. Section 5.6 describes three composition operations for combining interaction objects.

Representing relationships among conceptual objects   The appearance and behavior of interaction objects may be heavily dependent on the relationships between the corresponding conceptual objects. General approaches for representing relationships include the following:

- *Graph approach*. In the graph approach, each relationship is represented by an arc connecting the interaction objects representing the conceptual objects involved in the relationship. Figure C.1 illustrates the graph approach for one-to-one, many-to-one, and many-to-many relationships in which arcs connect signal interaction objects. Different types of arcs may be used to indicate different types of relationships.

- *Value-based approach*. In the value-based approach, related interaction objects contain a common value. Figure C.2 illustrates the value-based approach for one-to-one, many-to-one, and many-to-many relationships. In this example, relationships are represented by integer values. A variation of the value-based appraoch for representing relationships is a common identifying characteristic, such as color, border design, background design, or line thickness.

- *Position approach*. Figure C.3 illustrates how relationships can be represented by position. In this approach, interaction objects that are related are physically adjacent to each other. In some cases, objects must be replicated in order to be positioned adjacent to each of the several objects to which they are related, as is illustrated in Figures C.3(e), and C.3(f).

- *Chart approach*. Figure C.4 illustrates how a matrix can be used to represent a relationship class involving two object classes. One-to-one relationships [Figure

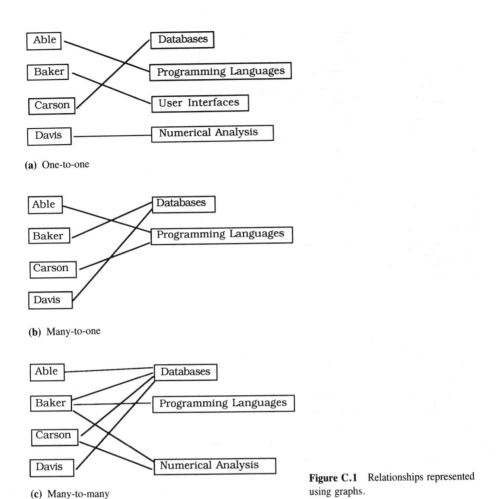

(a) One-to-one

(b) Many-to-one

(c) Many-to-many

Figure C.1 Relationships represented using graphs.

C.4(a)] have a single notation in each row and in each column. Many-to-one relationships [Figure C.4(b)] have multiple notations in some columns and a single notation in each row. Many-to-many relationships have multiple notations in each of several rows and columns [figure C.4(c)]. Pie charts [Figure C.5(a)] are used when the sum of values of objects is unity. Line charts [Figure C.5(b)] and bar charts [Figure C.5(c)] are used to represent many-to-one relationships. Multiple bars and lines in the same chart can be used to represent several many-to-one relationship classes involving a common object class [Figure C.5(d)].

Appendix A discussed relationships between objects in the same object class. These types of relationships occur frequently and can be represented in may ways not possible for relationships between objects in different classes.

Able	1
Baker	2
Carson	3
Davis	4

Databases	3
Programming Languages	1
User Interfaces	2
Numerical Analysis	4

(a) One-to-one

Able	2
Baker	1
Carson	2
Davis	1

Databases	3
Programming Languages	1

(b) Many-to-one

Able	1
Baker	2,4,5
Carson	3,6
Davis	7

Databases	1,2,3
Programming Languages	4,7
Numerical Analysis	5,6

(c) Many-to-many

Figure C.2 Value-based representations of relationships.

Graph approach. Figure C.6 illustrates a graph approach for representing a hierarchy, a common form of relationship among objects in the same object class in which there is exactly one path between each pair of objects. This approach is frequently used for business organization charts, scientific taxonomies, files and directories, and search spaces for solutions to game problems.

Value-based approach. Figure C.7 illustrates two tables representing the same hierarchy as Figure C.6. Value-based approaches are seldom used because of the cognitive processing humans must do in order to construct the hierarchy mentally from this tabular form.

Position approach. Figure C.8 illustrates two popular layouts. The Venn diagrams of Figure C.8(a) are used to represent sets while the outline form [Figure C.8(b)] is frequently used for text and speech outlines as well as for table of contents for large documents.

Chart approach. Figure C.9 illustrates the matrix representation of the hierarchy of Figure C.6. While this approach is compact and convenient for automatic processing, it suffers from the same excessive cognitive processing problems as the tables of Figure C.7.

Total orderings are usually represented using either a position approach (Figure C.10), often called an ordered list, or a special type of value-based approach where the

Able	Programming Languages
Baker	User Interfaces
Carson	Databases
Davis	Numerical Analysis

(a) One-to-one

Able	Programming Languages
Baker	Databases
Carson	Programming Languages
Davis	Databases

(b) Many-to-one (option 1)

Baker, Davis	Programming Languages
Able, Carson	Databases

(c) Many-to-one (option 2)

Figure C.3 Relationships represented by position.

Able	Databases
Baker	Databases, Programming Languages, Numerical Analysis
Carson	Numerical Analysis, Databases
Davis	Programming Languages

(d) Many-to-many (option 1)

Able	Databases
Baker	Databases
Baker	Programming Languages
Baker	Numerical Analysis
Carson	Databases
Carson	Numerical Analysis
Davis	Programming Languages

(e) Many-to-many (option 2)

Able, Baker, Carson	Databases
Baker, Davis	Programming Languages
Baker, Davis	Numerical Analysis

(f) Many-to-many (option 3)

Figure C.3 (continued)

	Databases	Program. Languages	User Interfaces	Numerical Analysis
Able		x		
Baker			x	
Carson	x			
Davis				x

(a) One-to-one

	Databases	Program. Languages	User Interfaces	Numerical Analysis
Able		x		
Baker	x			
Carson		x		
Davis	x			

(b) Many-to-one

	Databases	Program. Languages	User Interfaces	Numerical Analysis
Able	x			
Baker	x	x		x
Carson	x			x
Davis		x		

(c) Many-to-many

Figure C.4 Relationships represented by charts.

order is represented by an integer indicating the object's rank position in the total ordering (Figure C.11).

Partial orderings can also be represented using each of these four approaches. The graph approach results in a lattice. The other approaches need to replicate objects which are related to more than one superior object.

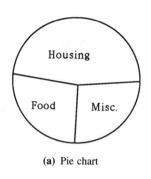

(a) Pie chart

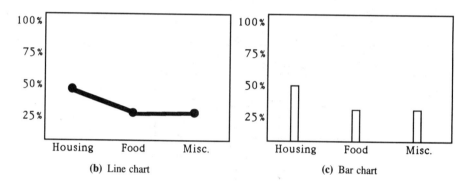

(b) Line chart

(c) Bar chart

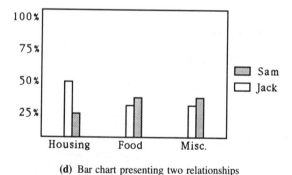

(d) Bar chart presenting two relationships

Figure C.5 Using charts to represent relationships.

When using the graph approach, reflexive relationships always have an arc from each object to itself. This never occurs with irreflexive relationships.

Rather than represent two directed arcs between pairs of related objects where the relationship is symmetric, a single, unordered arc may be used.

When a transitive relationship is represented, only a basic set of relationships is usually visible, rather than displaying all transitively derived relationships. Any valid

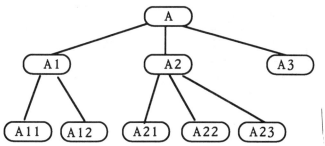

Figure C.6 Graphic representation of a hierarchy.

A	A1
A	A2
A	A3
A1	A11
A1	A12
A2	A21
A2	A33
A2	A23

A1	A
A11	A1
A12	A1
A2	A
A21	A2
A22	A2
A23	A2
A3	A

Figure C.7 Value-based representation.

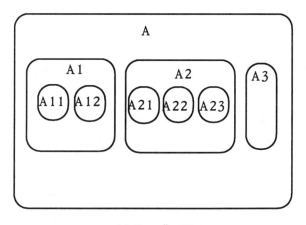

(a) Venn diagram

A
  A1
    A11
    A12
  A2
    A21
    A22
    A23
  A3

(b) Outline form

Figure C.8 Position-based representation.

	A	A1	A2	A3	A11	A12	A21	A22	A23
A		x	x	x					
A1					x	x			
A2							x	x	x
A3									
A11									
A12									
A21									
A22									
A23									

Figure C.9 Chart representation of hierarchy.

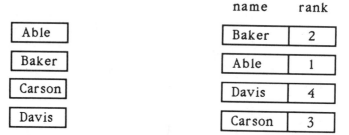

Figure C.10 Position representation of a total ordering.

Figure C.11 Value-based representation of a total ordering.

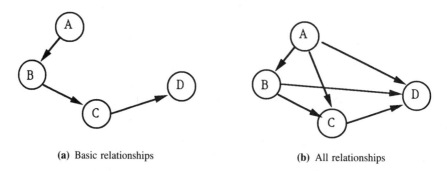

(a) Basic relationships

(b) All relationships

Figure C.12 Transitive relationships.

relationship can be derived by combining pairs of relationships from this basic set (Figure C.12).

The approaches for representing relationships between the same classes of objects are said to be *compatible* if the relationships can be represented in the presentation space without having to duplicate the interaction objects of any conceptual object involved in the relationships. Algorithms for the assignment of compatible representations for multiple relationships among the same class of conceptual objects is an open research problem.

Appendix D

Constructing Interaction Objects

This appendix describes a variety of tools for constructing interaction objects, including:

- Editors
- MICKEY
- The Petoud-Pigneur system
- Prototyper™
- TAE PLUS®
- NeXT™ Interface Builder™
- Peridot
- QUICK
- ITS

These tools were selected because they represent a wide range of approaches and methods for constructing user interfaces.

D.1 ARTISTS USE EDITORS TO CONSTRUCT THE APPEARANCE OF INTERACTION OBJECTS

Graphics artists use a variety of special-purpose text, bit-map, graphics, animation, and sound editors to construct libraries of clip art. Interaction object designers select and edit pieces of clip art for use as interaction object appearance and presentation.

Bit-map editors   Graphic artists use bit-map editors to design the appearance of an interaction object. A *bit map* is a two-dimensional matrix of dots (Figure D.1) that the human eye perceives as a picture. Using a bit-map editor, a graphics artist moves the cursor to the desired position in the two-dimensional matrix and indicates the color of the corresponding dot. Other editing commands available on some bit-map editors include shifting the entire bit-map up, down, left, and right. Artists may also rotate, flip, create, delete, save, and retrieve bit maps. Two bit maps may be combined by performing Boolean operations such as AND or OR as illustrated by the black and white bit maps in Figure D.1.

A scanning device can be used to digitize a picture or illustration and produce a bit map. Designers use a cropping operation to trim unwanted edges from bit maps produced by scanning devices.

Graphics editors   Bit-map editors are easy to use, but quickly become tedious when used to design simple geometric figures. Painting and drawing editors such as MacPaint and MacDraw enable graphics artists to create interaction object appearances quickly by selecting icons representing simple geometric figures; placing them onto a drawing "canvas"; and stretching, shrinking, rotating, flipping, and repositioning them. Many of the figures in this book were created using the MacDraw graphics editor.

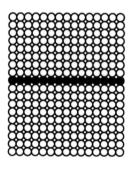

Bit Map A

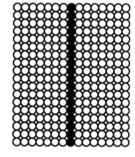

Bit Map B

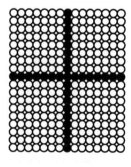

A or B

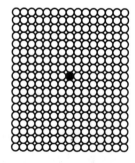

A and B

Figure D.1   Bit map Boolean operations.

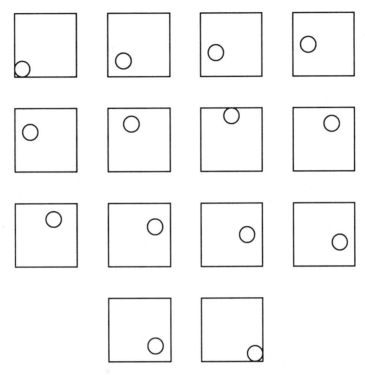

Figure D.2 Animation by movement.

Animation editors Animation can be achieved by displaying a sequence of images, each slightly different from the previous image. An animation editor enables graphics artists to specify a sequence of positions to simulate movement [Figure D.2]. An evolving or changing interaction object is simulated by displaying a sequence of slightly different images as illustrated in Figure D.3.

Sound editors Interaction object designers can also use sound to present information to users. Sound engineers use a sound sampler to capture and record sound as a sequence of digital representations. Sound engineers use sound editors to select prerecorded sounds from a sound library and modify those sounds. Typically sound libraries contain a variety of buzzer, bells, bongs, chirps, squeaks, sirens, creaks, and other interesting sounds which can be replayed on request.

Figure D.3 Animation by changing shapes.

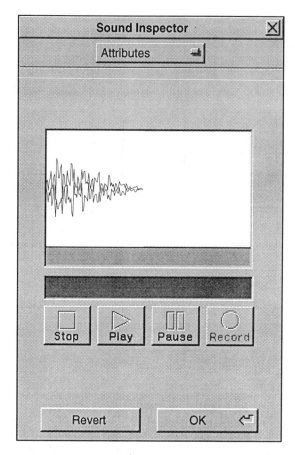

Figure D.4 NeXT sound editor. (Reprinted by permission of NeXT Computer, Inc.)

Sound designers generate and create new sounds using music synthesizers. Musicians compose musical scores which include sounds similar to those produced by musical instruments in addition to new sounds not possible with traditional musical instruments.

The NeXT computer's user interface builder displays a wave form representation of a sound (Figure D.4) to the interaction object designer, who may then cut, copy, and paste sound fragments to construct a variety of sound sequences of varying length. Sounds, including voice sentences, can be recorded, edited, and saved for future use.

Special-purpose editors such as those described can be used to construct separate aspects of the presentation of interaction objects. Interaction object editors integrate many of the capabilities of these special-purpose editors.

D.2 MICKEY GENERATES DEFAULT INTERACTION OBJECTS USING HINTS EMBEDDED IN THE APPLICATION CODE.

MICKEY, an experimental system developed at BYU by Dan Olsen, creates a user interface from information embedded within the application procedure definitions.

Figure D.5 illustrates MICKEY's approach for constructing default interaction objects. MICKEY Maker examines a Pascal program containing comments describing the appearance of the user interface and generates default interaction objects. The Pascal program is then compiled.

Figure D.6 illustrates part of the Pascal code for an application containing four procedures: deposit, withdraw, openAccount, and closeAccount. The programmer has inserted comments to the Pascal program. These comments are used by MICKEY to specify

- the menu name (Request),
- the name of each menu option (Deposit, Withdraw, Open account, and Close account),
- the label name for each data box in a dialog box to be displayed when the corresponding option is selected from the menu. In the example, the data boxes within the dialog box for the DEPOSIT option within the REQUEST menu are

Enter your account number
Enter amount of transaction
Your new balance will be

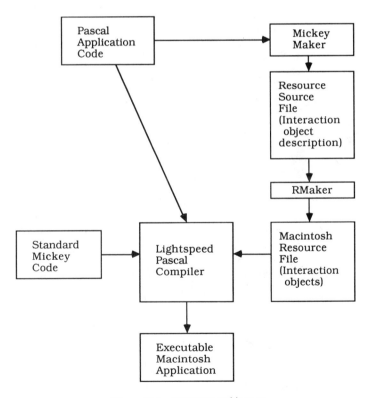

Figure D.5 MICKEY architecture.

- when the user interface is terminated. When the user selects Quit option from the menu, MICKEY will terminate the user interface.

Figure D.6 illustrates the Pascal code with programmer comments which is processed by MICKEY to generate the default interaction objects illustrated in Figure D.7.

```
unit InterfaceDef;
interface
 uses
  MickeyServe, MKW;

 type
  Stuff = record
     AccountNumber (* Name='Enter your account number' *)
     :integer;
     Amount (* Name='Enter amount of transaction' *)
     :integer;
     NewBalance (* Name='Your new balance will be' *)
     :integer;
   end;

 type
  Str21 = string[21];
  Stuff2 = record
     AccountNumber (* Name='Enter your account number' *)
     :integer;
     OwnerName (* Name='Enter your name' *)
     :Str21
   end;

procedure Deposit ((* Menu=Request Name='Deposit' *)
          DepositInfo:Stuff);

procedure Withdraw ((* Menu=Request Name='Withdraw' *)
          WithdrawInfo:Stuff);

procedure OpenAccount ((* Menu=Request Name='Open account' *)
          OpenInfo:Stuff2);

procedure CloseAccount ((* Menu=Request Name='Close account' *)
          CloseInfo: Stuff2);

var
  Quit (* Menu=Request Name=Quit *)
  :Boolean;
    {If this is set to true, then the user interface should terminate.}
```

Figure D.6 Example of Pascal declarations containing hints to Mickey for constructing interaction objects.

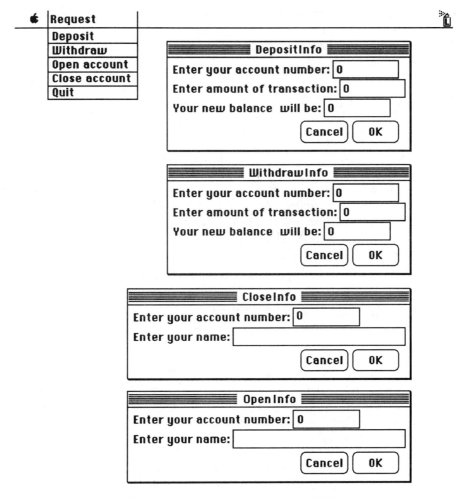

Figure D.7 User interface generated by MICKEY.

The programmer should note that Quit is not a procedure, but instead a variable. When the MICKEY run-time procedure detects that the user has selected Quit, the MICKEY run-time procedure will terminate.

MICKEY runs on the Macintosh. A more advanced version, called MIKE, runs under UNIX (Olsen, 1986, Olsen, 1989). MIKE supports a graphic editor for modifying the behavior and appearance of interaction objects.

While combining hints for interaction object construction within the source code may be convenient for the programmers designing interaction objects, it may not be convenient for interaction object designers who are not programmers. By factoring these hints out of the application source code and placing them in a separate file, it is easier for interaction object designers to modify the hints directly.

In the experimental system developed by Yue and Larson at the University of Minnesota, function declarations within the application code are interactively presented to the interaction object designer, who specifies the type of interaction object to be associated with the function. The user interface designer may choose any of several types of interaction objects, including data boxes, menus, and command lines.

D.3 THE PETOUD-PIGNEUR SYSTEM GENERATES INTERACTION OBJECTS FROM DATABASE DESIGN.

Database designers frequently use the entity-relationship data model during database design to describe entities (similar to relational database tables or file records), their attributes (similar to record fields or table columns), and relationships among entities (often represented by pointers between records or by tables with common values for columns). A description of the application's data structure expressed as an entity-relationship diagram, such as that illustrated in Figure D.8, is entered into the experimental system developed by Petoud-Pigneur, (1989).

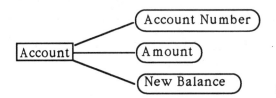

Figure D.8 Entity-relationship diagram.

Functions define the instruction set of the application. Each function has a name, processing rules, and input and output messages, and is usually related to an object in the entity relationship diagram. Figure D.9 illustrates descriptions of functions expressed using a high-level specification language called IDA/ISL, which is also entered into the Petoud-Pigneur system

The Petoud-Pigneur system generates a window for each entity type and for each relationship type. The initial relative position of the windows is based on the graphical layout of the entities and relationships. Each window contains signal objects, (showing the name of the attribute of the associated entity or relationship type) and data boxes (for display of attribute values). Functions are presented as buttons. The button is enabled only when the function it represents is capable of being activated. An alert box is generated for each possible failure of a function and is displayed whenever that failure occurs. Figure D.10 illustrates the (nonalert box) interaction objects automatically generated from the entity-relationship diagram of Figure D.8 and the IDA/ISL specification of Figure D.9.

As in MIKE, the interaction object designer uses a direct manipulation Editor to edit and adapt the generated user interface.

```
The function DEPOSIT
    generates an Account
        if (AccountNumber exists)
        otherwise error 1: The account number is invalid
    applies the following rules
```

Figure D.9 Example IDA/ISL.

1. If AccountNumber does not exist then error 1.
2. Amount is added to NewBalance

<u>receives</u> AccountNumber, Amount, NewBalance

The function WITHDRAW
<u>generates</u> an Account

    <u>if</u> (AccountNumber exists and Amount < NewBalance
    <u>otherwise</u> error 1 The account number is invalid
                error 2: Insufficient funds in your account

applies the following rules

1. If AccountNumber does not exist then error 1
2. If Amount > NewBalance then error 2
3. Amount is subtracted from New Balance

<u>receives</u> AccountNumber, Amount, NewBalance

The function OpenAccount

<u>generates</u> an Account
    <u>if</u> Account Number does not exist
    <u>otherwise</u> error 3 Account number already assigned

applies the following rules

1. If AccountNumber exists then error 3
2. Set NewBalance to zero

<u>receives</u> AccountNumber, NewBalance

the function CloseAccount

<u>deletes</u> Account

    <u>if</u> AccountNumber exists and NewBalance = 0
    <u>otherwise</u> error 1 the account number is invalid
                error 4 The account still contains funds

applies the following rules

1. If AccountNumber does not exist then Error 1
2. If NewBalance > 0 then Error 4

<u>receives</u> AccountNumber

Figure D.9 (continued)

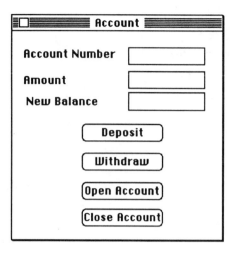

Figure D.10 Automatically generated default layout.

D.4 DESIGNERS USE PROTOTYPER TO GENERATE INTERACTION OBJECTS BY DEMONSTRATION

Interaction object designers may use several tools with graphical user interfaces to construct interaction objects. Prototyper, TAE+, and Interface Builder are three such tools. These tools, however, differ in two major aspects: (1) the manner in which interaction objects are composed to create composite interaction objects and (2) the degree to which designers may change the appearance of interaction objects without having to reenter the relationships between interaction objects and the underlying application functions.

Prototyper™, commercially available from Smether Barnes, is used to design and prototype standard Macintosh interaction objects, including dialog boxes, radio buttons, icons, static text, edit text, check boxes, buttons, lists, rectangles, lines, and scroll bars.

D.4.1 Constructing Composite Composite Interaction Objects

Figure D.11 illustrates the dialog box for specifying composite interaction object information. The designer enters the title of the window and selects a window type. Suppose the designer enters the name "window," chooses the highlighted window type, and then clicks the OK button. The dialog box disappears, replaced by the selected window with a palette of icons to its left (Figure D.12). Suppose the designer selects the static text icon (the capital T with white background) and indicates the position and size of the static text box within the window (Figure D.13). The designer next double clicks the static text box to cause a property sheet to appear. The property sheet is used by the designer to specify additional properties of the static text box, including its title and the

** File Edit Layout Info Special Font Style**

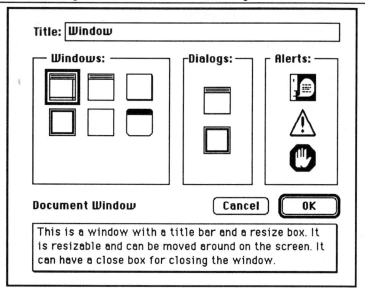

Figure D.11 Dialog box for window information. (Courtesy of SmetherBarnes)

** File Edit Layout Info Special Font Style**

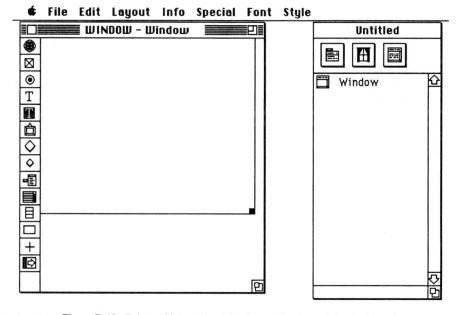

Figure D.12 Palette of interaction object icons. (Courtesy of SmetherBarnes)

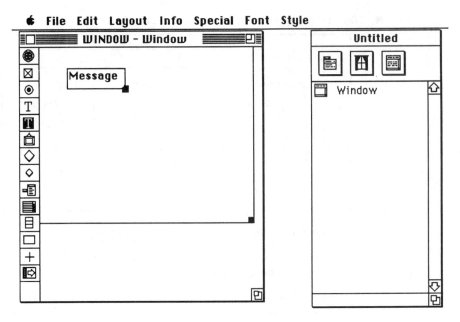

Figure D.13 Creating a static text box. (Courtesy of SmetherBarnes)

message to be displayed within the static text box (Figure D.14). After clicking the OK button, the dialog box disappears and the window reappears with the static text box containing the static message. After the interaction object designer has completed the

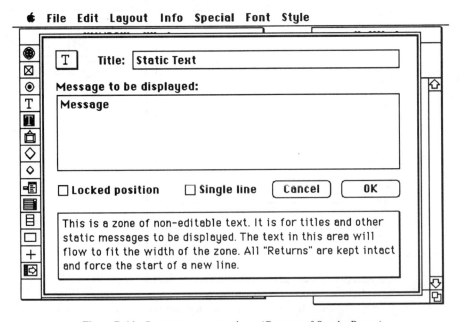

Figure D.14 Prototyper property sheet. (Courtesy of SmetherBarnes)

design, he or she may switch to the simulator mode in which the designer can simulate the user interface and demonstrate it to prospective users.

D.4.2 Connecting Application Functions with Interaction Objects

Prototyper generates commented Pascal source code for any of several Pascal compilers which run on the Macintosh. A programmer then inserts the application functions to the generated code. The interface designer may use Prototyper to modify the user interface and regenerate only the corresponding portions of the code. The programmer then needs to reinsert the application functions into the regenerated portion of the code, but does not need to reinsert application functions into the nonregenerated code.

D.5 TAE PLUS CONNECTS COMPONENT INTERACTION OBJECTS INTO COMPOSITE INTERACTION OBJECTS

TAE PLUS is a commercially available interaction object specification tool developed for NASA. Designers create panels (windows) and items (interaction objects) within panels by selecting item types from a menu and positioning them within the panel. Property sheets containing item specific options are presented to the designer who specifies additional attributes for items.

D.5.1 Constructing Composite Interaction Objects

Like Prototyper, TAE PLUS enables designers to construct composite interaction objects. However, the process of creating a composite interaction object, called a panel, is somewhat different from the process of painting a window in Prototyper. When using TAE PLUS, designers "connect" a simple interaction object to a panel by either (1) entering the panel name directly into a data box in a connect property sheet or (2) by entering the panel name indirectly into the data box by clicking the desired panel. User interface designers are thus able to connect several simple interaction objects to a panel. All interaction objects within a composite interaction object can be made to appear or disappear at the same time.

D.5.2 Connecting Application Functions with Interaction Objects

TAE PLUS automatically generates a user interface execution engine which consists of an event loop and several event handlers, one for each item in the user interface. Programmers must insert application-specific functions into the appropriate event handler code. Unlike Prototyper 3.0, no modifications made to a generated code will be incorporated into a regenerated version by TAE PLUS. To include custom modification into a regenerated code, the programmer must "cut and paste" the modification from the old code to the new code.

D.6 NEXT INTERFACE BUILDER LINKS INTERACTION OBJECTS WITH APPLICATION OBJECTS

D.6.1 Constructing Composite Interaction Objects

Like Prototyper, NeXT's Interface Builder displays a palette of icons to the interface designer. Each icon represents an interaction object class. The user interface designer constructs the appearance of the user interface by selecting an icon from the palette and dragging it to the desired position on a window.

D.6.2 Connecting Application Functions with Interaction Objects

While other user interface builders such as TAE PLUS and Prototyper then generate code to which programmers insert application specific functions, NeXT Interface Builder takes a different approach. If an application object class does not exist, the interaction object designer declares an application-specific object class by specifying the class name, the name of its methods, and the names of "outlets." After creating an instance of the application object, the programmer links the application object and interaction objects together as follows:

- To specify when a function within the application object should be invoked, the designer performs three tasks: (1) connect the interaction object with the desired application object by drawing a line between the two objects, (2) select the desired event associated with the interaction object, and (3) select the application function to be invoked from a menu of application functions (methods) associated with the application object.
- To specify data flow among interaction objects and application objects, the designer performs two tasks: (1) connect the application object to the interaction object with which the data will be exchanged by drawing a line between the visual representation of the two objects (Figure D.15) and (2) select the desired outlet name from a menu of port names associated with the application object.

Figure D.15 Displaying a connection. (Reprinted by permission of NeXT Computer, Inc.)

If the interaction object designer changes the components of a composite interaction object, he or she only needs to connect the new interaction object with the appropriate parts of the application object. Connections remain unchanged for existing interaction objects.*

If the object class has not been defined, Interface Builder generates an object class template which can be modified by the programmer. The NeXT Interface Builder also supports a simulator mode.

D.7 PERIDOT GENERATES INTERACTION OBJECTS BY DEMONSTRATION AND INFERENCE

Prototyper, TAE PLUS, and Interface Builder enable user interface designers to build user interfaces out of preprogrammed interaction objects, but they do not help the designer create the graphics that are an important part of direct manipulation user interfaces. Peridot partially overcomes this problem by enabling user interface designers to create a variety of interaction objects with specific behaviors.

Peridot (Programming by Example for Real time Interface Design Obviating Typing) (Myers, 1987; 1988) is an experimental system developed at Carnegie Mellon University. Peridot allows the designer to draw the appearance and demonstrate the behavior of a parameterized interaction object. First the dialog designer draws the appearance. Then the designer demonstrates typical user action and relates these actions to special parameters called active values. Peridot guesses or infers what behavior should occur in the general case.

An *active value* controls each part of an interaction object that can change. When an active value is modified, the interaction object is informed so that it redisplays itself, and the appropriate application functions are notified of the change in value. Active values provide a way for interaction objects and application functions to interact, yet still be independent of each other.

Figure D.16 illustrates the steps an interaction object designer follows to create a scroll bar that displays both the portion (first part, last part, etc.) of a file that is visible in a window and the amount of the file visible. In this example, there are two active values; ScrollPercent and WhereInFile, which correspond to the amount of the file and which part of the file are visible to the user. The interaction object designer's job is to demonstrate to Peridot the appearances of a scroll bar and relate those appearances with the ScrollPercent and WhereInFile active values. Peridot will then create the code to handle the actions it infers when the appearance is changed by the user. For this example, the interaction object designer performs the following demonstration steps:

1. Figure D.16(a). The background graphics are created.
2. Figure D.16(b). The gray bar is created to represent the situation when the user can see the entire file. The interaction object designer enters a value of 100 for the

---

*Rather than use lines to connect interaction objects to functions, interaction object designers using UIMX™, a user interface management system from Visual Edge™ available from Hewlett-Packard, indicates the application function by entering its name into a property sheet associated with the interaction object.

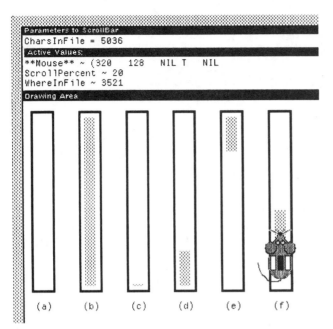

D.16 Peridot. (© 1987 IEEE. Reprinted by permission from B. Myers, *Creating Interactive Techniques By Demonstration,* COMPUTER GRAPHICS & APPLICATIONS, Sept. 1987.)

ScrollPercent active value to tell Peridot that the full scroll bar indicates the entire file.

3. Figure D.16(c). The gray bar is modified to be very small. The interaction object designer tells Peridot that this indicates the situation when the user can only use a very small portion of the file by changing the value of ScrollPercent to 1. Peridot automatically creates a linear interpolation that modifies the height of the bar based on the value of ScrollPercent.

4. Figure D.16(d). The interaction object designer moves a small gray box to the bottom of the bar and specifies that this corresponds to the last of the file by entering the largest value for the WhereInFile active value.

5. Figure D.16(e). The interaction object designer moves the small gray box to the top of the bar and specifies that this corresponds to the first of the file by entering zero for the WhereInFile active value. Peridot automatically creates the program that scrolls the contents of the window when the user moves the gray box up or down in the scroll bar.

To ensure that Peridot deduces the correct inferences, Peridot always displays the results of inferences and the corresponding change in appearance immediately. The designer must verify that the inference is correct. If the interaction object designer decides that the inference is wrong, the inference is undone.

Peridot notifies application functions about changes in active values. In this way, the user can change the appearance of an interaction object, which in turn changes an active value, which in turn notifies the appropriate application function. The interaction object designer selects one of the following options which causes Peridot to notify the application whenever

1. The active value is set.
2. The active value changes.
3. The active value changes by more than a threshold.
4. An interaction is complete (such as a mouse button in released after a move).
5. Never notify the application when an event occurs.

Because the mouse is used by the designer to demonstrate behavior of an interaction object, a simulated mouse is used as part of the demonstration. The interaction object designer can reposition the simulated mouse, cause any of the buttons on the simulated mouse to be pressed and/or released, and cause a mouse button to be clicked an arbitrary number of times as part of the demonstration behavior. Peridot can infer what part of an interaction object to drag based on where the mouse is placed on the object (center, corner, middle).

The interaction object designer can edit interaction object behavior and appearance by causing an existing behavior to be redemonstrated. The interaction object designer can demonstrate a new behavior, and then indicate whether the new behavior should run in parallel or replace the old behavior. All old behaviors affecting an active value can be removed.

Peridot demonstrates that it is possible to build the appearance and behavior of interaction objects by demonstration. The designer's interface to Peridot was itself developed using Peridot. However, Peridot is limited to the types of inferences in which it is preprogrammed to make. It lacks the ability to learn to make new types of inferences. This difficult problem is still in the research stage.

D.8 USER INTERFACE DESIGNERS USE SIMPLE PROGRAMMING LANGUAGES TO CONSTRUCT INTERFACE OBJECT BEHAVIOR

QUICK (Douglas, Doerry, & Novick, 1990; Douglas, Doerry, & Novick, 1991) is a user interface design kit for nonprogrammers to construct interaction objects. The user interface designer creates the appearance of each interaction object by using a bit-map editor or drawing tool. Each interaction object can be manipulated by the user in four ways:

Click the interaction object once.
Click the interaction object twice.
Drag the interaction object to a new location.
Drop the interaction object.

The user interface designer specifies actions to execute when a user performs each of these four operations. These actions are specified by a very simple language containing the following commands:

```
Animate <list of objects>
Flash <object>
Highlight <object>
Unhighlight <object>
If <test> <then> <else>
For-each <list of objects> <code>
Set-attribute <object> <attribute> <value>
Say <list of sounds>
Move <object> <location> (move the object along a
     predefined path to the desired location)
Trigger-action <object> <action>
```

It is possible to construct applications containing several interaction objects such as the following:

Example D.1

The following application was developed as a beginning-level tool for teaching foreign languages. The student is asked to imagine that he or she is aboard a sinking ship. The task is to stock the lifeboat with various items like a life vest, a map, water, and so on. The application starts by asking the user, in whatever language is being taught, to place one such object in the lifeboat. If the user succeeds, the system announces success, and proceeds to ask the user to place the next object in the lifeboat. If the user puts the wrong object in the lifeboat, or fails to place the object in the lifeboat, the object moves back to its initial position and the system announces failure. When the last item is in the lifeboat, the application is finished. Figure D.17 shows a view of the running application, which was created in approximately one-half hour (not counting the time to digitize sounds and draw the images). ■

D.17 QUICK application. (Reprinted by permission from Proceedings of the ACM SIGGRAPH Symposium on User Interface Software and Technology, Snowbird, Utah, Oct. 3–5, 1990.)

D.9 USER INTERFACE STYLE EXPERTS PROVIDE RULES USED TO GENERATE DEFAULT INTERACTION OBJECTS BY ITS

The Interactive Transaction System (ITS) project at IBM Research in Yorktown Heights (Bennett et al., 1990) uses rules to transform an abstract style-independent specification into a concrete, style-specific interaction objects. Composite interaction objects are represented by tree structures in which each node has both application attributes, such as data elements names and types, and style attributes, which include the appearance and dynamics of the interaction object. Rules are used to supply and modify values for style attributes. For example, rules may be used to specify the size and shape of basic interaction objects, their placement with respect to other interaction objects, and border and background attributes. Some rules may even determine the visibility or invisibility of dynamic interaction objects. Different rules can be used to generate multiple "views" of composite interaction objects to be displayed at the same time. Style rules are specified by user interface specialists. The use of rules has the following benefits:

- Rules can be more expressive than direct manipulation specification. Context, conditionality, and iteration can be expressed easily using rules.
- Rules can be reused, while direct manipulation specifications may need to be reentered each time they are needed. Decisions about when to use rules can themselves be captured as rules.
- Consistency can be enforced by common rules. For example, titles should be in 8-point Times Roman font throughout the interface.
- Rules can be shared among interaction object designers to form a shared basis of knowledge .

Appendix E

Windowing Systems

This appendix describes two popular windowing systems, Microsoft Windows and the X Window System.

E.1. MICROSOFT WINDOWS

Microsoft Windows is a popular window manager which runs under MS-DOS™. Several applications, including spread sheets, word processors, database management systems, and other business applications which execute under Windows are commercially available.

The Microsoft Windows Software Development Kit supports the following tools for the user interface developer:

- Interactive resource editors for generating interaction objects. The three major editors are

  - Icon editor for drawing icons, cursors, and bit maps.
  - Font editor for creating customized fonts.
  - Dialog editor for creating dialog boxes. Dialog boxes may themselves contain a variety of interaction objects, called controls, including check boxes (from which

the user may select one or more choices), radio buttons (from which the user may select exactly one choice), pushbuttons (rectangles with rounded edges containing text), horizontal and vertical scroll bars, list boxes (for menus), text (serving as static labels), frames (rectangle borders), and icons.

- Compiler for processing an application's interface to Windows™. This interface includes

  - A description of icons, fonts, and dialog boxes created by the dialog designer in a form that can be referenced by the application program.
  - A description of the application's memory and resource requirements. This information is needed so that Windows can act as a baby operating system controlling several applications executing in a time-shared manner.

- Run-time library containing modules which manage the execution of several application programs, manage the multiple windows on the computer's video screen, and manage the messages between application programs and the corresponding window managers.
- Linker and binders to bind application programs, run-time Windows library routines, and interaction object description files producing an executable Windows application.

Windows sends a message to the applications modules each time the user makes a change in a window. The appropriate application module consumes the message, performing actions such as computation and generation of one or more messages to Windows which in turn cause the contents of the application's window to change.

To build a Windows application, the programmer performs these tasks (Figure E.1):

1. Write the WinMain module which contains a message loop which continuously checks for messages of interest to the application. The WinMain and other window functions are placed in C language or assembly language source files.
2. Use the icon editor to create cursors, icons, and bit maps, and place them in a resource file
3. Use Dialog Editor to create dialog boxes (composite interaction objects) and place them in a resource file.
4. Write application modules and place them in module definition files.
5. Compile and link all C language and assembly source files.
6. Compile resource script files and add it to the executable file.

Version 3.0 of Windows has added significant features:

- A graphical user interface similiar in style to that provided by the Macintosh.
- Dynamic Data Exchange, a facility whereby users may copy a piece of one document into another document. Whenever the first document is modified, the modifications are reflected in copies within other documents.

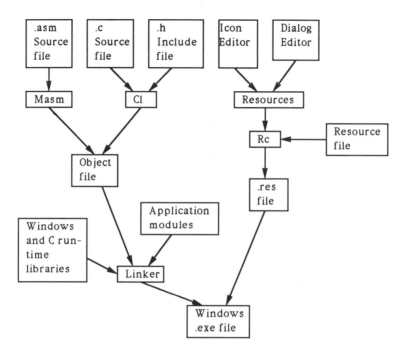

Figure E.1 Building a Windows application.

- Object Linking and Embedding, a facility whereby users can embed a piece of one document into another document, or link a piece of one document to another. Users may invoke the imbedded or linked document without exiting from the document containing the linked or embedded document.

Appendix D discusses the Prototyper, TAE+, and Interface Builder, user interface generators. There are at least two commercially available user interface generators which generate Microsoft Windows code: CASE:W from CASEWORKS and WindowMaker™ from Blue Sky Software. Both of these systems generate the WinMain module and skeleton application modules. Designers must extend each skeleton application module to perform application specific functions. Both systems have a rehearsal capability so users can preview the user interface without actually generating the code. Case:W has a regenerate capability in which designers may change the apperance of the user interface and regenerate the appropriate parts of the WinMain and skeleton application modules without losing the application-specific code manually inserted by application programmers. Recently Microsoft has introduced Visual Basic® which contains a user interface generator. Programmers may also insert functions into event handlers with each control generated by Visual Basic.

E.2 THE X WINDOW SYSTEM

The X Window System [Young, 1989] was developed at Massachusetts Institute of Technology. In X, a single process, known as a *server* controls all of the input and output

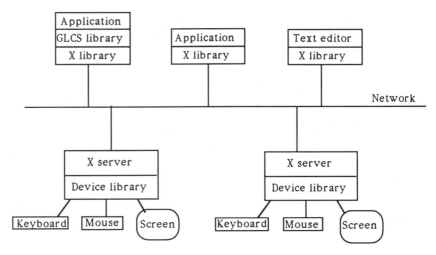

Figure E.2 X servers and applications communicate via network.

devices. An application is referred to as a *client*. Clients and servers (Figure E.2) communicate over a communication system using an asynchronous byte stream protocol. Typically, the server runs on a workstation and the client runs on a backend mini- or mainframe computer. Multiple clients may interact with a server, and a server may interact with multiple clients. In order to provide the speed necessary for graphics, the X protocol is asynchronous; neither the graphics server nor the application wait for acknowledgments from each other.

An X library, called Xlib, provides a procedural interface to the X protocol. An application calls procedures in Xlib which transmits messages to the X server which in turn manipulates windows displayed on a workstation screen.

As illustrated in Figure E.3, the X server supports an arbitrary hierarchy of rectangular windows. At the top of this hierarchy is the *root* window, which covers the entire screen. Each application has a hierarchy of windows, the top most window of each application being a subwindow of the root window. The window hierarchy models "stacks of papers" on a desktop.

Windows may overlay each other. A window hides the contents of the region of the underlying window which it overlaps. A window is not restricted in size or placement by the boundaries of its parent, but only that portion of the subwindow which is within its

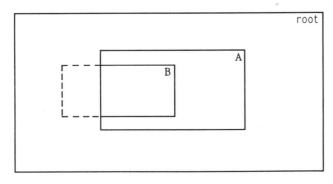

Figure E.3 Window B is a subwindow of A.

parent window is displayed, as illustrated in Figure E.3. Applications are not aware that windows overlap each other. The X server accepts display commands from applications and clips portions of windows that are obscured by other windows.

A hidden fragment of a window can become exposed in several ways. The parent window is enlarged so that a clipped portion of a subwindow now lies within the parent window. An overlying window is moved or shrunk so that more of the underlying window is exposed. A stack of windows are rotated, bringing the window at the bottom of the stack to the top of the stack so that it is exposed. When a window fragment becomes exposed, the X server sends an asynchronous event to the client indicating that the window and region have been exposed. It is the application's responsibility to redraw the exposed region or redraw the entire window. This requires that the client application maintain information about the current display and be able to redisplay that information.

The designers of the X Window System (Scheifler & Gettys, 1986 considered and rejected the following basic mechanisms by which the X server might restore window contents itself:

- The X server maintains a list of display commands, which can be reexecuted to display the exposed window. However, when executing the display list, the X server does not have any notion of when later output requests nullify earlier ones; the user sees a "fast forward" history of the window contents. Also, the display list becomes unmanageably long, causing the redisplay of the exposed window to take a significant length of time.

- The X server maintains an off-screen image (sometimes called a backing store) of the window, which is moved to the screen when the window becomes exposed. The memory needed to store multiple overlapping windows can become significant, requiring that workstations hosting an X server have significant memory.

Instead, the designers of the X Window System adopted the policy that the underlying applications must refresh all or part of a window when it becomes visible. The designers point out that many applications can take advantage of their own information structures to redisplay the contents of a window rapidly without the expense of maintaining a distinct display structure or backing-store in the server. For example, a text editor can redisplay directly from the source, and a VLSI (very large scale integrated) circuit editor can redisplay directly from the layout and component definitions. On the other hand, each application must be written in such a way that it is able to restore an exposed window at any time; this makes the design and implementation of applications more complex.

A library, called Xt Intrinsics, contains facilities to create, organize, and destroy widgets. *Widget* is the X terminology for interaction object. Xt Intrinsics also performs other bookkeeping tasks like translating event sequences from the graphics server into procedure calls to applications. The modules in Xt intrinsics are written using the C programming language and contain procedure calls to Xlib.

Other libraries, called tool kits and widget sets, contain modules which implement interaction objects. Types of widgets include menus, dialog boxes, and messages. Widget classes are organized into an IsA hierarchy such that widget classes inherit properties from other widget classes that are higher in the hierarchy. These properties may include both appearance attributes and behavior routines. Some appearance attributes like color, font, border width, size, and position can be customized. Additional behavior routines can be included with a widget class, making the widget class more specialized than the widget classes higher in the hierarchy from which it inherits behavior routines.

There are several widget libraries, including the following:

- Motif, available from the Open Systems Foundation
- Open Look, available from AT&T
- The Athena widget set developed by M.I.T.'s Project Athena

Other widget sets are being developed, including sets that contain widget classes for video, sound, and multimedia data types.

We will briefly describe the popular Motif widget set. The Core widget class contains declarations and code that are common to all widgets. An instance of the Core structure includes name, size, position, background, border color, and other attributes, as well as routines (called methods) for maintaining these attributes.

The Composite widget class is an ancestor for all widgets that can contain children. An instance of the Composite widget class contains a list structure in which children widgets are stored. The Composite widget contains routines (methods) for adding and deleting children. Composite widgets maintain a pointer to a geometry manager function that is responsible for the proper layout of the component widgets.

The Constraint widget class is a special Composite widget class which maintains constraints on widgets that are children of a Composite widget instance. Constraints might include the minimum and maximum number of children or the size and position of children. The Constraint widget contains methods for adding, deleting, and examining children subject to the prespecified constraints.

The Label widget class displays a character string. A Command widget is a subclass of Label widget with an additional caveat: when the user selects an instance of this widget class (usually by letting the left mouse button up while the cursor is inside the command box), a "callback" procedure is invoked. The callback procedure notifies the application program that the user has selected the command box.

When building a new widget class, the widget writer ignores the parts of a new widget class that are common to an existing widget class and concentrates on the differences. To create a new widget class, the widget designer selects an existing widget class which is similar to the new widget class. The designer makes a copy of the existing widget class and makes it subordinate to the original widget class in the widget hierarchy. Because a subordinate widget class can inherit attributes and methods from its superior class, the designer can remove all the attributes and methods from the subordinate widget class that are to be the same as those in the superior class. The designer can also add attributes and methods to the subordinate class, making the subordinate widget class more specified than its superior class.

Programming in X Windows can be very tedious. There is a trend to make the X window system less complex for the user interface designer by the use of user interface generators such as TAE PLUS, Xcessory™, UIMX, and OpenLook Express. These systems enable designers to draw the appearance of widgets graphically and generate the appropriate interaction object code automatically. Some of these user interface generators are discussed in Appendix D.

Appendix F

Schematic Editors

This appendix discusses schematic editors and various approaches for building the direct manipulation interfaces to these editors.

The following lists some of the frequently used schematic notations:

Notation	Use
Syntax diagrams	Programming language options
State transition diagrams	Control flow
Flowcharts	Control flow
Ladder logic diagrams	Manufacturing cell controller
Data flow diagrams	Data flow
Event response graphs	Interaction among objects
AND/OR trees	AI search algorithms
Grammar trees	Display and manipulate language grammars
Time lines	Animation design
Logic diagrams	Electronics design
Pert charts	Project management
Organization charts	General business

These notations are widely used to convey information. Schematics are easy for humans to draw by hand. They are compact; a single diagram conveys a large amount of meaning. The notations are frequently precise; each icon has a prescribed meaning.

The major disadvantage with schematic notations is that they are not immediately machine readable. Recognition of hand-drawn schematics is probably as difficult as automatic recognition of handwriting or spoken speech. An easier approach for capturing schematic notations is to provide an editor which is so easy to use that users can create schematics using the editor rather than to draw them on a blackboard.

Most schematic notations consists of the following:

- A set of nodes, each representing a state or object of interest to the user. Often the set of nodes is represented as a set of icons in a menu or palette.
- A set of links, each representing a type of relationship between two or more nodes. Often the links are represented as names or line types in a menu or palette.
- A capability to attach annotations of various types to the nodes and links.

A schematic editor supports the following functions:

- Create and position nodes within a schematic diagram. Often, the user selects a node to be created from a palette and drags it to the desired location.
- Link nodes together. Often, the user selects a type of link from a palette and identifies the nodes to be connected by the link.
- Insert annotations into links, nodes, and diagrams. The user selects the object to be annotated and uses a text editor to construct the annotation.
- Manipulate the diagram. Often the user may identify a portion of the schematic diagram to remove (cut), duplicate (copy), insert (paste), or reposition.
- Save the schematic for future use (save), retrieve a previously saved schematic (open), and create a new schematic diagram (new).

A schematic editor is quite different from a drawing editor. A drawing editor enables users to draw pictures of schematics but fails to generate an internal data structure that can be used for anything other than redisplaying the picture. A schematic editor creates both a picture and an underlying data structure which can be analyzed and interpreted by schematic specific software. For example, software can interpret a musical score and produce sounds, software can analyze logic diagrams for inconsistencies and generate software which simulates the corresponding electronic circuit. Many types of schematic editors have been and are being constructed. These schematic editors enable users to create schematic diagrams quickly, and use associated software to analyze, simulate, manipulate, and interpret schematic diagram.

We now focus our attention of software for generating schematic editors. A schematic editor generator is desirable for the following reasons:

1. A schematic editor generator would decrease the time and effort needed to build a robust schematic editor.

2. The schematic editors generated would have similar look and feel, enabling users to easily switch among schematic editors generated by the same generator.

We make the following decisions for each of the decision classes in the framework for designing user interfaces presented in Chapter 2:

1. *Structural decision class*. Assume that the structure consists of information about three sets: a set of node types, a set of link types which may connect nodes, and a set constraints on the types of nodes which can be connected by each link.
2. *Functional decision class*. Assume that in addition to the typical cut, copy, paste, save, new, and open operations, users may be able to reposition objects (with the lines representing the links stretching, shrinking, and repositioning appropriately), and perform schematic specific operations (such as simulate the logic represented by logic diagrams).
3. *Dialog decision class*. Assume that the user will use a direct manipulation dialog style in which node types and link types are selected from a palette, dragged, and dropped onto a canvas.
4. *Presentation decision class*. Assume that each node is represented by an icon, and each link is represented by a line with specified types of end points.
5. *Pragmatic decision class*. A specific operating system computer, and standard set of input/output devices is assumed.

The decisions which implementers are allowed to make follow:

1. *Structural decision class*. Implementers must specify the types of nodes, types of links, and the constraints on how links may connect nodes.
2. *Functional decision class*. Implementers may not specify any additional functions.
3. *Dialog decision class*. Implementers may not change the script.
4. *Presentation decision class*. Implementers may specify the appearance of each node type and link type.
5. *Pragmatic decision class*. Implementers may not make any decisions about this decision class.

Because implementers are restricted from making many of the decisions, a schematic editor generator is able to accept the limited decisions which implementers are allowed to make and generate the corresponding schematic editor.

Templa™/Graphica (Hekmatpour, 1990) enables schematic implementers to specify decisions about the structure and presentation. Templa enables a designer to specify the types of nodes, the types of links which may connect nodes, and constraints on the types of nodes which can be connected by each link. The designer also specifies the appearance of each node and link. Graphica, which uses the design information entered by the designer using Templa, configures itself to become the specific schematic editor. Graphica supports cut, copy, paste, save, new, and open and reposition operations. However, no schematic specific operations are supported currently by Graphica/Templa.

Unidraw (Vlissides & Linton, 1989) is an editor framework which runs under the X windowing system and Interviews (described in Section 9.5). While Unidraw does not generate schematic editors, it may be configured to become a schematic editor after the designer supplies the necessary structure, appearance, and behavior as follows:

The structure and appearance is specified by *components,* elements of the schematic domain. Components are represented by graphical icons such as electronic parts in a circuit layout or notes in written music. The designer of the schematic editor specifies the appearance and layout constraints of each component type.

Behavior is specified as a set of *commands* and *tools.* Commands define operations on components. Commands may include save, change value, duplicate components, and group components into composite component. Tools support the direct manipulation of components. Example tools include selecting components for editing, applying coordinate transformations on components, and connecting components. The schematic editor designer specifies commands and tools. Commands are often common to several schematic editors and may be inherited from generic commands available in the Unidraw framework.

Unidraw also generates external representations of schematics which may be used by application specific routines.

Karrer and Scacchi (1990) have identified the following requirements for extensible graph editors:

1. *Display update efficiency controls.* Algorithms that quickly update and display graphs are needed. Users do not want to work with graph editors that require many seconds, or even minutes, to redisplay a graph.

2. *Automatic layout algorithm support.* Such algorithms free users from manually placing nodes in aesthetically pleasing locations.

3. *Multiple-view support.* Some data need more than one view to be understood. For example, tree structures may be viewed as either trees or as Venn diagrams. In order to generate multiple views, multiple layout algorithms must be supported within a single graph editor.

4. *Undo Support.* Users should be able to undo one or more changes to the graph.

5. *User-defined data structure support.* The user should be able to define the underlying representation of the graph data. This enables the user to write other programs which access the graph data in an efficient manner.

6. *User-defined graphical support.* The editor should allow the user to specify the appearance of the nodes and arcs.

7. *Abstraction support.* For example, the user may replace a subgraph by a single node and then redisplay the subgraph by ''zooming in'' to the single node.

8. *Application interface support.* The user should be able to define interfaces to the graph data for other applications to access. For example, a database schema processor may need to access the graph data entered by a user via a database schema graph editor.

9. *Subgraph selection support.* To perform operations on a subset of a graph, there must be a method for selecting a subset and performing operations on the subset.

10. *Simulation/animation support.* It should be possible to execute or interpret the graph, perhaps resulting in the animation of the graph so the user can see the state of the graph execution/interpretation.

11. *Efficient user interface support.* Graph editors must have an extensible user interface.

12. *User-defined node and link types.* Users must be able to specify the types of nodes, types of links, and constraints on which types of nodes can be linked by the various types of links.

The Tree/Graph Editor (TGE) is a highly customizable graph editor developed at the University of Southern California based on the Interviews object-oriented user interface tool kit. TGE satisfies all of the foregoing requirements except for Undo. TGE is divided into two main parts: the base editor and the domain-specific editor. The user provides information which transforms the base editor into an editor that is suited for a specific application domain. Editors are created by essentially modifying the C++ class definitions for node, arc, graph, graph editor, node picture, arc picture, and graph picture. Extensible graph editors like TGE will play an increasingly central role in software developments, environments, and user interfaces.

Glossary

and/or tree: graphical representation of the productions of a grammar.

application: software that performs one or more domain-specific tasks.

application analyst: role played by individual(s) responsible for identifying the potential end users, defining the problem that end users need to solve, defining the domain-dependent tasks, and specifying the end users' conceptual model.

application conceptual model: describes the implementation of the objects and functions supported by the application.

application programmer: role played by individual(s) who implement nonuser interface portions of the application.

application programming interface (API): interface which defines the data structures and commands by which application functions and script execution engines interact with interaction objects.

audio designer: role played by individual(s) who develop the audio aspects of interaction objects, especially in multimedia applications.

author: designer and implementer of a multimedia title (application)

bit map: two-dimensional matrix of light or dark dots that the human eye perceives as a picture.

capture tools: tools for capturing or recording images, audio clips, and video clips for use in multimedia applications.

capture window: window receiving mouse input.

chronological backtracking: the systematic reversal of actions by undoing actions in the reverse of the order in which they were performed.

client: software module which implements decisions made in the structural, functional, and dialog decision classes.

client-server architecture: architecture consisting of two major components, the client and the server.

clip: audio or video segment which may be part of a multimedia application.

clipboard: memory buffer which can be accessed by multiple scripts. The operations cut, copy, and paste provide access to a clipboard and enable multiple, executing scripts to exchange information.

command processor: software which accepts a string of characters entered by the end user, determines the intent of the character string, and invokes the appropriate application functions.

command style dialog: user interface in which the user formulates and enters commands, usually using a keyboard for command entry.

commit point: a point during a dialog after which previous functions cannot be undone.

composite conceptual object: conceptual object which contains other conceptual objects.

composite interaction object: interaction object which contains two or more simple, editable, and/or other composite interaction objects.

computer-directed dialog: iterative dialog in which a request is presented to the user, who then responds by entering the requested information. Users often feel subordinate to the computer when using computer-directed dialogs.

conservational dialogs: type of user interface dialog provided by commands, question and answer, menus and form fill-in, and natural language dialogs.

context-free grammar: a set of production rules which describe a language in which a rule can be applied irrespective of the context of the nonterminal symbol being replaced.

conventions: guidelines defined by a vendor to make a user interface more specific and to provide a vendor "look and feel."

data box: interaction object into which the end user enters values.

data glove: a glove worn on a human's hand which senses the position and orientation of the hand.

dependency-directed backtracking: the reversal of actions by undoing only those actions which directly contributed to the undesired result.

derivation tree: parse tree.

design decision framework: a partitioning of a design problem into several smaller problems which can be solved individually.

design methodology: an ordering of decisions within a design decision framework.

device drivers: libraries of functions which cause an input or output device to operate.

dialog: specific set of semantic tokens exchanged during the execution of a script and the order in which those tokens are exchanged.

dialog decision class: decisions made when specifying the content and sequence of information exchanged between the user and applications during a dialog.

dialog designer: role played by individual(s) who design the metaphor the user interface presents to the end user and the dialog of information exchanged between the end user and the application.

direct manipulation dialog: style of user interface dialog in which the user operates directly on objects that are visible on the screen, performing rapid, reversible, incremental actions.

discrete value object: conceptual object containing a value from among a discrete set of values.

dispersement ratio: ratio of the output size to the output extent.

dynamic interaction object: composite interaction object in which the physical arrangement and visibility of its component interaction objects may change.

eager evaluation: class of algorithms which keep all slots of a rule graph up to date.

echo: lexical feedback.

editable interaction object: interaction object which accepts editable strings of alphanumeric characters from end users.

encapsulation: hiding of an agent's data structures and algorithms from other agents.

end user: role played by individual(s) who interacts with an interactive application.

end users' conceptual model: collection of objects, relationships, and functions which characterize an application from the end users' perspective.

ergonomics: study of how humans interact with physical devices.

event: message generated by the user, application functions, or the script execution engine in order to send a message to another agent.

event handler: process that waits for events and services them by performing predefined actions.

evolutionary user interface prototype: user interface prototype which is refined and modified until it satisfies the needs of the user and is then fielded and placed into production.

exploratory user interface prototype: user interface which is refined and modified until it satisfies the needs of the user, but then must be reimplemented before it is fielded and placed into production.

feedback: message to the user which confirms the acceptability of entered information.

finite state transition system: mathematical model of a system which accepts semantic tokens as input and performs actions based on that input.

focus window: window receiving keyboard input.

form fill-in: a composite interaction object consisting of several data boxes and the associated labels and user instructions.

form generator: processor which accepts form specifications and generates software which, when executed, displays one or more forms.

functional decision class: decisions made when constructing the functional aspects of the end users' conceptual model.

geometric structure: describes the relative position of the component interaction objects of a composite interaction object and the degree that they may be repositioned.

geometry manager: software which rearranges the geometric structure of an interaction object subject to prespecified constraints.

glue: constraints on the relative position of boxes within a composite interaction object.

graphics designer: role played by individual(s) who develop the visual aspects of interaction objects.

guidelines: general recommendations to be used with judgment and adapted to the specifics of the application.

help: messages containing useful information presented to the end user.

hypermedia system: execution engine that displays the text, graphics, images, audio, and video contents of nodes of information graphs.

hypertext system: execution engine that displays the textual contents of nodes in an information graph.

icon: pictorial representation of a concept, object, option, thought, idea, or command.

image model: model which describes the images to be displayed to the user via a windowing system. Two widely used image models are PostScript and pixels.

information tokens: units of information exchanged among multiple agents.

inheritance: ability of one object to reuse data structures and algorithms of another object without reimplementing them.

input signal interaction object: signal interaction object which accepts input from the user only.

interaction objects: objects which are presented to the end user to convey information and which are manipulated by the end user to enter information to the application. A software module which performs I/O to the end user on behalf of an application.

interactive Petri net: a formalism for describing concurrent dialogs.

interaction technique: interaction object.

interactor: interaction object.

interoperability: end user's ability to apply operating techniques of one user interface to another.

Interviews: a graphical user interface tool kit developed at Stanford University that defines interaction objects and composition strategies.

irreflexive relationship: relationship in which no object is related to itself.

ITS (Interactive Transaction System): user interface system developed at IBM which uses rules to transform an abstract style-independent specification into a concrete, style-specific interaction object.

keystroke analysis model: model used to predict the amount of time which a user needs to perform a sequence of actions.

Keystroke Analysis Tool (KAT): user interface evaluation tool developed at George Washington University which predicts the amount of time that an expert user needs to perform tasks using a user interface.

keyword-oriented command language: end user language consisting of character strings represented commands and parameters. Commands expressed in these languages are usualy entered by the end user via a keyboard.

lazy evaluation: class of algorithms which keeps only visible slots of a rule graph up to date.

lexical analysis: process which translates sequences of lexical tokens into sequences of semantic tokens.

lexical analyzer: processor which performs lexical analysis.

lexical token: keystroke, mouse movement, or mouse click entered by the user or a character, icon, or elementary sound presented to the user.

look and feel: manner in which the computer presents information to the user and the manner in which the user enters and manipulates information and requests.

MACHO: user interface containing *m*ultiargument *c*ommands *h*aving *o*ptions.

magnitude object: conceptual object containing a value which represents a position on a continuous scale.

many-to-many relationship class: relationships between objects in two classes in which an object in the second class may be related to more than one object in the first class and an object in the first class may be related to more than one object in the second class.

many-to-one relationship class: relationship between objects in two classes in which no object in the second class is related to more than one object in the first class, and at least one object in the first class is related to more than one object in the second class.

menu: displayed collection of options from which the user selects one or more choices.

menu formatter: processor which accepts menu specifications and generates the menu layout.

metamodel: modeling technique which contains a set of terms and concepts used by designers to describe object classes and relationships in conceptual models.

MICKEY: experimental UIMS developed by Brigham Young University that creates a user interface information embedded within the application procedure definitions.

MIKE: user interface management system from Brigham Young University which generates a log containing information used to evaluate a user interface.

model view controller architecture: user interface architecture made popular by the SmallTalk development environment.

Multiagent models: architectures in which the application is partitioned into several components, each performing a different activity within the application domain.

multitasking: a computer switches among several processing tasks, executing some instructions in each task before switching to another.

multithreaded dialog: the result of executing two or more scripts in an interleaved fashion.

natural language: end user formulates requests using English, Spanish, or some other language which the end user uses to converse with other humans. Natural language commands are usually entered via a keyboard.

NeXT Interface Builder: user interface generation facility on the NeXT computer.

nominal object: conceptual object containing an identifier of another conceptual object.

nontransitive relationship: relationships which are not transitive.

object class: set of objects of the same type.

one-to-one relationship class: relationships between objects in two classes in which no object in the first class is related to more than one object in the second class and no object in the second class is related to more than one object in the first class.

order-dependent scripts: scripts which require that semantic tokens be exchanged in a specific sequence.

order-independent scripts: scripts which permit semantic tokens to be exchanged in partially or totally arbitrary sequences.

output extent: number of objects in the smallest rectangle which contains the objects actually used to display the output of a command.

output signal interaction object: signal interaction object which only presents output to the user.

overlapped windows: multiple windows placed on the screen so that they give the end user the impression of being stacked on top of each other.

parallel processing: multiple CPUs, each operating in parallel, processing different tasks.

parse tree: the representation of a script as a tree structure with internal nodes representing production rules of a grammar.

partial order: relationship which is reflexive, antisymmetric, and transitive.

partial relationship: a relationship between two classes in which at least one object in the first class is not related to any object in the second class.

PERIDOT (programming by example for real time interface design obviating typing): experimental system developed at Carnegie Mellon University which enables the dialog designer to draw the appearance and then perform actions with an interaction object. PERIDOT guesses or infers what behavior should occur in the general case.

Petoud-Pigneur system: user interface generator which generates a window for each entity type and for each relationship type in an entity-relationship schema representation of the data of an application.

Petri net: see interactive Petri net.

pixel: short for picture elements, points which make up a graphics image.

polymorphism: the ability of different agents to react differently to the same message.

postconditions: statements associated with a function within an object class such that the statement must be satisfied after the function has been performed.

pragmatic decision class: decisions made when determining issues of gesture, space, and hardware devices.

preconditions: statements associated with a function within an object class such that the statement must be satisfied before the function can be performed.

presentation decision class: decision made when specifying interaction objects which make up the end users' interface.

prompt: message displayed to the user to remind or encourage the user to perform some action.

property sheet: form fill-in containing the names of attributes and values which can be modified.

Prototyper: a commercially available user interface generator used to design and prototype standard Macintosh interaction objects.

QWERTY keyboard: standard arrangement of keys used on most keyboards. QWERTY refers to the positions of the six keys on the upper left-hand side of the keyboard.

radio button: an option in a menu. Radio buttons are similar to the set of push buttons which are a part of the tuning device used with many car radios.

RAPID (rapid prototyper of interface design): a software-based design environment for the rapid prototyping of small control panel interfaces.

recognizer: lexical analyzer.

reflexive relationship: relationship in which each object is related to itself.

relationship: typed association between two objects.

room: a three-dimensional generalization of a window.

rule graph: graphical representation of a set of rules.

rule: constraint describing how one value is derived from other values.

scene: a segment of a multimedia application which consists of one or more clips.

schematic editor: editor used to create both a picture and an underlying data structure which can be analyzed and interpreted by schematic specific software.

script: special program which describes the exchange of information tokens among agents.

script authoring tool: software used by user interface designers to construct scripts.

script execution engine: executes a special program called a script to produce one of several dialogs described by the script. While processing a script, the script execution engine controls the exchange of semantic tokens among interaction objects and application functions.

Seeheim architecture: user interface architecture in which the application, dialog control, and presentation aspects of an application are in separate components. The Seeheim architecture was developed by user interface experts at a 1985 conference in Seeheim, Germany.

selection interaction object: interaction object which presents a small number of options to the user, who selects one of the options.

semantic dialog: sequence of semantic tokens exchanged between interaction objects and applications during the execution of a script.

semantic token: smallest set of lexical tokens exchanged between the user and application that can have a formally defined meaning.

semantic warning message: a warning message displayed to the user informing the user of the potential effects of the operation about to be performed, and asking the user to confirm that the operation should be executed.

Serpent: UIMS developed at Carnegie Mellon University's Software Engineering Institute. Serpent uses an interface definition language similar to a database schema to define the structure of data to be shared by the user interface and application functions.

server: library of I/O routines which implement the presentation aspects of the user interface.

signal interaction object: interaction object which transmits a predefined message between the end user and a dialog processor or application function.

simple conceptual object: type which describes a domain of possible values, and a value which is an encoding of information which characterizes the object. Some designers use the term attribute or field to refer to a simple conceptual object.

snapping: automatic movement of a point or object from the position that the user entered to the nearest permitted location.

spatial structure: geometric structure.

standards: rules developed by official standards organizations and considered to be mandatory.

state charts: a variation of state transition diagrams in which a node may itself represent a state transition graph.

state transition graph: directed graph frequently used to illustrate a finite state transition system.

state tree: state transition graph organized in the form of a tree.

static interaction object: composite interaction object in which the physical arrangement of its component interaction objects do not change.

structural decision class: decisions made when constructing the structural aspects of the end users' conceptual model.

symmetric relationship: relationship between two objects such that the relationship holds in both directions.

SYNGRAPH: an early user interface generator based on grammars.

TAE PLUS: a user interface management system developed for NASA which runs under UNIX.

Templa/Graphica: system enabling a schematic designer to specify the types of nodes, types of links which may connect nodes, and constraints on the types of nodes which can be connected by each link.

terminator: lexical token indicating that the user has completed manipulating an interaction object.

tiled windows: nonoverlapping windows.

title: multimedia application for use by the general public.

total order: relationship in which every pair of objects participates in the relationship.

total relationship: a relationship between two classes in which each object in the first class is related to some object in the second class.

transitive relationship: relationship such that if one object is related to a second object and the second object is related to the third object, then the first object is related to the third object.

undo function: function which cancels the effect of a previously executed function.

unidraw: editor framework developed at Stanford University which may be configured to become a schematic editor.

user-directed dialog: iterative dialog in which the user indicates the next type of information or command to be entered, and then enters the information or command. Users perceive that they control the computer when using user-directed dialogs.

user interface: the operations and manipulations performed by humans to interchange information with computerized applications.

user interface authoring tool: software which is used to author or create a description of a user interface.

user interface development environment: collection of guidelines, libraries, and tools for designing, building, and evaluating user interfaces.

user interface evaluator: role played by individual(s) who predicts whether or not a proposed interface design satisfies established standards, guidelines, and conventions. The user interface evaluator also determines the effectiveness of the user interface by determining its quality, usability, and robustness.

user interface execution engine: manages and controls the dialog between an end user and one or more applications by processing user interface specifications and producing user interface dialogs.

user interface management system (UIMS): (1) run-time execution engine which executes or interprets user interface specifications and produces the dialog of information exchange between users and applications. (2) collection of software tools used to design, represent, prototype, execute, and evaluate user interfaces.

user interface prototype: quickly developed and easily modified working model of the user interface.

user interface styles: major classifications of user interfaces. Five major user interface styles are command, question and answer, menu and form fill-in, natural language, and direct manipulation styles.

user interface system: software and hardware which implements a user interface.

user interface tool kit: collection of interaction objects which display information to users and solicit information from users; library of I/O routines which implement the presentation aspects of the user interface.

valuator: interaction object which can accept any of a continuous range of values.

WIMP: user interface consisting of *w*indows, *i*cons, *m*enus, and *p*ointing devices.

window: (1) region of the display screen used to display the interaction objects associated with a single application, (2) a data structure, and a unit of executable code to which messages can be sent.

window fragment: portion of a window overlaid by another window.

window manager: software which manages windows displayed on a screen.

WYSIWYG (what you see is what you get): a type of direct manipulation for positioning, orienting, stretching, shrinking, and sizing the visual components.

Bibliography

APPLE COMPUTER. *User Interface Guidelines: The Apple Desktop Interface*. Reading, MA: Addison-Wesley, 1987.

BASS, LEN and JOËLLE COUTAZ. *Developing Software for the User Interface*. Reading, MA: Addison-Wesley, 1991.

BASS, LEN, ERIK HARDY, REED LITTLE, and ROBERT SEACORD. "Incremental development of user interfaces." In *Engineering for Human-Computer Interaction*. Amsterdam: North Holland, 1990, pp. 155–175.

BENBASAT, IZAK, and YAIR WAND. "A structured approach to designing human-computer dialogues." *Int. J. Man-Machine Studies,* Vol. 21 (1984), pp. 105–126.

BENNETT, WILLIAM E., STEPHEN J. BOIES, JOHN D. GOULD, SHAREN L. GREENE, and CHARLES F. WIECHA. "Transformations on a dialog tree, rule-based mapping of context to style." *Proceedings of the ACM User Interface Software and Technology,* Williamsburg, Virginia, November 13–15, 1989, pp. 67–85.

BLOX/TEMPLATE "Getting Started with BLOX," Number 0252-0142-00, July 1986. Template Graphics Software, One Woodfield Lake, Suite 102, Schaumburg, Illinois 60173.

BROWN, MARLIN C. *Human-Computer Interface Design Guidelines*. Norwood, NJ: Ablex, 1988.

BROWN, JUDITH R., and STEVE CUNNINGHAM. *Programming the User Interface: Principles and Examples*. New York: John Wiley, 1989.

BUXTON, WILLIAM. "Lexical and pragmatic considerations of input structures." *Computer Graphics* (January 1983), pp. 31–37.

332

CARD, S., T. MORAN, and A. NEWELL. "The keystroke-level model for user performance time with interactive systems." *Communications of the ACM*, Vol. 23, No. 7 (July 1980), pp. 398–410.

CARD, S., T. MORAN, and A. NEWELL. *The Psychology of Human-Computer Interaction*. Hillsdale, NJ: Erlbaum, 1983.

CERI, STEFANO, and GIUSEPPE PELAGATTI. *Distributed Databases Principles & Systems*. New York: McGraw-Hill, 1984.

CHAKRAVARTY, INDRANIL, and MICHAEL F. KLEYN. "Visualisms for describing interactive systems." In *Engineering for Human-Computer Interaction*. Amsterdam: North Holland, 1990.

CHEN, P. P. "The entity-relationship model: Towards a unified view of data." *ACM Trans. Database Systems*, No. 1 (1976), pp. 9–36.

CLARKSON, MARK A., "An Easier Interface." *BYTE* (February 1991), pp. 277–282.

DEWAN, PRASUN, and ERIC VASILIK. "An approach to integrating user interface management systems with programming languages." In *Engineering for Human-Computer Interaction, pp. 493–514. Amsterdam: North Holland, 1990*.

DOUGLAS, SARAH, ECKEHARD DOERRY, and DAVID NOVICK. "QUICK: A user-interface design kit for non-programmmers." *Proceedings of the ACM User Interface Software and Technology*, Snowbird, Utah, October 3–5, 1990, pp. 47–56.

DOUGLAS, SARAH, ECKEHARD DOERRY, and DAVID NOVICK. "QUICK: Exploring the Middle Ground in User Interface Design Tools," *Proc. 24th Hawaii International Conference on System Sciences,* Jan. 8–11, 1991, Hawaii.

ELMASRI, RAMEZ, and SHAMKANT B. NAVATHE. *Fundamentals of Database Systems*. Redwood City, CA: Benjamin/Cummings, 1989.

FLECCHIA, M. A., and R. D. BERGERON. "Specifying complex dialogs in ALGAE." *Proc. CHI 87* (1987), pp. 2210–2234.

FOLEY, JAMES. "Transformations on a formal specification of user-computer interfaces." *Computer Graphics*, Vol. 21, No. 2, (April 1987), pp. 109–113.

FOLEY, JAMES, CHRISTINA GIBBS, WON CHUL KIM, SRDJAN KOVACEVIC. "A knowledge-based user interface management system." *Proc. CHI '88* (Conference Proceedings), Human Factors in Computing Systems, May 15–19, 1988, Washington D.C., pp. 67–72.

FOLEY, JAMES, WON CHUL KIM, SRDJAN KOVACEVIC, and KEVIN MURRAY. "Defining Interfaces at a High Level of Abstraction." *Software,* (January 1989), pp. 25–32.

FOLEY, J., and A. VAN DAM. *Fundamentals of Interactive Computer Graphics*. Reading, MA: Addison-Wesley, 1990.

GOLDBERG, A. and D. ROBSON. *Smalltalk-80: The Language and Its Implementation*. Reading, Ma: Addison-Wesley 1983.

GOODMAN, DANNY. *The Complete HyperCard Handbook*. New York: Bantam Computer Books, 1987.

GREEN, M. "Report on dialogue specification tools." In Gunther E. Pfaff, ed., *User Interface Management Systems, Proceedings of the Workshop on User Interface Management Systems,* Seeheim, FRG, November 1–3, 1983, pp. 9–20. New York: Springer-Verlag, 1983.

GREEN, M. "The University of Alberta user interface management system." *Computer Graphics,* Vol. 19, No. 3, (July 1985), pp. 205–213.

HAREL, DAVID. "Statecharts: A visual formalism for complex systems." *Science of Computer Programming* Vol. 8 (1987) pp. 231–274.

HARRISON, M. and H. THIMBLEBY. *Formal Methods in Human-Computer Interaction. Cambridge: Cambridge University Press, 1990*.

Bibliography

HARTSON, H. REX, and DEBORAH HIX. "Human-computer interface development: Concepts and systems for its management." *ACM Computing Surveys,* Vol. 12, no. 1 (March 1980), pp. 5–92.

HEKMATPOUR, SHARAM. *Templa Graphica: A Generic Graphical Editor for the Macintosh™.* Englewood Cliffs, NJ: Prentice Hall, 1990.

HILL, RALPH D. "Event-response systems—A technique for specifying multi-threaded dialogues." *Proc. CHI '87,* pp. 241–248.

HILL, RALPH D. "Supporting concurrency, communication, and synchronization in human-computer interaction—The sassafras UIMS." *ACM Transactions on Graphics,* Vol. 5, no. 3 (July 1986), pp. 179–210.

JACOB, ROBERT J. K. "Using formal specifications in the design of a human-computer interface." *Comm. of ACM,* Vol. 26, no. 4 (April 1983), pp. 259–264.

JACOB, ROBERT J. K. "A specification language for direct-manipulation user interfaces." *ACM Trans. on Graphics,* Vol. 5, no. 4 (October 1986), pp. 283–317.

JARKE, MATTHIAS, and YANNIS VASSILIOU. "A framework for choosing a database query langauge." *ACM Computing Surveys,* Vol. 17, no. 3 (September 1986), pp. 313–340.

KARRER, ANTHONY, and WALT SCACCHI. "Requirements for an extensible object-oriented tree/graph editor. Proceedings of the ACM SIGGRAPH Symposium on User Interface Software and Technology, Snowbird, Utah, October 3–5, 1990, pp. 84–91.

KRASNER, GLENN E., and STEPHEN T. POPE. "A cookbook for using the model-view-controller user interface paradigm in smalltalk-80." Journal of Object-Oriented Programming August/September 1988, pp. 26–49.

LINTON, MARK A., JOHN M. VLISSIDES, and PAUL R. CALDER. "Composing user interfaces with interviews." *Computer,* Vol. 22, no. 2 (February 1989), pp. 8–22.

LUTHER, ARCH C. *Digital Video in the PC Environment.* New York: McGraw-Hill, 1989.

MEIER, BARBARA J. "ACE: A color expert system for user interface design." *Proceedings of the ACM SIGGRAPH Symposium on User Interface Software,* Banff, Alberta, Canada, October 17–19, 1988, pp. 117–128.

METZ, STEPHEN V., ROSE MAE M. RICHARDSON, and MOHAMMED NASIRUDDIN. "RAPID: Software for Rapid Prototyping of Control Panel Interfaces." Proc. 31st Human Factors Society Annual Meeting, Oct. 19–23, 1987.

MILLS, C., and A. I. WASSERMAN. "A transition diagram editor." In *Proc 1984 Summer Usenix Meeting,* June 1984, pp. 287–296.

MYERS, BRAD A. "Creating interaction techniques by demonstration." *IEEE Computer Graphics and Application,* Vol. 7, (no. 9) (September 1987), pp. 51–60.

MYERS, B. A. *Creating User Interfaces by Demonstration.* Boston: Academic Press, 1988.

OLSEN, D., W. BUXTON, R. EHRICH, D. KASIK, J RHYNE, and J. SIBERT. "A context for user interface management." *IEEE Computer Graphics and Applications,* Vol. 4 (December 1984), pp. 33–42.

OLSEN, DAN R., JR., "MIKE: The menu interaction kontrol environment." *ACM Transactions on Graphics,* Vol. 5, No. 4 (October 1986), pp. 318–344.

OLSEN, DAN R., JR. "A Programming Language Basis for User Interface Management." *Proc. CHI '89,* 1989, pp. 171–176.

OLSEN, DAN R., JR., and ELIZABETH P. DEMPSEY. "SYNGRAPH: A graphical user interface generator." *Computer Graphics,* Vol. 17, no. 3 (July 1983), pp. 43–50.

OLSEN, DAN R. JR., and BRADLEY W. HALVERSEN. "Interface usage measurements in a user interface management system." *Proceedings of the ACM SIGGRAPH Symposium on User Interface Software,* Banff, Alberta, Canada, October 17–19, 1988, pp. 1102–1108.

OPEN SOFTWARE FOUNDATION. *OSF/Motif™ Style Guide*. Englewood Cliffs, NJ: Prentice Hall, 1990.

PETOUD, I. and Y. PIGNEUR. "An automatic and visual approach for user interface design," In *Engineering for Human-Computer Interaction*, Amsterdam: North Holland, 1990, pp. 403–420.

REISNER, PHYLLIS. "Formal grammar as a tool for analyzing ease of use: Some fundamental concepts." In J. C. Thomas and M. L. Schneider, eds., *Human Factors in Computer Systems*, New York: Ablex, 1984, pp. 53–78.

REISNER, PHYLLIS. "Formal grammar and human factors design of an interactive graphics system." *IEEE Transactions on Software Engineering*, Vol. SE-7, no. 2 (March 1981), pp. 229–240.

RUMBAUGH, JAMES. "State Trees as Structured Finite State Machines for User Interfaces." *Proceedings of ACM SIGGRAPH Symposium on User Interface Software*, Banff, Alberta, Canada, October 17–19, 1988, pp. 15–29.

SCHEIFLER, ROBERT W., and JIM GETTYS. "The X Window System." *ACM Transactions on Graphics*, Vol. 5, no. 2 (April 1986), pp. 79–109.

SENAY, HIKMET, LUCY MORAN, PIYAWADEE SUIKAVIRIYA, JAMES D. FOLEY, and JOHN L. SIBERT. "Tools for improving user-computer interfaces," Report GWU-IIST-88-22, Washington, D. C.: George Washington University, July 1988).

SHNEIDERMAN, BEN. *Designing the User Interface*. Reading, MA: Addison-Wesley, 1986.

SHNEIDERMAN, BEN. "Multiparty grammars and related features for defining interactive systems." *IEEE Transactions on Systems, Man, and Cybernetics*, Vol. SMC-12, no. 2 (March/April 1982), pp. 148–154.

SMITH, S. L., and J.N. MOSIER. "Guidelines for designing user interface software," Technical Report MTR-10090, The Mitre Corporation, Bedford, MA, 1986.

SOWA, J. F. *Conceptual Structures, Information Processing in Mind and Machine*. Reading, Ma: Addison-Wesley, 1984.

STALLMAN, RICHARD M. and GERALD J. SUSSMAN. "Forward reasoning and dependency-directed backtracking in a system for computer-aided circuit analysis." *Artificial Intelligence*, Vol. 9, no. 2 (1977).

TENNANT, HARRY R., KENNETH M. ROSS, RICHARD M. SAENZ, CRAIG W. THOMPSON, and JAMES R. MILLER. "Menu-based natural language understanding." 21st Annual Meeting of Association for Computational Linguistics, 1983, pp. 151–158.

ULLMAN, JEFFREY D. *Principles of Database Systems*, Rockville, MD: Computer Science Press, 1980.

VLISSIDES, JOHN M. and MARK A. LINTON. "Unidraw: A framework for building domain-specific graphical editors." *Proceedings of the ACM SIGGRAPH Symposium on User Interface Software and Technology*, Williamsburg, VA, November 13–15, 1989, pp. 158–167.

WASSERMAN, ANTHONY I. "Extending state transition diagrams for the specification of human-computer interaction." *IEEE Transactions on Software Engineering*, Vol. SE-11, no. 8 (August 1985).

WEBSTER, DALLAS E. "Mapping the design information representation terrain," *Computer* Vol. 21, no. 12, (December 1988), pp. 8–23.

WELLNER, PIERRE D. "Statemaster: A UIMS based on state charts for prototyping and target implementation." *Proc. CHI '89* May 1989, pp. 117–182.

YOUNG, DOUGLAS A. *X Window Systems Programming and Applications with Xt*. Englewood Cliffs, NJ: Prentice Hall, 1989.

Index

A

Agents, 127–29
And/or tree, 160–65, 316
Animation editor. *See* Editor, animation.
API. *See* Application conceptual model, programming interface.
Application conceptual model, 37
    programmer, 18, 74
    programming interface, 106
Attribute, 40
Audio, 80–81

B

Backtracking:
    chronological, 182–83, 192
    dependency-directed, 184, 192
Bass, Len, 196
Benbasat, Izak, 143

Bennett, William E., 309
Bergeron, R. D., 205, 222
Bit map. *See* interaction object, bit map.
Bit map editor. *See* editor, bit map.
BLOX/TEMPLATE, 152
Body suit, 109
Brown, Marlin C., 108
Buxton, William, 26

C

Calder, Paul R., 99, 188
Callback, 76
Card, S., 230
Ceri, Stefano, 248, 269
CASE:W, 312
Chakravarty, Indranil, 165
Chen, P. P., 39
Chronological backtracking. *See* Backtracking, chronological.

Clarkson, Mark A., 121
Client-server architecture, 125–26, 130–31, 312
Clipboard, 70, 120, 128
Command box. *See* Interaction object, command box.
Command dialog style, 5, 7, 22
Command processor, 3, 12, 22
Composite conceptual object. *See* Conceptual object, composite.
Computer-directed dialog, 10–11, 22
Conceptual object, 40–43, 53–55
  composite, 42–43, 95–102
  simple 40–44
Concurrent dialog. *See* Dialog, concurrent.
Conservational dialog style, 8
Constraint, 38, 54, 76, 124, 174, 186–92, 220–24
Context-free grammar. *See* Grammar.
Control. *See* interaction object.

D

Data box. *See* Interaction object, data box.
Data glove, 109
Dempsey, Elizabeth P., 169
Dependency-directed backtracking. *See* Backtracking, dependency-directed.
Derivation tree. *See* Parse tree.
Design decision framework, 22
Deterministic state transition system. *See* State transition system, deterministic.
Device drivers, 112–13, 131
Dewan, Prasun, 214
Dialog:
  box, *See* Interaction object, dialog box
  concurrent 69–70, 208, 217–19
  decision class, 26–32, 34–35, 125–28
  designer, 18, 21–22, 30, 64–65
  multithreaded 69–70, 147–50, 206–8, 211
Direct manipulation dialog style, 8-10, 22
Doerry, Eckehard, 86, 307
Douglas, Sarah, 86, 307

E

Eager evaluation, 184
Earcon, 30

Ease of use, 1
Echo, 78, 110
EDGE user interface system, 165
Editor:
  animation, 291, 293
  bit map, 291–92
  graphics, 292
  schematic 316–20
  sound, 291, 293–94
Elmasri, Ramez, 258
Encapsulation, 210
End user, 17, 74
End users' conceptual model, 6, 21, 26, 36–55
Event, 75, 200–208, 212
  loop, 203
  queue, 75
Evolutionary user interface prototype, 232
Exploratory user interface prototype, 232
Eye tracking, 109

F

Feedback, 32–33
Field. *See* Attribute.
Finite state transition system. *See* State transition system.
Flecchia, M. A., 205, 222
Foley, James 26, 219, 252
Forms, 3, 5, 12–13, 22
Function, 38, 41, 50–52, 54–55
  redo, 123
  undo, 122–23
Functional dependency, 262–63
Functional design decision class, 22, 27, 31, 34–35, 125–28

G

Geometry manager, 191–92
Gettys, Jim 314
Gibbs, Christina, 219
GKS, 120
Goldberg, A. 127
Goodman, Danny, 152, 216
Grammar, 153–72, 220–24
  multiparty, 159

Graphics designer, 17–18, 21, 74
Green, M., 126, 205
GUI, 10

H

Halverson, Bradley W., 233
Handwriting recognition, 94–95
Hardy, Erik, 196
Harel, David, 144
Harston, H. Rex, 1
Hekmatpour, Sharam, 318
Help, 33, 123, 141–44
Hill, Raph D., 205, 222
Hix, Deborah, 1
Holographic display, 109
Hypercard, 210–12, 214, 216–17, 232

I

Image model, 119–20
Inheritance, 211
Interaction object, 30, 35, 73–110, 112
    bit map, 92, 291–92
    command box, 92, 282
    composite, 78, 95–102, 110
    data box 12, 91, 281
    dialog box, 96
    dynamic composite, 102
    editable, 78, 915
    exclusive setting menu, 85–86, 110,
        281–82
    nonexclusive setting menu, 96
    selection, 78, 83–90, 110
    signal, 78-82, 110, 281, 298
    toggle switch, 84–85, 281–82
    valuator 86–87
Interaction technique. See Interaction object.
Interactive Transaction System, 309
Interactor. See Interaction object.
Interface Builder, 226, 304–5
Interoperability, 6
Interviews graphical user interface tool kit,
    188-91, 320
IsA relationship, 48-49, 243–80
IsMemberOf relationship, 49–50, 243–80
IsPartOf relationship, 43, 47–48, 243–80

J

Jacob, Robert J. K., 138
Jarke, Matthias, 5

K

Karrer, Anthony, 319
Keystroke Analysis Tool, 230–31
Kim, Won Chul, 219
Kleyn, Michael F. , 165
Krasner, Glenn E., 127, 208
Kovacevic, Srdjan, 219

L

Larson, Mike, 339
Lazy evalution, 184–86
Lexical analysis, 76–77
Lexical analyzer. See Lexical recognizer.
Lexical recognizer, 76–77
Lexical token, 28, 30, 76–77, 109
Linton, Mark, 99, 188, 319
Little, Reed, 196
Look and feel, 6
Luther, Arch C., 81

M

Macintosh, 10
    Interface toolkit, 102
Many-to-many relationship class. See
    Relationship class, many-to-many.
Many-to-one relationship class. See
    Relationship class, many-to-one.
Meier, Barbara J., 228
Menu, 3, 5, 12
    Exclusive setting. See Interaction object,
        exclusive setting menu.
    Menu dialog style, 8, 22
    Meta model, 39, 55
Metz, Stephen V., 229
MICKEY, 226, 294–98
MIKE. See MICKEY.
MicroMind Director, 236–37
Newell, A., 230

Microsoft Windows. *See* Windowing
  systems, Mircosoft Windows.
Mills, C., 152
Model view controller architecture
  127–28
Mole, 108
Moran, T., 230
Mosier, J.N., 108, 228
Motif windowing system. *See* Windowing
  system, Motif.
Multimedia, 233–39
Multithreaded dialog. *See* dialog,
  mutithreaded.
Multivalued dependency, 273–76
Murry, Kevin, 219
Myers, Brad A., 305

N

Natural language, 8, 22, 39
Navathe, Shamkant B., 258
NeXT, 294, 304
Nondeterministic state transition system. *See*
  state transition system, nondeterministic
Normalization, 255, 258–63
Novick, David, 86, 307

O

Object, 38-40
Object class, 40–41
Object-oriented approaches, 131
Olsen, Dan R., Jr., 15, 169, 233, 294, 297
One-to-one relationship class. *See*
  Relationship class, one-to-one.
One-to-many relationship class. *See*
  Relationship class, many-to-one.
Open Domain, 226
OpenLook windowing system. *See*
  Windowing system, OpenLook.

P

Parse tree, 156–58
Partial relationship class. *See* Relationship
  class, partial.

Pelagatti, Giuseppe, 248, 269
PERIDOT, 305–7
Petoud, I., 298-99
Petri net, 174, 217–19
PHIGS, 120
Pigneur, Y., 298-99
Polymorphism, 211
Pope, Stephen T., 127, 208
Postcondition 51–52, 54
PostScript 119
Pragmatic decision class, 26, 31–32, 35,
  125
Precondition, 51–52, 54
Presentation decision class, 26, 30–32, 34–
  35, 125–28
Presentation Manager. *See* Windowing
  systems, Presentation Manager.
Prompt, 32
Property sheet, 104, 107
Prototyper, 300–303

Q

Question and answer dialog style, 7, 22
QUICK, 86–87, 215, 307–8
QWERTY, 31

R

RAPID, 152
Redo function. *See* Function, redo.
Reisner, Phyllis, 223, 230
Relationship, 38, 43, 45–50, 240–42
  IsA. *See* IsA relationship.
  IsPartOf. *See* IsPartOf relationship
  IsMemberOf. *See* IsMemberOf
    relationship.
Relationship class, 45
  antisymmetric, 240–42
  compatible representation, 290
  equivalent, 47
  irreflexive, 240–41, 288
  many-to-many, 46–47, 55, 282
  many-to-one, 46–47, 55, 282
  nontransitive, 240–41
  one-to-one, 46–47, 55, 282
  partial, 45–46, 55

partially ordered, 242, 287
reflexive, 240–42, 288
symmetric, 240–41, 288
total, 45–46, 55
totally ordered, 242, 285
transitive, 240–42, 288
Robson, D., 127
Room, 121
Rubout, graphical, 170–71
Rule, 173–86, 192, 220–24
Rule graph, 174–86
reversible, 181–84
Rumbaugh, James, 141

S

Scacchi, Walt, 319
Scheifer, Robert W., 314
Script:
authoring tool, 15–16
execution engine, 15–16, 57–58, 60, 72, 77–78, 109, 121–22
order-dependent 65–68
order-independent 68
Seacord, Robert, 196
Seeheim architecture 126–27, 130–31, 212
Semantic tokens, 28, 32, 76–77,109
Senay, Hikmet, 230
Serpent user interface system, 196–200
Shared memory, 129, 131, 191–200, 212
Shneiderman, Ben, 230
Simple conceptual object. See Conceptual object, simple.
SmallTalk, 127–28, 131, 208–10, 212
Smith, S. L., 108, 228
Snapping, 187
Sound editor. See Editor, sound.
Sowa, J. F., 39
Speech:
recognition, 8, 30, 92–94
synthesis, 8
SQL, 12
Stallman, Richard M., 184
State charts, 144–50, 152
State transition system, 132–52, 220–24
deterministic 137
Moore, 138
Mealy, 138
nondeterministic, 137

State tree, 140–41
Structural design decision class, 26–27, 31, 35, 125–27
SUITE user interface management system, 214–15
Supernode, 144–47
Sussman, Gerald J., 184
SYNGRAPH user interface generator, 169–72, 172

T

TAE Plus, 226, 300, 303–4, 315
Task analysis, 38
TeleUse user interface management system, 214–15
Templa/Graphica, 318
Toggle interaction object. See Interaction object, toggle switch.
ToolBook, 210
Total relationship class. See Relationship class, total.
Transition graph, 134–36
Tree:
parse. See Parse tree.
derivation. See Derivation tree.
and/or. See And/or tree.
Tree/Graph Editor, 320

U

UIMX, 226, 315
Ullman, Jeffrey D., 258
Undo function. See Function, undo.
Unidraw, 319
UNIX, 12, 114, 169
User-directed dialog, 11, 22, 174–80
User interface:
authoring tool, 3–4
development environment, 225–39
evaluator, 18-19, 22
execution engine, 4–5
guidelines, 6, 226–29, 239
life cycle, 19–22
management systems, 3, 15, 22, 121–31
protoype, 22, 232
tool builder, 18
tool kit, 3, 13–16, 22, 125

V

Valuator. *See* Interaction object, valuator.
VanDam, A. ,26
Vasilik, Eric, 214
Vassiliou, Jannis, 6
View controller, 197–200
Vlissides, John M., 99, 188, 319

W

Wand, Yair, 143
Wasserman, Anthony I., 138, 152
Webster, Dallas E., 39
Wellner, Pierre D., 144
WIMP, 10
Window 112–13, 131
  fragments, 119
  manager, 14, 22, 113–21

overlapped, 116
tiled, 116
WindowMaker, 312
Windowing system, 3, 112–14
  Microsoft Windows, 102, 114, 130, 310–12
  Motif, 114, 315
  OpenLook, 114, 315
  Presentation Manager, 102, 114, 130

X

Xcessory, 315
X Window System, 102, 114, 130, 191, 312–15

Y

Young, Douglas A., 312